The Imperative of Reliability

SRLT

NORTHWESTERN UNIVERSITY PRESS

Studies in Russian Literature and Theory

The Imperative of Reliability

Russian Prose on the Eve of the Novel, 1820s–1850s

Victoria Somoff

NORTHWESTERN UNIVERSITY PRESS / EVANSTON, ILLINOIS

Northwestern University Press
www.nupress.northwestern.edu

Printed in the United States of America

ISBN 978-0-8101-3442-3

The Library of Congress has cataloged the original, hardcover edition as follows:

Somoff, Victoria, author.
The imperative of reliability : Russian prose on the eve of the novel, 1820s–1850s / Victoria Somoff.
pages cm. — (Northwestern University Press studies in Russian literature and theory)
ISBN 978-0-8101-3057-9 (cloth : alk. paper) — ISBN 978-0-8101-6821-3 (ebook)
1. Russian prose literature—19th century—History and criticism. 2. Russian fiction—19th century—History and criticism. I. Title. II. Series: Studies in Russian literature and theory.
PG3093.S66 2015
891.78309—dc23

2014038245

In memory of my mother and father

Contents

Acknowledgments		ix
Introduction	The Novel in Prose	3
Chapter One	Framing the Truth: Discourse as the Object of Discourse in the 1820s–30s	21
Chapter Two	In Search of Lost Voice: The Tale Collector in the Prose Cycle	42
Chapter Three	The Limits of Optic Power in the Society Tale	62
Chapter Four	Types, Doubles, and the Fantastical Sources of Narrative Realism	88
Chapter Five	No Need for Dogs or Women: Transparent Minds in Turgenev	111
Chapter Six	Waking Up to the Novel: The Dream Origin of Goncharov's *Oblomov*	139
Afterword and Afterward	Tolstoy's *After the Ball*	159
Notes		173
Works Cited		217
Index		233

Acknowledgments

I have been fortunate to have had truly remarkable teachers, both in Ukraine and here in the United States, and want to acknowledge and thank them here: my professors at Donetsk National University in Ukraine, Vladimir Viktorovich Fedorov and Mikhail Moiseevich Girshman—for teaching me early on that an artistic work cannot be derived from any context, no matter how subtly this derivation is understood.

My teacher, friend, and constant interlocutor Vladislav Prostsevichus—for his insistence that I remain true to this dictum and for his most demanding criticism during my work on this book.

I would also like to honor the memory of the late UC Berkeley folklore professor Alan Dundes who welcomed me to American academia and gave me an unforgettable and inimitable example of intellectual and personal generosity.

I owe a special debt of gratitude to my UC Berkeley mentor Irina Paperno, whose immense scholarly and pedagogical expertise has shaped my understanding of the profession. My most sincere appreciation goes to my other professors in the UC Berkeley Department of Slavic Languages and Literatures who inspired me with their scholarship and teaching: Lisa Little, Olga Matich, Anna Muza, Eric Naiman, Anne Nesbet, Harsha Ram, Alan Timberlake, and the late Viktor Markovich Zhivov.

This book benefited greatly from formal and informal conversations with Luba Golburt, Joachim Klein, and Leslie Kurke, as well as with the members of the Historical Poetics Working Group: Kate Holland, Ilya Kliger, Michael Kunichika, and Boris Maslov.

I would also like to express my deep admiration and gratitude to the late Lev Vladimirovich Loseff and to his wife, Nina Pavlovna.

On a personal note, I am thankful to my friends, near and far, who shared with me the good times, not so good times, and some critical times during my work on this project: Valentina Apresyan, Polina Barskova, Laura Edmondson, Felixa Eskey, Irene Fondriest, Luba Golburt, Regina Groisman, Mikhail Gronas, Yuliya and Yaroslav Halchenko, Laura Hercod, Anzhelika Khyzhnya, Yuliya Komska, Julie Lirot and Jaime Combariza, Mila Nazyrova, Olga Nikiforova, Lynn Patyk, Jane Shamaeva, and Zhenya Teytelman.

My very special thanks go to Avram Brown, who provided impeccable editorial assistance throughout my work on the book and to the editorial staff of Northwestern University Press for their exceptional professionalism and efficiency.

I would also like to thank the members of my family: my cousin Inna Bleykhman, for sisterhood; my stepmother Dora Polunovskaya for her grandmotherly love for my children; my father-in-law Ivan Somoff for his unwavering support; and Zhiravard Avagova for being the best nanny ever and for becoming family.

I am grateful to my husband, Gregori Somoff, for giving me an opportunity to pursue my vocation, for his endless love and care, and for reading and editing all my writings. To my children, Ivan, Dimitri, and Natalia—I can't put into words how much your warmth, wit, and exuberance sustain, amaze, and inspire me.

This book is dedicated in memory of my mother Natalia Nesterenko (1935–1988) and my father Felix Bleykhman (1934–2013), who together gave me my earliest and deepest experience of a love that is absolutely reliable.

The Imperative of Reliability

The Novel in Prose

> I would like so much to write a novel; but no,
> I cannot . . .
> —Aleksandr Pushkin

THE FIRST CHAPTER of Pushkin's *Eugene Onegin* (*Evgenii Onegin*) appeared in 1825 with the subtitle "a novel in verse." Pushkin famously emphasized the second constituent of his work's generic makeup: "I am now writing not a novel but a novel in verse—a hell of a difference [*roman v stikhakh—d'iavol'skaia raznitsa*]."[1] At the same time, the novel *in prose* remained a desirable but unattainable venture for Pushkin, who acknowledged his difficulties in mastering novelistic narration: "I would like so much to write a novel; but no, I cannot: I have three of them started; I start splendidly but then do not have enough patience, and cannot manage [*ne slazhu*]."[2]

The prose work that Pushkin did "manage" to complete in the early 1830s—*Tales of the Late Ivan Petrovich Belkin* (*Povesti pokoinogo Ivana Petrovicha Belkina*)—constitutes a cycle of five tales (*povesti*) rather than a novel. In 1841 Mikhail Lermontov took a similarly circuitous route toward longer-form narrative when he abandoned his unfinished novel *Princess Ligovskaia* (*Kniaginia Ligovskaia*) and turned to the compositional form of the prose cycle for *A Hero of Our Time* (*Geroi nashego vremeni*).

These two major writers' twin paths toward novelistic discourse were highly representative of Russian literary developments of the 1820s–30s. The prominent literary historian Boris Eikhenbaum demarcates the late 1820s as Russia's "turn toward prose" (*povorot k proze*): "After 1828, Russian prose began to develop rapidly, and by the mid-1830s we already have a long list of prose writers: besides Pushkin and Gogol, there were also Bulgarin, Marlinsky, Senkovsky, Pogorel'sky, Zagoskin, Odoevsky, Dal', Vel'tman, Grech, Kalashnikov, Lazhechnikov, Polevoi, Masal'sky, Begichev, Stepanov, Voskresensky, Mashkov, and so on."[3] This decisive turn notwithstanding, throughout the 1840s–50s, Russian writers continued to experience difficulties both with generic taxonomies and longer-sustained narratives.

In 1841 Nikolai Gogol subtitled his major prose work *Dead Souls* (*Mertvye dushi*) a *poema*—a mirror counterpart, as critics suggested, to Pushkin's celebrated "novel in verse." Ivan Turgenev destroyed *Two Generations* (*Dva pokoleniia*)—his first unsuccessful attempt at a novel—and subtitled what is now considered to be his first novel, *Rudin* (1856), a "novella" (*povest'*). Both Gogol and Turgenev had appeared on the literary scene with, again, prose cycles: *Evenings on a Farm near Dikan'ka* (*Vechera na khutore bliz Dikan'ki*, 1831) and *A Sportsman's Sketches* (*Zapiski okhotnika*, 1852) respectively. In 1849 Ivan Goncharov published a piece in the *Contemporary* (*Sovremennik*) entitled "Oblomov's Dream" ("Son Oblomova"), introduced as "an episode from an unfinished novel." The novel into which this "Dream" was eventually incorporated, *Oblomov*, was completed some ten years later.[4]

The generic ambiguity, if not "monstrosity"—to invoke Henry James's famous characterization of Tolstoy's *War and Peace* (*Voina i mir*)—of the masterpieces of Russian prose became a marker of a distinctly Russian literary-historical development, and the Russian novel's unconventional form has been explored by scholars in a variety of ways. Nonetheless, somewhere—midway, perhaps, between the generic complexity of *Eugene Onegin* and that of *War and Peace*—lies the birthplace of the Russian novel, the unmistakable novel *in prose*. Numerous manuscripts of projected novels, abandoned, destroyed, and generically transformed in the 1830s–50s, attest to the fact that writers of this period viewed the back roads and byways they took (often, quite rewardingly) toward novelistic discourse as a matter of artistic necessity rather than virtue, deeming the novel—the novel in prose—a touchstone for Russian literature's aesthetic prospects.[5]

And yet, it was less than twenty years after the publication of *A Hero of Our Time* that the Russian novel was startlingly, suddenly abundant, incarnate in Turgenev's *Rudin* (1856), *A Nest of the Gentry* (*Dvorianskoe gnezdo*, 1859), and *Fathers and Sons* (*Otsy i deti*, 1862); Goncharov's *Oblomov* (1859); and most prominently, Dostoevsky's *Crime and Punishment* (*Prestuplenie i nakazanie*, 1866) and Tolstoy's *War and Peace* (1865–69). As Richard Freeborn succinctly remarks, the novel in Russia "grew from a virtually experimental form into a genre of such prominence that by the end of the 1860s it not only exerted a dominant influence in Russian literature but had begun to acquire that international reputation which has since given it a leading place in any history of the nineteenth-century European novel."[6] The transition from the shorter and often experimental prose forms predominant in the 1820s–50s to the full-fledged and soon to be internationally renowned novels of the 1860s–70s took place with remarkable quickness. How do we account for this "great leap forward," representing as it does one of the most significant events in Russian literary history? How did this evolution of narrative forms take place? These are the questions my book endeavors to explore.

Scholars analyzing western European literary traditions have advanced a number of theories of the novel's genesis. The influential "rise of the novel" paradigm was inaugurated by the classic study of Ian Watt, who viewed the genre of the novel as a literary response to the sociohistorical development of early modern Europe, the "vast transformation of Western civilization since the Renaissance."[7] Since the publication of *The Rise of the Novel* in 1957, Watt's approach has been variously modified and challenged by subsequent historians of the novel. The principal direction taken up in criticisms of Watt's model consists in the loosening, blurring, and decisive crossing of the borderlines—national, sociopolitical, and linguistic, among others—within which, according to Watt, the genre of the novel first "rose" in world literature. More recent approaches to the novel's genealogy aim to dispense with the "seductions of first-hood" (Diana de Armas Wilson), allowing instead for the genre's multiple and alternative "rises" at various points in time and space.[8] As a consequence, the geographic scope of studies of the novel has been dramatically expanded, and scholarly attention to literary traditions that do not conform to the western European model has increased.[9]

The Russian novel seems to represent one such alternative "rise." It may be no exaggeration to say that the basic constituents of Watt's model simply do not obtain in mid-nineteenth-century Russia when the novel made its sudden appearance: Russia had neither an influential middle class, nor an extensive reading public, nor a developed literary marketplace. In a recent study, William Mills Todd III emphasizes the stark differences, in socioeconomic and sociohistorical terms, between Russian and Western literary development:

> In most cases it is the institutional circumstances of the Russian novel that most distinguish it from, say, the English, French, or American novel of the time. . . . As late as 1863, Dostoevsky would estimate that only one Russian in five hundred had access to . . . nontraditional literary culture. Sales and circulation figures suggest it was closer to one in a thousand. In assessing this cultured elite, the terms *bourgeois* and *middle class* must be used with extreme caution, as Russia remained a predominantly rural society.[10]

It is for this reason that Todd transposes the "rise" of the novel paradigm into the "ruse" of the Russian novel. The fact that Russian writers launched an internationally reputed novelistic tradition in spite of the deficiency of this tradition's purported sociohistorical prerequisites calls for an interpretive shift, one that might bring alternative factors of the genre's genealogy into play.

To be sure, beginning with Watt's own notion of "formal realism," the sociology of the novel has been closely intertwined with its epistemological concerns and narrative form. Contemporary studies of the novel oscillate between social and literary analysis, situating themselves, to use Alex Woloch's formulation, "at an imprecise juncture between form and history."[11] Consequently, the sociohistorical dimensions of the novelistic form remain central to the inquiry into the origins and advance of the western European novel both as a genre and as a literary institution.[12] According to Michael McKeon, who himself in *Origins of the English Novel, 1600–1740* undertook one of the most thorough reevaluations of Watt's methodological assumptions, critiques of Watt's model have generally "aimed not to refute the relevance of the historical context but to complicate Watt's version of it."[13]

As applied to "belated" novelistic traditions, such critiques aim to overcome the Eurocentrism implicit in the Watt paradigm, but nevertheless continue to seek particular correlations between the sociohistorical circumstances of the culture under study and the genre of the novel as it took shape in western Europe.[14] The predominant interpretive stance in investigations of deferred novelistic "rises" consists in examining them within the dynamics of cultural and literary exchange. In one influential non-Eurocentric account of the novel, the Brazilian scholar Roberto Schwarz discusses the problematic nature of superimposing the European novel and liberal Enlightenment ideas onto the realities of Brazil's slave-owning economy. At one point, Schwarz comments on the striking similarities between socioeconomic circumstances in Brazil and Russia, commonalities that, in his opinion, informed the similar ways in which the novel emerged and advanced in the two countries: "In Russia, too, modernization would lose itself in the infinite extent of territory and of social inertia, and would clash with serfdom and its vestiges."[15] According to Schwarz, Russian novelists, like their Brazilian contemporaries, "became world-historical" precisely by exploiting, rather than denying, their marginality: "Sustained by its historical backwardness, Russia forced the bourgeois novel to face a more complex reality."[16]

There is no disputing the profound and wide-ranging European impact on the development of nineteenth-century Russian literature, and this topic continues to preoccupy students of Russian literary history.[17] At the same time, one of the central analytical tasks in the investigation of a "descendent" literary phenomenon—the rise of the novel in Russia in our case—is to isolate and examine the very process itself which enabled Russian authors to embrace, assimilate, and ultimately, in unprecedented ways, transform the achievements of the European novel. In studies of the Latin American novel, subsequent reevaluations of Schwarz's model consistently raise a methodological issue that exceeds the context of Brazilian literary history, and has significance for a theoretical framework of cultural exchange in general. Namely, critics of Schwarz's model note that the "imported" properties can take root in a given context if (and only if) appropriate conditions exist to enable their reception and assimilation. In the absence of such conditions of intelligibility in a receiving system, these properties, be they ideas or artistic forms, may prove to be unviable or simply invisible.[18]

In the late nineteenth century, the prominent Russian literary scholar Aleksandr Veselovsky, a methodological pioneer in historical poetics, addressed the same problem in the course of his polemics with the migration theory in folklore studies. Without diminishing the enormous significance of contacts and influences among various populations, Veselovsky asserted: "The influence of a foreign element is always conditional upon its internal agreement with the level of that milieu in which it happens to be active. Everything contrasting too sharply with this level will remain incomprehensible, or will be understood in a particular way, in line with its surroundings. . . . Influence is more a matter of breadth than of depth, more of providing material than importing new ideas."[19] Accordingly, the impetus for the "new idea" of the novel in Russian prose should be sought neither in the European novelistic tradition; nor in the sociohistorical and institutional circumstances of nineteenth-century Russia, inauspicious as these were to the advance of the novel; nor in the interplay, however intricate and multifaceted, between the two. Rather, it was this overwhelming impetus that drove the manner in which Russian writers "turned the fragility of their institutional status to their own advantage" (as Todd put it)[20] as well as the ways in which they appropriated and transformed—or ignored and dismissed—European literary traditions. This third, and primary, operative factor in the rise of the Russian novel conceptually precedes this event's tangle of influences and sociohistorical circumstances and, therefore, has to be defined and substantiated on different grounds.

In order to account for this factor, my study provisionally suspends considerations of sociohistorical dynamics and the workings of cultural and literary exchange alike, and gives undivided attention to the emergence and development of the *discursive perspective* that engenders and sustains novelistic narration. Commenting on Lermontov's search for a narrative position for *A Hero of Our Time*, Eikhenbaum, having discussed two viable options, specifically, external narration and *Ich-Erzählung* (first-person narration), points out that the fully authoritative—self-reliant—novelistic perspective was not yet available to Russian prose of this period: "As for a third form in which narration does not need any motivation, and is conducted by an all-knowing author who is as if flying above his characters, this form appeared and was established in literature much later. . . . This form was not possible for Lermontov."[21] Building on Eikhenbaum's remark, I propose to situate the cause of writers' 1820s–50s difficulties with a "novel in prose" in their as-yet unacquired ability to get hold of a discursive perspective befitting the author of a novel. The authors' search for and discovery of this perspective—from the initial difficulties noted by 1820s–50s writers and critics to the moment when a distinctly novelistic narration was first discovered in original Russian fiction—thus constitute the substance of the novel's "rise" as it is understood in this study. Within this premise, my account of the rise of the Russian novel acquires specific literary-historical and theoretical parameters: to discern and examine the various discursive perspectives explored by prose writers in the 1820s through the 1850s, and to "capture" the moment when the novelistic authorial position was first discovered in Russian prose—on the eve of, and in anticipation of, the startlingly rapid advance of the full-fledged novel of the 1860s and 1870s.[22]

By choosing the word "reliability" as a metaphor to designate the vector and driving force of the emergence, succession, and transformation of prose forms in the 1820s–50s and, in particular, the transition from shorter prose forms specifically to the novel, I indicate an entity (a person, object, idea, etc.) that has no need of being verified, confirmed, or measured by external standards, but rather can be safely and completely trusted and depended upon. Applied to literary history, the concept of the reliability imperative denotes the writer's quest for a narrative position that is fully self-sufficient in and of itself regardless of the referential relationship between the text and the world outside it. It is precisely this position that differentiates fictional narrative from all other orders of discourse and that was first established in literary prose with the birth and advance of the novel.

The borderline of fictionality is the central concern of Dorrit Cohn's *The Distinction of Fiction*. Cohn takes it to be a consensus among the most diverse approaches to the problem of fictional referentiality that "in fictional poetics, though the concept of reference has recently been reinstated, its qualification by such terms as *fictive, nonostensive*, or *pseudo-* sufficiently indicates its nonfactual connotations, even if it denotes components of the fictional world taken directly from the world of reality."[23] As distinct from all other kinds of discourse, the commitment to verifiable documentation is suspended in fiction, which thus becomes immune to judgments of truth and falsity.

On the literary-historical "end" of scholarly inquiry into fictionality, Catherine Gallagher argues that fiction only became "distinct" with the appearance and advance of the novel. Opening up the "rise of the novel" paradigm to what she describes as the "rise of fictionality" in early eighteenth-century Europe, Gallagher examines the newly emergent English novel against preceding prose genres—explicitly incredible romances and libelous societal allegories: "The romances exalted particular courtly lords and ladies, turning them into exemplars of the virtues, whereas the *chroniques scan-*

deleuses, as the later libelous satires à la Manley were called, mocked the romance conventions and reversed their judgments. Neither form, however, sought to dispense with referential truth claims about specific individuals."[24] According to Gallagher, the novel became the very first non-referential prose genre; consequently, "the novel discovered fiction."[25] My choice of the term "reliability" as defining authorial status in fictional discourse can thus be placed in opposition to "referentiality" to the world outside the text, which is inescapable (in a form of either correspondence or contradiction) in all other narrative domains.[26]

One example of the debate on the status of the narrative agent in the fictional text can be seen in the ongoing conversation (at times a quite heated one) among prominent students of the novel about the relationship between novelistic authority and societal power. In *The Novel and the Police*, D. A. Miller applies Foucault's analyses of disciplinary institutions to the novel, arguing that novelistic discourse fulfills society's ideal of an unseen but all-seeing (panoptical) and pervasive monitor. According to Miller, the novelistic author's surfeit of power inconspicuously raises societal power structures to a level of efficiency that society itself is unable to attain through its officially designated enforcement agencies. This privileged narrative voice cannot be personified in any way, but rather "institutes a faceless and multilateral regard."[27] Cohn, who also examines the ocular and cognitive potencies of fictional texts, fundamentally disagrees with Miller's and other scholars' panoptically inspired approaches to the novel and argues for a qualitative difference between the author of the novel and all other kinds of power-wielders, be they ideological, political, penitentiary, or domestic. As evidence of the "uniquely privileged and entirely unreal"[28] powers exercised in the novel, Cohn offers the transparency of novelistic characters' hearts and minds: there is no plausible real-world somebody—whether individual or institutional—capable of directly accessing another human being's thoughts and feelings.[29] Transparency of the characters' minds thus becomes the most forceful and definitive evidence of novelistic non-referentiality.

The presentation of a character's consciousness—the hallmark of novelistic authority—is at the core of my inquiry into the rise of the Russian novel. Examination of Russian prose of the first half of the nineteenth century reveals that writers of the time experienced their authority in presenting characters' inner life as problematic and in need of justification. In the tale (*povest'*) and the cycle of tales[30]—the dominant prose genres of this period—the narrator either employs all manner of "documentary" materials (diaries, personal notes, intimate letters), or else attempts to catch the character "unaware" in a moment of spontaneous self-expression. Nevertheless, the character's inner speech and thoughts remain unavailable within the generic confines of the novella since they remain inaccessible even to the most perceptive witness and even in the most skillfully executed ambush. In the course of prose writers' explorations and experimentation, both *Ich-Erzählung* narration and external observation emerged as thoroughly inadequate in their capacity to present a character's consciousness.[31]

For instance, in Mikhail Lermontov's *Princess Ligovskaia*—one of the abandoned novels of the 1830s mentioned above—the narrator stumbles upon profound limitations that hinder his ability to interpret what he sees with any degree of confidence, despite his surveillance-enabling near-invisibility and great capacity for face-reading. He discovers, among other things, that different feelings can be manifested in the same external sign: tears, for example, might be induced by any number of emotions, from joy to despair. The narrator's helplessness to present consciousness is featured prominently in episodes wherein a given observed character, overcome with feeling, covers his or her face, or turns toward a wall: these gestures, signifying a character's own inability to express himself, and thus the limits of *Ich-Erzählung* narration, remain interpretively unavailable to the outside observer as well. Ultimately, having come to understand the decisive difference between face- and mind-reading, the narrator admits that where the character's heart and mind are concerned, only "God knows." The fact that *Princess Ligovskaia* remained unfinished can be explained by the discrepancy between Lermontov's aspiration to write a novel—the author having included this generic designation in the work's subtitle—and the position of external observation, which proved inadequate to the achievement of access to character consciousness. In *A Hero of Our Time* (1841), written, so to speak, "instead" of *Princess Ligovskaia* (and with the character-name Pechorin transposed therefrom), the cyclical form of organization presents the hero's "blank" interiority as if encircled by external views on him and his own *Ich-Erzählung*, at the same time withholding any opportunity for the mediation of this reportage.

Literary-historical accounts of the presentation of inner life in the western European novel confirm that access to character consciousness was acquired by the novelistic author at a particular historical moment. In his classic "Forms of Time and of the Chronotope in the Novel," Mikhail Bakhtin argues that the genre of the novel and the narrative technique employed in it emerged in direct response to the need to represent spheres of life hidden from outside observation: "Public life and public man are by their very essence open, visible, and audible. Therefore, the particular positioning of a person who could observe or eavesdrop on this life (a 'third person') presents no special problem, nor do the particular forms necessary for making that life public. . . . But when the private individual and private life entered literature . . . these problems were inevitably bound to arise. . . . In the process of resolving this problem, the ancient novel emerged."[32]

Bakhtin discusses some of the most significant devices developed by the novel to narrate events and experiences occurring behind closed doors. From Apuleius's Lucius the Ass, with his "enormous ears"; to Le Sage's devil Asmodée, who removes Madrid's rooftops to reveal the goings-on thus exposed; to the prominent place of crime-based plots in the history of the genre; to the significance of such characters as the adventurer, the servant (the "eternal third" in the private life of his masters), the procurer and courtesan, the novel consistently discovers and enhances such narrative strategies as are best suited to observing and analyzing private life. However, none of these strategies are adequate to the task of presenting character consciousness. Even so bold a narrative device as lifting a city's rooftops, and granting the narrator thus full exposure of characters' private dealings, brings us no closer to these characters' inner thoughts and emotions, which are, as distinct from their facial, gestural, and verbal manifestations, invisible and inaudible: however many rooftops (including those of closets and boudoirs) are removed, hearts and minds remain opaque and unpresentable.[33]

Thus in Russian nineteenth-century novellas, as in early forms of the Western novel, the author is unable to present a character's inner (as distinct from merely private) life with any degree of authority. In *Transparent Minds: Narrative Modes for Presenting Consciousness in Fiction*, Cohn observes that it was only through the establishment of realism in narrative fiction that access to character consciousness was granted to the prose writer. Cohn envisions this chronological coincidence as paradoxical, deeming it "surprising . . . that the novelists most concerned with the exact representation of life are also those who place at the live centers of their works this invented entity whose verisimilitude it is impossible to verify. . . . Narrative fiction attains its greatest 'air of reality' in the representation of a lone figure thinking thoughts she will never communicate to anyone."[34] Clearly, the common understanding of realism that Cohn employs in referring to "exactness" and "verisimilitude" does not suffice to elucidate that characteristic—presented consciousness—that she herself pinpoints as central to narrative realism.

Constructed verisimilitude—achieved through temporal, spatial, and linguistic particularity in the representation of both inner life and the external world—remains central to contemporary definitions of narrative realism, whether these construe the realist aesthetic as an aspect of ideology, rhetoric, or the "reality effect." However, transparency of minds cannot be conceptualized either as "naive" or constructed attempts at verisimilitude since this transparency is absolutely unavailable in real life.

Similarly, the term "omniscience," routinely employed to describe the narrative perspective in the realist novel, is utterly ineffective in elucidating the problem of the presentation of consciousness in fiction.[35] This term obscures rather than highlights the historical and typological boundary between the position of external observation (actualized, as noted, in pre-realist forms of the European novel and in the Russian fiction of the first half of the nineteenth century) and the transparent rendition of characters' hearts and minds—a boundary critical for substantiating the presentation of consciousness as a key constitutive trait of the realist novel. The difference between the stances of "omniscience" and external observation is only one of degree: the former expands, magnifies, or perhaps (to use Miller's term) "pulverizes" external observation to a state of depersonalized ubiquity. However, access to a character's consciousness calls for a narrative perspective qualitatively different from that of external observation, one that cannot be conceptualized as either its continuation or enhancement.

My concentration on that period in Russian literary history when the exclusive narrative stance of the novelistic author was not an aesthetic given but rather still *in the making* enables me to bring together the historical enigma of the "rise" of the Russian novel and the theoretical paradox of narrative realism formulated by Cohn. The "startling swiftness" (Freeborn) of the development of Russian prose renders it uniquely suited for interrogating the key issues of contemporary novel studies: when and how does the author acquire the authority to penetrate a character's heart/mind without relying on the elaborate, yet inadequate, narrative devices developed in pre-novelistic fiction and early forms of the novel? What are the discursive circumstances in which the narrator's audibly palpable presence gives way to the "unspeakable" (Ann Banfield) representation of character consciousness? Ultimately, how can the paradoxical connection between the transparency of figural minds and the establishment of realist aesthetics be substantiated?

Analyzing various approaches to the presentation of consciousness in texts written on the "eve" of the Russian novel, and the historical (dis)continuities evinced in these approaches, I aim to pinpoint those narrative situations wherein a character's mind at last becomes transparent to the emerging novelistic author. At the center of my book—and at the chronological midpoint of nineteenth-century Russian literary history—stands Ivan Turgenev's short novella *Mumu* (1852). That same year, Turgenev published the prose cycle *A Sportsman's Sketches*, and four years later, his first novel, *Rudin* (1856), which he subtitled "novella" (*povest'*) and which, up to the 1880 edition of his collected works, he categorized with his other writings of that generic designation. As Jane Costlow remarks, Turgenev "struggled with longer narrative, doubted his abilities in his first effort [as mentioned above, destroying *Two Generations*], and wavered throughout his career in knowing just how to name his longer prose: novellas or novels."[36] Turgenev's ultimate mastery of novelistic discourse provides a unique opportunity to feel palpably, within the text itself, those moments when the reliability-driven novella writer assumes a qualitatively new—novelistic—position.[37]

The protagonist of *Mumu*, the serf Gerasim, is deaf, mute, and illiterate. The only sound he is able to produce seems not human but rather animal, bovine, and is denoted as "mooing" (*mychanie*). Characteristically, Gerasim's face is also inexpressive, a direct result, the narrator tells us, of his deaf-muteness. With a speechless hero, the discrepancy between inner life and outer expression, between consciousness and its manifestations, reaches its apex: this mute hero's interiority lacks any means of articulation. Having chosen such a protagonist, the narrator can no longer rely on the stock devices developed in pre-novelistic prose for presenting the inner life of a speaking, hearing, facially expressive, and letter- and diary-writing character. In my reading of *Mumu*, I show how the narrator's efforts to overcome this self-imposed obstruction culminate in the discovery within the text of a new and qualitatively different narrative position—that of the novel author, empowered to render transparent the hearts and minds of his characters. This position would be consolidated and explored in Turgenev's own prose and the ensuing Russian realist novel.

The diachronic perspective assumed in my study has determined my close engagement with Mikhail Bakhtin's phenomenology of aesthetic experience developed in a range of works of the 1920s.[38] A fundamental concept of Bakhtin's aesthetic theory is the notion of authorial "outsideness" (*vnenakhodimost'*), variously translated also as "being-beyond," "extopy," and "extra-location." Bakhtin himself defined "outsideness" as the authorial exemption from the temporal and spatial—as well as the ethical and cognitive—constraints of the narrated world: "The author's fundamental, aesthetically productive relationship to the hero . . . is a relationship in which the author occupies an intently maintained position outside the hero with respect to every constituent feature of the hero— . . . space, time, value, and meaning."[39] This definition places Bakhtin's author concept among the theories of narrative that underscore the non-referential—"uniquely privileged and entirely unreal" (Cohn)—authorial status in fictional texts.

At the same time, as distinct from other approaches to the authorial stance in fictional discourse, Bakhtin views the author's exemption from the narrated world as the target of a uniquely oriented and diligently sustained *activity*. According to Bakhtin, the position of "outsideness" is not simply surrendered but must be conquered: "The author's position of being situated outside the hero is gained by conquest, and the struggle for it is often a struggle for life."[40] It is this "deadly combat" that, I believe, constitutes the domain of meaningful and responsible critical inquiry into the authorial stance in fictional narrative.

Given that "the novel discovered fiction"—as Gallagher and other historians convincingly argue—the periods in literary history in which the "rises of the novel" occurred feature the material most amenable for tracing the path toward authorial outsideness, and for recording the various ways in which the battle for this outsideness was won—or lost—both in select fictional texts and in overarching literary-historical developments.

Interest in Bakhtinian aesthetics has been on the rise since the discovery of his early manuscripts in the 1990s.[41] At the same time, while the philosophical, ethical, and artistic implications of "outsideness" have been debated by both philosophers and literary critics, this central notion of Bakhtin's phenomenology of verbal art has never been inscribed onto the living fabric of any literary history, Russian or otherwise. My study brings Bakhtin's notion of authorial outsideness to bear on the specific context of pre-novelistic Russian fiction and the rise of the Russian novel. In the course of their efforts to assume a reliable position of narration, writers left within their texts discernible trails, the succession and dynamic interconnections of which comprise the history of Russian prose in the first half of the nineteenth century. My readings of narrative fiction of the 1820s–50s, the formative years of original Russian prose, discern and explore the stages and shifts in the quest for reliable narration, from the framing narrators of the early nineteenth-century novella to the "risen" author of the realist novel.

The incredible swiftness with which Russian prose advanced from shorter forms to the novel, creating a compact and well-defined body of texts, allows us, I believe, to envision this trajectory in sharper and bolder outlines than would be possible in the case of traditions with a much more extended timeline of prose narrative in general and of the novel genre in particular. Thanks to the sharpness with which we can imagine this compressed trajectory in the Russian literary tradition, my inquiry into the emergence and rapid advance of the Russian novel yields reciprocal insight into the rise and development of the novel in the West.

The following brief episode from Russian literary history will both illustrate my interpretive and methodological premises and offer an example of one of the earliest textual manifestations of the quest for a reliable position of narration.

In 1831 Nikolai Gogol anonymously published his prose cycle titled *Evenings on a Farm near Dikan'ka*. The cycle consisted of eight stories, each attributed to a different narrator, and then collected and published by a certain Rudyi Pan'ko. Readers and critics immediately recognized the resemblance of the cycle's "mock" narrative personae to the host of authorial stand-ins in the novels of Sir Walter Scott; and subsequent criticism pursued this parallel. For instance, analyzing Gogol's narrative technique in *Dikan'ka Tales*, the prominent twentieth-century linguist and literary scholar Viktor Vinogradov is in total agreement with Gogol's contemporary Nikolai Polevoi: "If we compare the compositional functions performed by the provincials in

Walter Scott's introductions and by Rudyi Pan'ko in his role as publisher of *Evenings* and impresario to Dikan'ka's masters of rhetoric, we will have no doubt that these functions are directly related. . . . Polevoi numbered Gogol directly among [Russia's] 'little Walter Scotts.'"[42]

Vinogradov's (and Polevoi's) comments stop with Scott—any examination of Scott's *own* reliance on the framing technique and embedded narrators is left for students of the English novel; and whatever such investigations might uncover would certainly not be defined as resulting from the influence of a predecessor.[43] My study, in its broadest application, argues that Scott's employment of the mock authorship device and the employment of this device by Russian writers were motivated by needs and concerns of the same nature, concerns which thus manifested themselves in similar compositional forms. The widespread popularity of mock authorship and embedded narrators in both Russian prose (the numerous "little Walter Scotts" of the 1820s–30s) and in the earlier forms of the Western novel can be seen as a discursive effect of an authorial initiative undertaken in response to the reliability imperative. This initiative, both in European and Russian prose, consisted of *disowning* the utterance and attributing the text to an embedded narrative persona. The quest for a reliable and therefore fully authoritative position of narration first revealed itself, somewhat paradoxically, in the *renunciation* of authorship.[44]

This paradox forms the very core of the concept of narrative reliability as employed in this book. As the following chapters demonstrate in detail, the quest for a reliable narrative position unfolds precisely as the persistent and concentrated effort of *not* owning the utterance and, therefore, of *not* being identified with any of the speaking subjects. The delegation of authorship to an embedded narrator appears in this light as the simplest and most direct way to renounce textual ownership. The early European and Russian prose writers' framing of their narratives as someone else's "memoirs," "notes," or "anecdotes" anticipates and explicitly demonstrates Mikhail Bakhtin's foundational definition of novelistic discourse as "another's/someone else's word" (*chuzhoe slovo*, sometimes also rendered as the "alien word").

Understood as such, my concept of the reliability imperative differs radically from Wayne Booth's use of "reliability" in his widely employed tripartite model of the fictional text. In Booth's model, it is the *narrator's* cognitive and ethical attitudes that are at stake; the degree to which this attitude is congruent with the authorial stance determines the narrator's (un)reliability. The narrator can stand closer or farther away from the "implied author," and it is the reader's task—assisted by authorial textual signals—to measure the distance that separates the unreliable narrator from the author. In this view, the "implied author" functions as an unwavering and unfailing control gauge: he or she sets up the cognitive and moral parameters for the narrator's inadequacies, thereby establishing "a secret communion of the author and reader behind the narrator's back."[45]

My study is concerned with the literary-historical dynamics of *authorial* reliability and the process through which a fully reliable position of narration came to be discovered in Russian prose. Consequently, the object of my inquiry is this intense effort itself, rather than the ways in which the secure and stable author creatively generates and channels the reader's interest. The following chapters will show how the authorial quest for reliability informed the succession and transformation of compositional forms and narrative strategies—including the employment of reliable and unreliable narrators—both within specific texts and within the history of nineteenth-century Russian fiction.

The book proceeds along both historical and theoretical lines: on the one hand, it demonstrates how the quest for reliability on the part of the writers under discussion informed the emergence, interaction, and transformation of prose forms by closely examining the various positions of reliable narration discovered and tested by Russian writers in the 1820s and 1830s (Bestuzhev-Marlinsky, Odoevsky, Pushkin, Gogol, and Lermontov, among others), 1840s (the Natural School, early Dostoevsky), and 1850s (early Turgenev and Goncharov).

Ultimately, this is a study in historical poetics of narrative forms, namely, the realist novel. While extensive comparisons to patterns and developments in the history of western European prose are given throughout the book, my study focuses on one national tradition, Russian, and, proceeding by way of close readings of specific texts written within a specific historical epoch, explores the historical unfolding of narrative forms of literary prose. At the same time, these readings in Russian fiction allow for a new theoretical perspective on some major concerns of the study of prose genres, such as the literary-historical and structural relationship between the novella, the prose cycle, and the novel; the notion of narrative realism; and the paradoxical connection between the nineteenth-century novel's realist aesthetics and the "utterly unreal" transparency of this genre's characters.

Chapter 1 identifies an unprecedented situation in the production and perception of the utterance that arose in early modern European prose, as well as in Russian prose of the first half of the nineteenth century. I define this situation as that of the story-discourse convergence: both producer and perceiver of the nascent novelistic discourse find themselves in a position from which the object of representation and the representation itself concur in time and space; events do not precede their representation, but rather arise and develop with and within it. In the architectonics of discursive perspective thus configured, any textual action or "move" carries forward both events and their representation in such a way that, as a matter of principle, no boundary can be drawn between the two. I argue that this situation radically differentiated the emergent novelistic narration not only from preceding forms of literary prose, but also from all other orders of discourse, wherein events, whether factual or pseudo- or nonfactual, always antedate their representation in one way or another. The chapter considers some of the characteristic features evinced both in early forms of the European novel and in Russian novellas of the 1820s–30s—claims to authenticity (the "found manuscript" device), the frame composition, and transgressions of narrative levels, among others—as implications and textual symptoms of the story-discourse convergence.

Chapter 2 draws upon the hypothesis, formulated by the Russian formalists but essentially unacknowledged by literary historians, that the cyclical form of organization can be seen as precursor to the novel both in Russian and world literature. Juxtaposing Russian cyclical narratives of the 1830s (by Odoevsky, Pushkin, and Gogol, among others) with some of the most prominent western European examples of the genre, I demonstrate that in the Russian cycle, which features no explicit thematic focus nor rationale behind the selection of tellers or assemblage of tales, the tale collector comes center stage. Likewise, this narrative persona is underscored in Russian writers' engagement with the "found manuscript" tradition and, specifically, Sir Walter Scott's literary mystifications. The chapter argues that the tale collector's narrative stance is marked by the essential absence of communicative intention: collecting can be seen as the discursive mode most adequate for *non*-narrating, for conceptualizing the word as, in principle, "someone else's," as "reported" rather than uttered by him or herself. Drawing on Bakhtin's foundational definition of novelistic discourse as "another's/someone else's word," I propose that the tale collector's bereftness of communicative intention, or voice, a fundamental lack differentiating him or her from all other narrative personae—narrators, characters, and editors—actualizes the discursive perspective befitting the author of a novel.

Chapter 3 considers one of the most popular novella subgenres of the 1830s, the "society tale" (*svetskaia povest'*) and shows how, despite the literal and metaphorical presence of optical devices (microscopes, telescopes, etc.), as well as situations of spying, eavesdropping, and dissecting, the genre fails to perform the "autopsy of the human heart" to which it aspires. I situate the society tale among other genres of the 1830s, categorizing it, in particular, alongside another prominent novella subgenre of the time, the tale of the Caucasus. Ostensibly informed by quite different thematic and ideological concerns, these subgenres emerged and developed in Russian fiction of the 1830s, I maintain, in analogous response to the writerly search for narrative means to bridge the gap between external behavior and its underlying causes in the human heart and mind. The chapter further addresses the pronouncements of 1830s writers and their critics, both contemporaneous and subsequent, of Balzac as the predecessor of the society tale's artistic epistemology and, in particular, of Balzacian methods of characterization as the immediate literary influence on the society tale's predictive physiognomy. Engaging Fredric Jameson's examination of Balzac in his seminal work *The Political Unconscious* (while also polemically distancing my conclusions from some contained therein), I argue that Balzac's characterization is antithetical to the Russian society tale's epistemological and artistic impulses. Instead, I propose that *A Hero of Our Time*, the prose work Lermontov wrote upon abandoning *Princess Ligovskaia*, not only marks the author's decisive departure from the generic path of the society tale, but also stands as a nonimitative response to Balzacian narrative.

Chapter 4 juxtaposes romantic and naturalist discourses and the corresponding "schools" central to the Russian literary scene of the 1840s. Textual analysis of "physiological sketches" (from the collection *Physiology of Petersburg* [*Fiziologiia Peterburga*, 1845]) considered alongside fantastic novellas (by Odoevsky, Pogorel'sky, Somov, Vel'tman, Zagoskin, and others) reveals an unexpected affinity between romantic and naturalist poetics, most importantly, between naturalism's "epidemic craving for types" (Vinogradov) and the "doubles" abounding in romantic novellas. This affinity becomes particularly stark when "doubles" and "types" are considered not as particular character-forms, but rather as aspects of temporal and spatial organization actualized within romantic and naturalist discourses. I propose that, despite obvious differences and "school" rivalry (self-proclaimed by writers themselves, and subsequently endorsed by literary critics), romantic and naturalist poetics can be viewed as mutually complementary modes of authoritative narration. The chapter further postulates a definite—albeit inverse—correspondence between romantic writers' reliance on fantastic, credulity-straining plots (as opposed to naturalist writers' aversion to the fantastic) and the temporal and spatial specificity of events in the realist novel. This inversion, it will be argued, takes place between *siuzhet* and *fabula* (story and discourse): the emergent realist novel does not exile the fantastic—with the author, according to the common understanding of realism, now eschewing the implausible; rather, the nascent realist narrative *displaces* the fantastic onto the authorial position itself. From this perspective, realism emerges not from gradually increasing preoccupation on the part of writers with more conscientious, multifaceted representations of reality (or with fashioning such representations in the service of a "reality effect"), but rather as the result of a qualitatively new—new in its temporal and spatial organization—position of authoritative narration.

Chapter 5 examines, from the standpoint of the quest to reliably represent consciousness, two prose works that "bookend" the novelistic career of Ivan Turgenev: the novella *Mumu* (1852), written four year prior to Turgenev's first novel *Rudin* (1856), and the tale "The End of Chertopkhanov" ("Konets Chertopkhanova," 1874), which was written and incorporated into *A Sportsman's Sketches* (1852) more than twenty years after most of the other stories in the cycle, during which interval Turgenev had produced his major novels. My readings demonstrate how in both texts, the position of external observation is not only taken as far as it can narratively go, but also—albeit under two distinct sets of literary-historical circumstances—surmounted, thereby enabling unmediated presentation of figural consciousness. In *Mumu*, while on the level of narrated events, the protagonist's inability to express himself verbally is a specific physical trait, at the level of narration, this muteness manifests the incongruence between inner life and its outer manifestations that is the very core of the authorial attempt to access character consciousness. In this light, Turgenev's otherwise untypical hero models the dilemma accompanying the aspiration to narrate the inner life of *any* character, however articulate or informationally forthcoming. I argue that in *Mumu*, this situation, far from marking a narrative impasse, yields a unique resolution to the novella narrator's inability to represent consciousness. "The End of Chertopkhanov," otherwise sustaining the position of external observation in accordance with the rest of the cycle's tales, in one particular instance "betrays" its author's capacity for novelistic presentation of consciousness. This peculiar moment provides a uniquely advantageous opportunity to explore the discursive circumstances in which the fictional mind attains novelistic transparency.

Chapter 6 examines Ivan Goncharov's novel *Oblomov*, in which the transition from the short form (physiological sketch) to the novel occurs within the text itself. The landmark of this transition is the main character's dream, central both to the work's composition and the history of the novel's creation and publication. In 1849 Goncharov published a new piece in the *Contemporary* entitled "Oblomov's Dream: An Episode from an Unfinished Novel" ("Son Oblomova: Epizod iz neokonchennogo romana"). The novel itself appeared in print some ten years later, with "Oblomov's Dream" marking the end of part 1. I suggest that in *Oblomov*, it is the unique reliability status of the dream narrative that allows both author and hero to acquire a qualitatively new—novelistic—status. There being no criteria by which the contents of a dream can be judged either reliable or unreliable, the character's innermost experience becomes unimpeachably valid in comparison to his waking thoughts and feelings. The new status of the hero, achieved through the representation of the dream, stands as the major reason (aside from the obvious aspiration to later write a longer book) for Goncharov's anticipatory attribution of "Oblomov's Dream" to the novelistic genre. It was the dilemma of precisely what to do with this new hero that resulted in the almost ten-year delay in Goncharov's work on *Oblomov*: the post-dream narration had to be mastered on a qualitatively novel(istic) level. Drawing on research on the phenomenology of dream experience, I propose that the "dream origin" of the hero in *Oblomov* has crucial consequences for the life and death of its titular character, and furthermore accounts for the acknowledged peculiarity of Goncharov's work in the Russian novelistic canon of the nineteenth century.

The afterword offers an example of the continuing influence of the reliability imperative following the height of the "age of the novel" proper. I read Tolstoy's short novella *After the Ball* (*Posle bala*, 1903) as a narrative in which the authority of novelistic representation of consciousness is undermined by the increasing demands of the very quest itself for a position of absolute reliability.

Chapter One

Framing the Truth: Discourse as the Object of Discourse in the 1820s–30s

THE *POVEST'* (tale or novella),[1] the dominant genre in Russian prose of the 1820s and 1830s, consistently employed various and often quite intricate means to assure the reader that events narrated were not fictitious, but taken rather from "real life." This narrative strategy, characterizable as an authenticity claim, is readily apparent from a mere sampling of subtitles: Aleksandr Bestuzhev-Marlinsky's *Night on a Ship* (*Noch' na korable*, 1823) professes to be "From the notes of a guard officer on his way back to Russia after the campaign of 1814"; the same author's *The Clock and the Mirror* (*Chasy i zerkalo*, 1831)—"A page from a diary"; Vladimir Odoevsky's *Imbroglio* (1835)—"From a traveler's notes"; Orest Somov's *The Kikimora* (*Kikimora*, 1830)—"A story told by a peasant on the highroad"; and the same author's *Matchmaking* (*Svatovstvo*, 1832)—"From an old man's recollections of his youth."[2]

Claims to authenticity were also regularly made in early forms of the European novel, as many literary historians have noted. Jack Goody supplies the following examples from English prose of the late seventeenth and early eighteenth centuries: "Consider Defoe's attempts to establish the details of the time and place of the tale he is telling. And in fact the tale itself, in the case of *Robinson Crusoe* or *A Journal of the Plague Year*, did oscillate between truth and fiction, incorporating details of actual events. So too with time and place in Henry Fielding or Tobias Smollett. The epistolary mode, adopted by Aphra Behn in the late seventeenth century and later by Samuel Richardson in *Clarissa*, was perhaps another example of this claim."[3] Whether in western European or Russian prose, such assertions of authenticity were apparently not intended to induce readers to believe they were indeed encountering an original (or perhaps "translated") correspondence or genuine testimonial; nor did readers fall victim to such a belief, a few notable exceptions notwithstanding.[4] These claims to historical truth, consistently made in the newly emergent *fictional* genres, indicated a radical change within the concept of fictionality itself.

In "The Rise of Fictionality," Catherine Gallagher addresses this change as it pertains to early eighteenth-century English prose. Not objecting, as critics of Ian Watt's foundational paradigm commonly do, to the privileging of eighteenth-century England as a site for the emergence of novelistic discourse, Gallagher nevertheless disputes Watt's understanding of what exactly constitutes the substance of this "rise," deeming Watt's account deficient insofar as it explains "not the discovery of fiction, but its subordination to the reality principle, assuming that fiction was already an established and recognized thing that only needed to be brought down to earth by middle-class cultural hegemony."[5] She notes that the emergent novel differentiated itself not only from explicitly incredible stories (romances, fables, fairy tales, etc.) but also from the numerous late seventeenth- and early eighteenth-century credible narratives meant to be read as either factual or allegorical accounts of contemporary events and people. In pre-novelistic prose, plausible stories were spontaneously perceived as referring to the world outside the text; it was only the advent of the novel that brought "stories that were both plausible and received as narratives about purely imaginary individuals."[6] In the process of its development, the novel "discovered fiction" since, as Gallagher argues, fictionality as a concept "only became visible when it became credible."[7] Through the emergence and advance of the novel, the credible/incredible distinction became annulled as the index of fictionality.

Consequently, the essence of the novel's "rise" should be understood as the emergence of writers' and readers' aptitude for non-referential perception of narration. It is not that narrated events themselves became ever more credible (e.g., historically accurate, spatially and temporally specific, or particularly appealing to the reading public's real-life assumptions and expectations); rather, the very necessity of establishing a referential relationship—whether of contradiction or correspondence—between narrated events and the world outside the text became annulled in novelistic discourse, enabling the reader's experience of the irrelevance of the credibility factor. The sources of the new fictionality are thus to be sought not in the properties of the novelistic story, but rather on the level of discourse, namely, in the discovery of the position of narration that rendered inoperative the heretofore-unavoidable juxtaposition of narrated events and reality.

Viewed within the context of this newfound fictionality, claims to historical truth, whether in early forms of the European novel or Russian pre-novelistic prose, appear in a new light. Contrary to Goody's thesis that initiators of radically new forms of writing proclaimed their stories' authenticity to conceal these forms' fictional nature,[8] these truth-claims, which at the same time stand as *dis*claimers of authorship, stem from writerly uncertainty as to whether one's narrative is fictional *enough*, that is, whether one has succeeded in establishing and sustaining the position of narration that annuls the referential relationship between the text and the world outside it. In this chapter, drawing on underexplored aspects of Mikhail Bakhtin's "Discourse in the Novel" ("Slovo v romane")—namely, the tautological nature of his definition of novelistic narration as "discourse as the object of discourse"[9] (*slovo kak predmet slova zhe)*[10]—I will consider the claim to authenticity, alongside other major characteristics of emergent novelistic narration, as the textual symptom of a unique situation in the production and perception of the utterance that arose in early modern European prose, as well as in Russian prose of the first half of the nineteenth century. In this situation, the utterance itself, oral or written, became the object of representation within the bounds of the frame narrative—an event I posit as decisive for the emergence and development of non-referential discourse in literary prose.

Aleksandr Bestuzhev-Marlinsky's novella *Ammalat-Bek* (1832) provides an apt introductory example of how the claim to authenticity was configured in Russian fiction of the 1820s–30s. On submitting this work to Nikolai Polevoi, the editor of the literary periodical *Moscow Telegraph* (*Moskovskii telegraf*), Bestuzhev emphasized that *Ammalat-Bek* was based on real events having occurred during the recent war in the Caucasus: "This is a true story; on my own I've only added details" (*Eto istinnoe proisshestvie, i ia ot sebia pribavil tol'ko podrobnosti*).[11] To substantiate his claim, Bestuzhev subtitled the novella *A True Story of the Caucasus* (*Kavkazskaia byl'*) and went so far as to supply an extended commentary annotating its historical background. Here Bestuzhev meticulously cites all his sources, even taking care to note the rather insignificant cases in which he had departed from the facts: "The events described above are not made up. The names and personalities of the people involved have been preserved exactly: all that remains for the author of the novella is to say a few things about his modifications of the truth in certain details."[12]

At the same time, Bestuzhev appended to his letter a postscript addressed exclusively to the editor: "In order not to ruin novelistic suspense [*chtoby ne razrushat' zanimatel'nosti romanicheskoi*], this commentary can be published in the next issue."[13] Polevoi granted the author's request, and Bestuzhev's historical explanations and clarifications appeared not in the issue of *Moscow Telegraph* containing *Ammalat-Bek*, but separately, in the one following. Notably, Bestuzhev excluded this commentary from all editions of his collected works published during his lifetime. The publication history of *Ammalat-Bek* captures well the tension between the author's need to "prop up" his still incipient authority as fiction writer and his recognition, revealed in the request to publish the novella and its historical substantiation separately, that such dependence on factuality is contrary to the aesthetic needs of both writer and reader of fictional narrative.

The sources of information mentioned in Bestuzhev's commentary to *Ammalat-Bek* include not only military reports of the 1823 campaign in Dagestan but also oral accounts: personal testimonies of witnesses and participants, as well as collective memories crystallized in the form of legends, anecdotes, and "word of mouth" (*molva*)—as valid a source as strictly historical documents in justifying the novella's authenticity:

> As for the story's plot, the author received it entirely by word of mouth and did not deem it necessary to doubt any parts. . . . As for Ammalat's brutal [practice of] digging up [Russian generals'] graves, the author also did not depart a jot from [people's] reports. . . . All soldiers remember this to this day with indignation. . . . In conclusion, I should add that he was truly handsome and exceptionally gifted—all the anecdotes about his prowess in shooting and horse riding related in chapter 1 are still told in Dagestan.[14]

Bestuzhev's use of anecdotes is an example of 1820s–30s Russian prose writers' broad fascination with folklore, its various genres, themes, motifs, and images. Authors of this period who widely employed folkloric and ethnographic material include Odoevsky, Pogodin, Pogorel'sky, Polevoi, Somov, and, most prominently, Gogol. Like historical events, anonymous folk tradition served to supply these writers with an already legitimized narrative mode for them to "try on," test, and interrogate in their search for their own as yet unfounded aesthetic authority.

The penchant for authorial disclaimers reached its extreme in the practice of anonymous, pseudonymous, and mock authorship, all of which were extremely popular in early nineteenth-century Russian fiction. Prose works published anonymously or under pseudonyms and mock authors' names range from the earliest attempts to create original prose narratives at the beginning of the century all the way up to Pushkin's *Tales of the Late Ivan Petrovich Belkin* (1831). Examples include, among many others, Mariia Zhukova's *Vechera na Karpovke* (*Evenings on the Karpovka*; published anonymously in 1837), novellas by Aleksei Perovsky (writing as Antonii Pogorel'sky) and Orest Somov (posing as one Porfirii Baisky), the society tales of Elena Gan (published under the pseudonym Zinaida R-va), and a number of Gogol's early works—up to his mock-authored *Dikan'ka* cycle.

Discussing the pseudonyms of the early Gogol, Stephen Moeller-Sally remarks that "such masks were not uncommon in Russian literary life at this time, nor is it surprising that a young man just arrived from the provinces and unsure of his vocation would want to take the precaution of hiding his identity."[15] In a sense, Russian fiction of the 1820s–30s itself was a "provincial subject" (in relation to the West), still in search of its own authoritative voice, shyly concealing its ambitious experimentation under narrative masks. But there is more at work here than belatedness or "provinciality"; after all, in the early periods of the novel's development in the West, decidedly "metropolitan" authors likewise experienced, as noted by historians of European prose, an "uncertainty of vocation," evincing an unease with forms quite similar to that displayed by Russian writers in the 1820s–30s. Regarding the phenomenon of anonymous publication, James Raven remarks: "The overwhelming majority of the English novels of the eighteenth and early nineteenth centuries were published without attribution of authorship either on the title page or within the preface or elsewhere within the text. . . . Over 80 percent of all novel titles published in the 1770s and 1780s were published anonymously."[16] The disinclination to assume authorship can thus be attributed to an aesthetic concern shared by Western and Russian writers alike at the initial stages of the novel's development; these persistent claims to historical accuracy can be seen as stemming from the pursuit of reliability on the level of discourse, the quest for a narrative position that is fully authoritative in and of itself.

Perhaps the most notable manifestation of the claim to authenticity in the 1820s–30s Russian novella is the explicit presence of a narrator posited as a participant in or a witness of events, thus standing as living proof of the story's credibility. Concomitant with this practice is that the novella is typically structured as a frame narrative, whose framing narrator delegates his or her voice, or "gives the floor" as it were, to a framed narrator or narrator-participant. The most laconic marker of narrative embedding (and the most widespread, as evidenced by the examples cited above) is the novella subtitle, which simultaneously introduces a narrator-participant and frames his account. In a more extended version, the framing narrator appears as the receiver or finder of manuscripts, letters, or other "documentary" materials, which he has taken upon himself to make available to the reading public.

In Odoevsky's *Imbroglio*, the embedded narrative is presented as the testimony of a man induced to write only by force of his extraordinary experiences. The embedded narrator's lack of professional ambition attests to his trustworthiness: he is no littérateur, but rather a "mere traveler, a tourist" (*prostoi puteshestvennik, turist*)—someone who would presumably not bother to convey thus occurrences of his life had they not been truly remarkable and, most importantly, true. His simplicity of style and flaws of narration only underscore the story's authenticity:

> An acquaintance of mine described for me a strange incident that happened to him during his travels in Italy. My acquaintance is not an author and does

> not know how to tell a story eloquently and ornately; my hope is that for my readers, the incident itself shall substitute for the beauty of a story. I reiterate: my friend is not an author but a mere traveler, a tourist, who took up the pen in order to unburden his conscience.[17]

To confirm his credibility, the framing narrator might furthermore relate a rather involved backstory as to how he came upon the documents presented. In the tale "The Mute Girl, or Notes of a Recluse" ("Nemaia, ili zapiski otshel'nika"), from Zhukova's cycle *Evenings on the Karpovka*, the narrator accidentally stumbles upon an ancient manuscript in an old church:

> I approached an icon-case and began to examine it. When I touched the bottom, I felt it give way to the pressure of my finger. I pushed harder, and the little board, which had probably decayed over time, fell out, and along with it a bundle of papers. The priests knew nothing about it; after conferring upon this for a long time, they finally resolved to let me read it.[18]

In Aleksandr Vel'tman's *Radoi*, a journal is fortuitously discovered in a Turkish village, where its pages were serving as wrapping paper. The title and beginning of the manuscript are missing—already used by a local merchant to pack ground coffee. The remaining fragments of the manuscript's opening are offered to the reader in their authentically damaged condition, with ellipses designating lacunae in the text:

> kneel, and the other one would misbehave so that he might kneel beside his comrade; and in class and at the desk together, compose poems: Hooray! Vacation is here!—Together . . .[19]

In Nikolai Pavlov's *The Name-Day* (*Imeniny*, 1832), the framing narrator presents a manuscript given him by a friend as an excuse for the latter's misogyny, and to explain his limp:

> With these words, he unlocked a drawer of his desk, took out a small notebook, and gave it to me with a laugh: "Take it and read, you'll find it will come in handy: one of my acquaintances describes here a rather unusual incident." I kept the manuscript that I received from N.[20]

Here N.'s denial of his self-evident authorship of the manuscript is motivated on the homodiegetic level by his embarrassment as to the origin of his injury; but himself subdelegating narrative authority to an alleged "acquaintance"—such that when we finally hear the story, it comes from a narrator embedded now at a second remove—N. in effect marshals the same "credibility anxiety" employed by the novella's author to increase the sense of authenticity.

As in Vel'tman's *Radoi*, the fragmented state of the manuscript is adduced as if to bolster its realness and historical accuracy. The framing narrator admits he is unable to decipher the manuscript's conclusion due to ink stains on the last page, and substitutes ellipses for the illegible text:

> (At this point in the manuscript, many words could not be made out: they had been spattered with ink, apparently because the pen had been thrown onto the paper.) I once secretly observed how . . . cried furtively . . . there is . . . not enough room for him and me under one sun . . . we met . . . we both fell. He did not rise; I now walk with a limp.[21]

In both novellas, the fragmented form of the manuscript confirms its authenticity by stressing that the framing narrator has no pretensions to authorship—he refuses to provide what is missing, even for the sake of clarity and coherence. The employment of such fragments, with their presenter either unwilling or unable to decipher them or fill in their gaps, is a "hands-off" strategy commonly used to strengthen narratorial trustworthiness in Russian novellas of the 1820s–30s.

Often in this period the "artifact" finding its way into the narrator's possession is someone's correspondence. For instance, in Orest Somov's *Novel in Two Letters* (*Roman v dvukh pis'makh*, 1832), the framing narrator introduces two letters he has accidentally found; he does not know the surname of his (or the letters') hero—this going unmentioned in the correspondence itself—and does not wish to make one up. Once again, an artless style is said to attest to authenticity:

> I came by chance to possess these two letters written by Lev Konstantinovich . . . I don't know the last name, since both are signed simply *Leon*. I have endeavored neither to improve their style, which was somewhat careless, nor to translate the French phrases with which they abound. . . . I present these two letters to the world because they provide, if not an amusing account, at least a full one.[22]

The epistolary form—with the framing narrator preparing purportedly authentic, real-life letters for publication—was common in Russian novellas of the 1820s–30s. For instance, Bestuzhev's *Novel in Seven Letters* (*Roman v semi pis'makh*, 1824) and Pushkin's fragment *A Novel in Letters* (*Roman v pis'makh*, 1829) are structured similarly to Somov's work. The popularity of the epistolary form can be explained in large part by the letter's "natural" status as a ready-made narrative needing only to be "found."[23]

Other "real-life" genres that appeared to lend themselves readily to narrative embedding include diaristic or memoiristic notes (*zapiski*) and journals. Examples of early nineteenth-century novellas that rely on constructed personal documents are plentiful; to name a few: In Bestuzhev's *Ammalat-Bek* the reader is presented with Colonel Verkhovsky's letters and Ammalat-Bek's diaries. In Odoevsky's *Princess Zizi* (*Kniazhna Zizi*, 1839), the embedded narrator, the elderly Mariia Ivanovna, relates the life story of the heroine Zizi by leafing through her private letters. Evdokiia Rostopchina's *Rank and Money* (*Chiny i den'gi*, 1838) begins with the hero's letter to his sister, followed by excerpts from his diary. The formats of letters, journals, and diaries, whether private or intended for publication, were hardly a novelty in late eighteenth- and early nineteenth-century Russia; but they acquired a new significance in the frame novellas of the 1820s–30s, convenient as they were for the delegation of narrative authority.

The authenticity claim in Russian prose of this period also informed the archetypal features of the novella narrator, namely: the quality of being a good, compassionate listener; a commitment to faithfully record witnesses' and participants' testimonies; a tenacious memory enabling the reproduction verbatim (*slovo v slovo*) of the lengthy monologues of their interlocutors; and finally an immense and burning curiosity. Examples of narrators driven exclusively by this last impetus—to the point of sacrificing their own affairs and even well-being—abound in the novellas of the period. For instance, in Somov's *The Sign*, subtitled *The Story of a Traveler* (*Vyveska, rasskaz puteshestvennika*, 1829), the narrator, in order to have a valid reason for approaching a French barber whose life story he is dying to hear, is on the verge of having his blood drawn or having a healthy tooth extracted:

> My curiosity was strong; I indulged this tendency of mine by always blindly following its whims. . . . I do not know what I might have dared to do; perhaps—to what might an overwhelming passion not lead one!—perhaps I would have even resolved to let my blood be drawn without any need or have a tooth pulled just to satisfy my curiosity by making the acquaintance of the barber and learning of his adventures.[24]

The claim to authenticity also requires events and situations favorable to the narrator's acquisition of the necessary data. Thus, often the narrator is a traveler willing to set out anywhere at a moment's notice to obtain sought-for information. The common late eighteenth- and early nineteenth-century persona of the traveling writer—one who provides, earnestly or mockingly, an account of his own impressions and experiences on a journey—acquired a qualitatively new status in 1820s–30s novellas: mobility became a prerequisite for the authoritative and efficient presentation (i.e., the embedding) of *other* narrators' stories.[25]

One example of these attributes that falls outside the chronological span of this chapter is Ivan Turgenev's *A Sportsman's Sketches* (1852). Despite its status as temporal outlier, Turgenev's prose cycle continued, and in many ways consummated, the tradition of the early nineteenth-century frame narrative. In *A Sportsman's Sketches*, the narrator's mobility, in his constant search for game, as well as his capacity for sympathetic listening and faithful recording, lay at the core of the narrative organization of the tales in the cycle (all of which employ, in a more or less extended version, the embedding technique).

The framing composition was also prominent in early forms of the European novel. According to David Lodge: "The rise of the English novel in the eighteenth century began with the discovery of new possibilities of mimesis in prose narrative, through the use of characters as narrators—the pseudo-autobiographers of Defoe, the pseudo-correspondents of Richardson—thus making the narrative discourse a mimesis of an act of diegesis, diegesis at a second remove. These devices brought about a quantum leap in realistic illusion and immediacy."[26] Lennard Davis makes a similar albeit more radical assertion, positing the narrative frame as a primary compositional marker of the early novel, one that signified the new genre's rupture with preceding forms of literary prose: "Because novelists deny that they are creating an illusion, they are frequently forced into the position of claiming that they are only editor to some found document. This act of authorial disavowal helps establish the rim of prestructure which makes the novel a framed narrative, as opposed to the romance."[27] Thus Davis argues that the embedded narrator was not introduced to novelistic discourse as part of some sequential development (i.e., as a device for further authentication or "realistic illusion"), but rather emerged simultaneously with and within this discourse as its central constituent.

Several scholars have deemed Davis's conclusion peremptory; frame composition, they note, does not always jibe with a given writer's denial of his or her narrative's fictionality and with a text's identification as "novel" either by seventeenth- and eighteenth-century readers or by hindsight-equipped posterity.[28] On a broader level of disagreement, Davis's analysis has been criticized for reducing the scope and scale of the transformative historical changes of the early modern period. According to Michael McKeon, for instance, Davis's version "render[s] invisible all other expressions of the epistemological revolution of the seventeenth century—most notably the rise of the new philosophy of empiricism, the long and complicated revolution in historiography, and the crisis in biblical exegesis."[29] In McKeon's own influential view of the novel's rise, early novelists' claims to historicity, and the novel's participation in the fact/fiction discourse generally, should be seen as one expression of the larger, ultimately all-encompassing concern of "how to tell the truth in narrative"[30]—a concern that, according to McKeon, became central not only to literary but also social, scientific, and religious domains in the late seventeenth century.

At the same time, McKeon's complex and nuanced examination of the epistemological crisis of the seventeenth century brings into sharper relief the particular position of emergent novelistic narration vis-à-vis the fact/fiction dichotomy, a position unique among discursive practices. As I argued above, drawing on Gallagher's examination of the "rise" of novelistic fictionality, the heretofore-mandatory establishment of a referential relationship between narrated events and the world outside the text became, for the reader of the novel, annulled. I would maintain that this release from the requirement to interrogate an utterance's relationship to reality—obligatory in other communicative situations, and in previous forms of literary prose—constitutes a principal difference between nascent novelistic narration and other (scientific, historical, religious, etc.) discourses of the early modern period. This fundamental distinction retains its validity despite the overall instability, convincingly explicated by McKeon, of social and generic categories in the seventeenth and early eighteenth centuries. It is evident that the utterance's attribution to reality is a prerequisite for discrimination between the "factual" and the "fictional"; in the absence of this prerequisite, the very question of the utterance's correspondence to or contradiction of that reality becomes extraneous. Thus it would seem that the narrative epistemology of the emergent novel cannot be adequately examined alongside other discursive practices of the time, but should be approached from a different analytical perspective.

In such a perspective, I believe, the framing composition takes center stage. Literary scholars have noted that the phenomena of non-referential narration and the framing narrator are not diffused along the timeline of the development of artistic prose (whether in western Europe or over a century later in Russia); rather, they coincide historically or, at a minimum, distinctly overlap. To account for this coincidence, I propose to dissociate the frame composition from the problematics of the fact/fiction dichotomy (which is inadequate to address non-referential narration) and to examine instead a correlation between narrative embedding and the very essence of novelistic fictionality, that is, the annulment of the utterance's attribution to reality.[31] Namely, further exploring Gallagher's assertion that the difference between old (pre-novelistic) and new kinds of fictionality is to be sought from the perspective of the utterance's perception, I would argue that any utterance whose source can be (however provisionally) situated in time and space engenders, on the part of the perceiver, this utterance's attribution to reality, and an ensuing evaluation of either correspondence to or contradiction of that reality.

The temporal and spatial cohesion of the speaking subject necessitates a similarly unified localization on the part of the perceiver, and the resulting misalignment in space-time between speaker and perceiver enables the cognitive and axiological evaluation of the utterance in accordance with the perceiver's assumptions and expectations. The utterance may be deemed true, false, or something in between, but the very possibility of such judgment derives from the architectonics of its perception—the utterance's attribution to reality. Such attribution stems not from the content of the utterance, but rather from the position of the perceiver him or herself: the perceiver's *own* temporal and spatial localization (itself enabled by the coherency of the speaker's position) compels the inevitable attribution of the utterance's content to reality.

In the frame narrative, the impulse to situate the source of narration within a coherent temporal and spatial context—an impulse inevitably realized in utilitarian discourse—is blocked. The "composite" arrangement of such a telling, its being made up of framing narrator and narrator-participant, hinders the localization of the speaking subject in time and space; consequently, the reader loses the basis for his or her own localization and, with it, the hitherto compulsory anchoring of narrated events to reality. Whether these events correspond to or contradict the reader's beliefs or expectations, *at the moment of their perception* (i.e., reading), the perceiver's experience consists in that of the annulment of the utterance's attribution to reality—annulment enabled by the lack of a very position from which to undertake such attribution. It is likely the unmistakable experience of their *own* release from temporal and spatial localization that accounts for early readers' mistrust of the new narratives' factuality—even that of otherwise "believable" texts—despite writers' assertions that their stories were historically accurate.

Furthermore, the emergence of the character-narrator—an autobiographer, memoirist, correspondent, or witness—within the bounds of the frame narrative enabled an unprecedented circumstance in the production and perception of the utterance. Namely, there occurred a situation in which the *utterance itself*—an autobiography, memoir, journal, letter, or oral story—became the object of representation. As a result of this coincidence, both producer and perceiver of the novelistic utterance found themselves in a position from which narrated events and the event of narration itself seemed concomitant in time and space; events did not precede their narration, but rather occurred and developed with and within it.

This particular situation in the history of literary prose, both Russian and western European, finds its immediate theoretical validation in Mikhail Bakhtin's approach to the specificity of novelistic discourse. According to Bakhtin's classic formulation, the object of novelistic representation is language itself; a novel character is, first and foremost, a speaking subject:

> The fundamental condition, that which makes a novel a novel, that which is responsible for its stylistic uniqueness, is the *speaking person and his discourse* . . . . The speaking person and his discourse in the novel is an object

> of *verbal* artistic representation. A speaking person's discourse in the novel is not merely transmitted or reproduced; it is, precisely, *artistically represented* and thus—in contrast to drama—it is represented *by means of* (authorial) *discourse.*[32] (Emphasis in original)

Novelistic discourse is "non-direct speaking";[33] it is discourse about discourse; or discourse that has another discourse (or more precisely, *another's* discourse) as the object of representation. In this light, the early modern novel's frame composition, in which a character-narrator relates, orally or in writing, his or her own story can be seen as the most explicit demonstration of Bakhtin's thesis. Bakhtin himself discusses the framed narrator as one of the basic forms for organizing discourse in the novel, and he supplies examples from Russian fiction of the 1820s–40s to support and illustrate his argument.[34] Bakhtin also observes that prose genres featuring embedded narrators—"the confession, the diary, travel notes, the biography, the personal letter," and others—"play an especially significant role in structuring novels, sometimes by themselves even directly determining the structure of a novel as a whole—thus creating novel-types named after such genres."[35] Precisely these generic forms are prominently represented among exemplars of both the early European novel and the Russian novella of the first half of the nineteenth century.

As developed in literary theory, Bakhtin's insights along these lines, and his appeal for a principally different approach to novelistic narration generally, have served to foreground especially the heterogeneity of novelistic discourse, its stratification (social, professional, linguistic, etc.), and multi-accentual nature. Bakhtin's own terminology—from heteroglossia, hybridization, double-voiced word to polyphony and dialogism—has stood above all to emphasize the novel's non-unitary nature and the interaction of different languages (each representing a "particular way of viewing the world")[36] within the novelistic utterance. At the same time, the essentially tautological nature of Bakhtin's formulation—"discourse as the object of discourse"—implies not only the existence of (at least) two discourses—one being represented, the other performing the representing—but also these discourses' synchronous, simultaneous development: their complete and utter convergence in time and space.

It is precisely this total coincidence that differentiates even the most nuanced "transmission," or "reproduction" of another's speech, from its artistic representation—a principal difference, Bakhtin insists, between the modality of the word of another in the novel vs. utilitarian speech genres. And yet the predominant methodological orientation toward the novel's heterogeneity, that reigning conception that seeks to draw boundaries, however intricate and interpenetrating, between discourses, cannot fully explicate the consequences of these discourses' synchronous unfolding.

Beyond studies of the novel, several theorists have called into question the methodological validity of the story vs. discourse model of narrative analysis (known by a variety of parallel terminological dichotomies beginning with the Russian formalists' *fabula* and *siuzhet*). This model remains today virtually unchallenged in the practice of literary interpretation, but thirty years ago, for instance, Barbara Herrnstein Smith argued that it inevitably posits the conceptual primacy of events, or "story," over the narration of events, and thus cannot be meaningfully applied, first of all, to fictional narratives, for which "there evidently are *no* sets and sequences of events that, already arranged in some particular way, could be spoken of as *re*-arranged" in the course of narration.[37] Jonathan Culler, similarly questioning the "studies of point of view that have dominated American narrative theory in the past,"[38] proposes to view the story, or *fabula*, "not as the reality reported by discourse but as its product."[39] Culler does not dismiss the two-level model altogether, but argues for the simultaneous unfolding of story and discourse, their mutual conditioning rather than consecution.

Neither Smith nor Culler sees any contraindications for extending their views on story-discourse mutuality to a variety of, and ultimately all, narratives. Culler supports his thesis with examples from fiction (*Oedipus Rex* and George Eliot's *Daniel Deronda*), the case studies of Freud, and tales of personal experience (Labov's "natural narratives"), demonstrating that in all these communicative situations, the story emerges both as prior to and independent of discourse—that is, as its cause—and, simultaneously, as the effect or outcome of discursive developments. Likewise, Smith maintains that in all verbal transactions, fictional and nonfictional alike, the story is generated, first and foremost by a teller himself or herself, through processes of "inferring, construing, projecting, hypothesizing, imagining, anticipating, and so forth,"[40] which activities occur simultaneously with the event of narration:

> For like our imaginings of events that never occurred, our knowledge of past events is usually not narrative in structure or given in story-like sequences: on the contrary, that knowledge is most likely to be in the form of general and imprecise recollections, scattered and possibly inconsistent pieces of verbal information, and various visual, auditory, and kinesthetic images—some of which, at any given time, will be more or less in or out of focus and all of which will be organized, integrated, and apprehended as a specific "set" of events only in and through the very act by which we narrate them as such.[41]

My emphasis on story-discourse convergence as the foundational characteristic of emergent novelistic fictionality resonates strongly with these scholars' search for a framework that has at its core the mutual conditioning of narrated events and events of narration. At the same time, I would argue that story-discourse simultaneity in fictional narrative differs radically from that extant in "serious" or "natural" narrative, wherein events, whether factual or (as in lies or daydreams) pseudo- or nonfactual, always antedate their representation in one way or another. Despite the fact that, as Smith convincingly argues, real-life events and experiences become a "story" only in the course of their narration, the very attribution of this evolving story to reality functions as an essential operative component in the production and perception of nonfictional narrative, a component with profound implications for the "inferring, construing, projecting, hypothesizing, imagining, anticipating, and so forth" through which the story is generated in the course of narration by both teller and audience.[42] Discussing Freud's case studies, Culler asserts (following Freud himself) that while it is not possible in practice to isolate an actual occurrence in a patient's life from the "story" as it emerges in the course of psychoanalytic interpretation, it is also impossible, for patient and analyst alike, to reconcile oneself to this indeterminacy:

> Freud . . . recognizes that the reader or analyst can never calmly accept this conclusion [that what actually happened is unknowable] when he has engaged with a narrative. There is no happy compromise, for the force, the ethical import of a narrative, always impels the reader or analyst toward a decision. The ethical and referential dimensions of narrative, that is to say, make such questions of compelling interest, even though the theorist recognizes that the attempt to opt for one perspective rather than another will still give one the same narrative.[43]

Culler's assertion is valid, I believe, for any nonfictional narrative: however vague, elusive, and ultimately irretrievable the reality of an event, both speaker and audience of a nonfictional utterance are inevitably driven ("compelled") by the imperative to distinguish its "what" and "how," that is, the event and the discursive means of its rendering in a specific here-and-now communicative situation. This activity becomes annulled only in fictional discourse, wherein narrated events do not precede the event of their narration. The definitive voiding of the "ethical and referential dimensions of narrative" (Culler), so far from constituting a mere absence, engenders a perspective of utterance formation and reception qualitatively different from all other communicative situations. In this chapter and throughout the book I attempt to account for the implications of this unparalleled situation in the production and perception of the utterance. Specifically, I will view story-discourse simultaneity as a prime operative factor in the development of the novelistic form and as a major analytical resource for the history and theory of the novel.

In literary-historical perspective, the story-discourse convergence differentiated nascent novelistic fictionality from preceding forms of literary prose, which were "referential." Non-referential perception of the utterance, which Gallagher posits as the hallmark of novelistic fictionality, is grounded, first and foremost, in the simultaneity of events and their narration, a synchronicity that was established with and within the frame composition. Indeed, the perceiver's attribution of an utterance to reality (and the resulting judgment as to its correspondence to or contradiction of that reality) implies his or her capacity to distinguish the "content" of the utterance from the narration of this content. But when the utterance itself becomes the object of representation, such a differentiation is irrelevant; given the simultaneity of story and discourse, events (whether historically accurate, credible, or explicitly improbable) no longer precede their narration.

One of the most glaring effects of the story-discourse non-differentiation can be seen in a characteristic of the early modern novel that has received considerable scholarly attention: heightened writerly awareness of the artfulness of one's creations, especially that deliberate and strategic transgression of boundaries between textual and extratextual levels that narratologists term metalepsis.[44] In a study devoted entirely to the workings of this phenomenon, Debra Malina observes that metaleptic tendencies (the obtrusive narrator; synchronization of the time of narrated events with that of their narration or reading; "entrapment" of the reader in the text; etc.) are apt to intensify during periods of substantial change in the conception of fictionality; she notes that such prose writers of the English eighteenth century as Swift, Fielding, and Sterne especially "indulged" in metalepsis.[45]

The metaleptic effects so prominent in the early novel likely stem from the architectonics of the production and perception of the utterance, by which differentiation between story and discourse was rendered extraneous. In discourse thus configured, any textual action or "move" advanced both events and their narration, such that it was impossible to draw a boundary between the two. This experience of non-differentiation between story and discourse gave authors "permission" (or perhaps even encouragement) to deliberately blur the boundaries between narrative levels. The metaleptic effects can thus be seen as a writerly response to the irrelevance of the story-discourse distinction, and as a "symptom" of this experience.

Another such symptom, but one bearing the opposite tendency of *downplaying* artifice, is the authenticity claim, the writer's denial of his or her connection to the narrative. These two writerly initiatives, both prominent in early forms of the novel, can be viewed as mutually complementary responses to the strange experience of story and discourse having converged; to the concomitant absence of some "point of application" that would be strictly, exclusively authorial. In the face of this absence, the author undertakes to locate him or herself either "everywhere," as in the "self-conscious" novel (Alter); or, as in the "factual" novel (Davis), nowhere, effectively "disowning" the utterance. Still, like the fact/fiction dichotomy discussed above, the notion of metalepsis cannot suffice to explicate the underlying processes that engender these textual effects: metalepsis conceptualizes the interpenetration of story and discourse, their non-differentiation, as the continuous transgression of a boundary, and thus relegates what is properly understood as story-discourse simultaneity or convergence (a crucial development in the production and perception of the utterance) to a matter of consecution.

In Russian fiction of the 1820s–50s, we find another textual effect of that convergence of narrated events with the event of narration that arose when the utterance itself became the object of representation within the bounds of the frame narrative; namely, numerous examples, of which only a few are cited below, show the framing narrator breaking out of his proclaimed role as mere observer, sympathetic listener, or faithful recorder, and becoming more and more engaged in events he or she initially only intended to frame. Ultimately, such narrators find themselves *characters* in their own stories, with boundaries between frame and embedded story blurred.

The simplest manifestation of this involvement consists in the framing narrator's compulsion not merely to publish available documents, but to actively search for any missing data, to compare the testimony (written and oral) of different characters, to correlate various pieces of "evidence," and so on. Often, eager to obtain all necessary information, the narrator "gives the floor" to a lengthy succession of interpolated narrators, exploiting the technique of narrative embedding to its maximum and producing a compositional effect sometimes metaphorically dubbed a "Chinese box" or, more appropriately for our subject, a "Russian nesting doll." Odoevsky's novella *The Apparition* (*Prividenie*, 1838) is a fitting—perhaps even crowning—example of this framing technique. The novella is organized as a story within a story within a story within a story: the narrator, Irinei Gomozeiko, relates a story he has heard from another person, who had in turn heard the prehistory of this story from someone else (his landlady) and himself participated in its denouement.[46] On top of all this, there is an "I" who narrates the whole proceeding: an anonymous fellow passenger with Gomozeiko and others in the coach where the recorded conversation takes place.

In Vel'tman's novella *Radoi*, the framing narrator, upon rescuing, as mentioned, a Russian-language manuscript from being repurposed to wrap the goods of Turkish merchants, does not allow himself simply to assume that the manuscript is a journal in the sense of personal diary—might it not be a misplaced submission of fiction to a literary journal?

> Here the manuscript ended. But what strange circumstances: rereading it when it was already prepared for publication, I . . . fell to thinking: "Is this a

journal of someone's life, or just a journal [or magazine] story in the full sense of the word?"[47]

After a moment of hesitation, the narrator does find evidence of the manuscript's authenticity: specifically, he recalls his own chance meeting with one of its characters, a Serbian named Radoi. The uncertainty of the manuscript's status—is it truly a confessional account, or a fictional *Ich-Erzählung*?—encourages and intensifies the narrator's own implication in the events narrated; in the end, his own witness—his having personally encountered one of the journal's characters—is called upon to, as it were, certify it. Thus does the narrator step out of the frame of his story and into its world, becoming a character in an account that seemed at first to have nothing to do with him personally, and that he had simply intended to "prepare for publication."[48]

The novella *The Convent Girl* (*Monastyrka*, 1830) by Antonii Pogorel'sky (the pen name of Aleksei Perovsky) offers another example of narratorial intervention and immersion into the story world. The text begins as a traditional frame narrative, with a traveler-narrator fortuitously coming upon a batch of letters written by a Smol'nyi Convent graduate. Three of these missives are then presented to the reader verbatim as material proof of the narrator's reliance on documentary sources. But soon after finding the letters, the narrator becomes acquainted with their author, the former convent girl Aniuta, who expands the story behind and beyond the events described in the letters. Other witnesses provide information Aniuta could not have known firsthand:

> Soon thereafter I met the author of the letters. She conveyed to me all the adventures of her life and allowed me to publish them. Some other participants in these adventures added parts that had been missing in her telling; and this is how the book that is now being offered to the public was put together.[49]

The framing narrator of *The Convent Girl* thus distributes his evidentiary materials among secondary narrators—a common framing technique; but in the course of establishing his story's authenticity, he also winds up taking a far bolder, even life-altering step. In the final pages of the novella, where the current whereabouts of the main characters are related, the reader discovers that while tracking down information for his story, the framing narrator (here finally identified as Antonii Pogorel'sky) met one of the story's characters, Gapochka, and eventually married her, thereby becoming a relative, neighbor, and confidant of the main character of his story, the convent girl Aniuta:

> There Agaf'ia Alekseevna Pogorel'skaia, whom you, dear readers, knew under the name of Gapochka, lives with her husband. After this introduction, you will surely conclude that Gapochka has married me, and you would not be wrong in your supposition. We have been living happily together for three years now.[50]

In *The Convent Girl*, the narrator-character conversion evinces a certain symmetrical or "bookend" distribution: the novella starts with a traveling narrator relating an account of his main character from an authorly distance, and ends with this narrator a part of his characters' lives, albeit standing at a remove of three years elapsed since the events of the story. A similar "post factum" plunging of the narrator into the story world occurs in Odoevsky's *Princess Zizi*: after hearing Zizi's life story, the narrator meets his heroine at a masquerade and falls in love with her. Somov's novella *The Sign* offers an example in which the framing narrator becomes a character whose participation in events narrated is not only acknowledged in the epilogue, but decisive to the outcome of the plot. Before presenting the French barber Achilles' *Ich-Erzählung* story, the narrator assures us of its authenticity:

> Here is his story almost word for word, with the omission of only some interjections when, carried away by his telling, he would do something wrong; and some brief outbursts against his boys when the water was too cold or the pliers too hot, etc.[51]

Achilles reveals his past adventures and also the source of his present grief: the father of his beloved Celina does not want the young couple to marry. The barber's story ends here; the narrative, however, continues. Back at the hotel where he is staying, the narrator encounters a peer of France he happens to know, and he asks this influential acquaintance to help the barber. The peer is eager to oblige; the stubborn father's resistance is overcome, and Achilles and Celina join hands in matrimony—a happy resolution possible only due to the narrator's intrusion into the course of narrated events: "I congratulated the young couple and bid them farewell, there occurring to me the sweet thought that I was, if indirectly, still a cause of their happiness."[52] In *The Sign*, then, the initially clear-cut division between frame and embedded narrative is ruptured when part of the frame becomes integral to the story itself.

In Odoevsky's novella *The Apparition*—the quintessential example, as noted, of the framing technique in Russian prose—the narrator's change of status is even more pronounced. The narrator presiding over the work's nucleus—that is, embedded at the deepest level, fourth out of four—is an "old man" relating a "true story" (*istoriiu istinnuiu*) from his youth, when he was one in a group of servicemen billeted in a castle. Encouraged by their hostess, a charming countess, they dress up as ghosts in order to play a trick on her son; this ends tragically when the young man, half-asleep and afraid of the dark, fires his gun and kills his own mother, who had thrown a sheet over herself as one of the phantoms. The story is ghastly, as the narrator admits, but there is nothing unnatural, he insists, in the course of its events. The "old man" is a positivist and an admirer of Voltaire; the point of his narrative is to undermine what he laments as the current fashion for "scary" or "romantic stories" (*strashnaia istoriia*; *romanticheskaia istoriia*), which he dismisses as "ravings" (*bredni*). Apparitions, that is, have rational (albeit in this case lugubrious) explanations:

> We left the mournful house where we had spent so many pleasant days. I still do not know how it all turned out; at least if I've never seen a ghost, I nevertheless have been one myself, and that counts for something. All ghost stories are like this. [Regarding this incident], people have made up, I'd wager, God knows what, but as you see, it was a simple matter.[53]

However, when the narrator finishes his story, "a certain young man," who had been "listening with great attention" but so far remained silent, suddenly speaks up:

> You have related this event with great precision; I know about it myself since I belong to the family in which it occurred. But there is one thing you do not know, namely, that the countess is in good health to this day, and that it was not she who led you to the son's room, but a real ghost that dwells in the castle still.

Now it is the narrator's turn to fall silent:

> The narrator went pale. The young man continued: "There was much talk about this incident; but nothing could explain it. What is notable, though, is that all those who have told the story of this incident died two weeks after doing so." Having uttered these words, the young man took his hat and left the room. The narrator went paler still.[54]

His account having received this crucial amendment, the "old man's" credibility is undermined; he is transformed from narrator of a story he has just told to character therein, the sense of demotion emphasized by his state of speechlessness. Now he is subject to all the risks potentially befalling a character in events still ongoing:

> Some days later we learned that our mocker of ghosts had taken ill, and very dangerously so. His physical sufferings were accompanied by fanciful dreams. It constantly seemed to him that a pale woman in a white veil was trying to drag him from his bed, and just imagine—added Irinei Modestovich in a tragic voice—in exactly two weeks, the guests in Mar'ia Sergeevna's drawing room were fewer by one![55]

And so, while the narrator of Pogorel'sky's *The Convent Girl* deliberately inserts himself into the story world after the denouement of events, and the narrator of Somov's *The Sign* voluntarily leaves his frame to bring about a happy ending, Odoevsky's *The Apparition* features a narrator-into-character conversion that is inadvertent, but the most ominous and final of them all. Here events narrated "with great precision" turn out to have been misunderstood, and the "old man" is forced to reexamine his participation in them. This is a narrator thus deprived of his narrating (or framing) privileges by the surfacing of a superior, more authoritative frame—that provided by a "young man with a convincing, cold voice."[56] Along with his change of status, moreover, the "old man" experiences a transformation in worldview: the "impenitent Voltairean" whose "only belief is that two times two equals four"[57] is converted into a visionary tormented by "fanciful dreams."

My last example of the shakiness of a narrator's footing is another of Odoevsky's novellas, *The Sylph*, subtitled *From the Notes of a Reasonable Man* (*Sil'fida, iz zapisok blagorazumnogo cheloveka*, 1836). The novella begins with seven letters written by a young man named Mikhail Platonovich who, having settled on the estate of his late uncle, pursues a relationship with his neighbor's daughter Katia, eventually proposing marriage. At the same time, he becomes fascinated with the books on mysticism and alchemy he has discovered in his uncle's house. As a result of one of Mikhail Platonovich's mystical experiments, a rose in a vase filled with water opens to reveal a tiny beautiful woman, a sylph. After the hero's path into magic has been recounted via his letters, there follows another missive, this one written to the narrator by Katia's father, Gavrila Sofronovich, who expresses therein his suspicion that something is amiss with his daughter's fiancé: Mikhail Platonovich has locked himself in his house, and spends his days staring at a vase filled with clear water. The next part of the narrative is titled "The Story" ("Rasskaz"), and represents the account of the framing narrator, the "reasonable man" of the novella's subtitle. Having consulted a doctor regarding Mikhail Platonovich's bizarre behavior, this individual decides to take action; but his account is interrupted by "Excerpts from Mikhail Platonovich's Journal" ("Otryvki iz zhurnala Mikhaila Platonovicha"), which once again provide the young man's perspective on events, recording his visions, revelations, and conversations with the sylph.[58]

The "Journal" becomes incomprehensible, and the narrator resumes his account of his and the doctor's fight for Mikhail Platonovich's sanity. With the help of bouillon baths, special mixtures, and fancy food and drink, they eventually succeed. The recovered Mikhail Platonovich marries Katia as originally planned; in their final recorded conversation, the narrator gets the impression that Mikhail Platonovich might be on the verge of sliding back into his internal spiritual world, but as the former comments, "this was his last flare-up" (*eto byl ego poslednii pripadok*); since then he has been "a man like any other" (*chelovek kak drugie*) and finds lasting satisfaction in his bouillon baths.[59] Thus in *The Sylph*, once Mikhail Platonovich as narrator-participant (i.e., in his capacity as letter-writer and diarist) has been deprived of a unique viewpoint, he no longer has anything to narrate. His relegation solely to the status of character coincides with his having become a typical, fully decipherable person; that is, concomitant with his loss of narratorhood is the loss of his very interiority.

These and other patterns of the narrator-character conversion to a great degree determine the variety and peculiarity of narrative strategies, compositional forms, and vicissitudes of the plot in the Russian novella of the first half of the nineteenth century. Like the metaleptic tendencies observed in the European novel, these transferences in Russian pre-novelistic fiction between the framed and the framing, between characters and narrators, story and discourse, were informed by that story-discourse convergence established when the utterance became the object of representation. In the next chapter, I will argue that the prose cycle, a favorite mode of organizing discourse in Russian fiction of the 1820s–50s, offered a qualitatively new, in relation to both narrators and characters, discursive position from which to sustain the experience of story-discourse simultaneity—namely, that of the tales' *collector*.

Chapter Two

In Search of Lost Voice: The Tale Collector in the Prose Cycle

THE PROSE CYCLE became a widely popular compositional form in the first half of the nineteenth century, as attested most readily by the remarkable proliferation of tale-sharing *evenings* in Russian fiction of the time: *Evening on a Bivouac* (*Vecher na bivuake*, 1823) and *Evening at the Caucasian Waters in 1824* (*Vecher na kavkazskikh vodakh v 1824 godu*, 1830) by Aleksandr Bestuzhev-Marlinsky; *The Double, or My Evenings in Little Russia* (*Dvoinik, ili Moi vechera v Malorossii*, 1828) by Antonii Pogorel'sky; *An Evening on the Khoper* (*Vecher na Khopre*, 1834) by Mikhail Zagoskin; *Evenings on the Karpovka* (1837) by Mariia Zhukova; and, best-known of all, *Evenings on a Farm near Dikan'ka* (1832) by Nikolai Gogol. Other cyclical narratives abound, including Osip Senkovsky's best-selling *Fantastic Travels of Baron Brambeus* (*Fantasticheskie puteshestviia Barona Brambeusa*, 1833), Vladimir Odoevsky's *Motley Tales* (*Pestrye skazki*, 1833), and the two most celebrated examples: Aleksandr Pushkin's *Tales of Belkin* (1835) and Mikhail Lermontov's *A Hero of Our Time* (1841).[1]

Vladimir Odoevsky's literary career provides a worthy example of the appeal of the prose cycle from the 1820s through the 1850s. Odoevsky's two major works, *Motley Tales* and *Russian Nights* (*Russkie nochi*, 1844), are organized as cyclical narratives.[2] Moreover, several of Odoevsky's tales were conceived as "down payments" as it were on prospective cycles that were never completed. For instance, the novella *Orlakh Peasant Girl* (*Orlakhskaia krest'ianka*, 1842) was published with the subtitle "from the cycle *The Possessed*" (*iz tsikla "Besnuiushchiesia"*).[3] Another of Odoevsky's cycles, *Notes of a Coffin-Maker* (*Zapiski grobovshchika*), inspired by Pushkin's *Tales of Belkin*, was to include thirteen tales, of which only three were ultimately written.

Boris Eikhenbaum, the first to note the prominence of cyclization in Russian fiction of the 1820s and 1830s,[4] envisioned the cycle as a "laboratory" for working out the genre of the novel in Russian fiction: "It was impossible to sit down and write all at once a Russian novel in four parts with an epilogue; the novel had to be pulled together out of tales and sketches in some way or other connected with one another."[5] Viktor Shklovsky, the other key member of the Russian formalist school, assigned to the cyclical narrative an analogous role, albeit one performed on a much larger scale, namely, that of the history of world literature: "The collection of tales was the predecessor of the modern novel; this is not to claim a causal relationship between the two, but rather an affirmation of a chronological fact."[6] To prove his thesis, Shklovsky drew up an extensive list of narratives, from Apuleius's *The Golden Ass* to *The Thousand and One Nights* to Boccaccio's *Decameron* that employ, in a variety of configurations, the two major techniques of cyclization: "framing" (*obramlenie*) and "threading" (*nanizyvanie*).

These formalists' insights on the role of the prose cycle in the genesis of novelistic discourse in Russian and world literature have received surprisingly little scholarly attention. Referencing Eikhenbaum and Shklovsky in her study of the evolving tradition of women's prose fiction, Josephine Donovan notes that "the major theorists and historians of the rise of the novel—Ian Watt, Michael McKeon, and J. Paul Hunter, for example—have overlooked the framed-novelle as a progenitor of the novel."[7] Donovan herself endorses the Russian scholars' view on the prose cycle as precursor to the novel. Her book identifies the framed-novelle as the "dominant genre in prose fiction in the late medieval to early modern period"[8] and argues that the cycle's built-in propensity for dispersing an authoritarian point of view, enabled by the genre's inherent dialogical structure, played a decisive role in the emergence of the novel in western European prose.

Both Shklovsky and Donovan envision the cycle-to-novel transition as occurring incrementally, as the boundaries separating tales within the cyclical narrative—Shklovsky's "internal stitches" (*vnutrennie skrepy*)[9]—are dissolved. Analyzing the patterns of narrative embedding in *Don Quixote*, Shklovsky points to the frame narrative's gradual development toward plot unification: "It can be stated in general that within the history of the novel, both devices—framing and the linking of episodes—were developing toward an ever closer integration of inserted material into the main narrative of the novel."[10] Donovan asserts that the explicit structural tension between frame and embedded stories, which allows for the coexistence of diverse and often antagonistic narrative perspectives within the prose cycle, is mitigated in the novel's compositionally cohesive textual body: "The novel as it finally took shape in the eighteenth century is characterized by its focus on one or a group of individuals whose voice dominates—to whose story digressive narratives are subordinated. This indeed is the distinguishing difference between the novel and the framed-novelle."[11]

According to this view of the development of the cyclical narrative, we would expect to find in the Russian tradition, wherein the prose cycle anticipates the emergence of novelistic discourse most markedly and immediately, a pronounced tendency toward homogeneity and the merging of the cycle's thematic and structural components. Yet an examination of prose cycles in Russian fiction of the late 1820s and 1830s does not bear such expectations out. On the contrary, mature prose cycles—for instance, Gogol's *Evenings on a Farm near Dikan'ka*, Odoevsky's *Motley Tales*, and Pushkin's *Tales of Belkin*—exhibit the exact opposite tendency, namely, that of the amplification of thematic and structural boundaries (Shklovsky's "internal stitches"), both among embedded tales and between the tales and narrative frame.

To highlight these characteristics of the Russian cyclical narratives, I would undertake to juxtapose them—solely to bring these characteristics into sharper relief—with perhaps the most prominent examples of the genre in the western European tradition: Boccaccio's *Decameron* and Chaucer's *Canterbury Tales*.[12] In both works, the narrative frame provides an occasion, or motive, for an exchange of stories: in *Decameron*, the outbreak of bubonic plague justifies the flight of ten young Florentines from urban chaos to the surrounding countryside; in *Canterbury Tales* a pilgrimage to the shrine of Saint Thomas Becket at Canterbury Cathedral prompts a storytelling contest among a party of thirty or so travelers. The unity of the narrative situation facilitates numerous interactions between frame narrative and embedded tales, of which I will provide only a few prominent examples. In *Decameron*, the number of tales is determined in advance (ten per day over ten days), and a particular theme, assigned for each daily series, ensures the tales' explicit thematic linkage (their enormous generic and stylistic diversity notwithstanding). In *Canterbury Tales*, a similarly rigorous preliminary arrangement is introduced in the "General Prologue," but is thwarted by the pilgrims' responses to the tales and their interactions with one another. Though Boccaccio's order-imposing frame contrasts with the frame of Chaucer, which is "disordered by design,"[13] both works feature a unified and elaborate framing story and explicit linkages, associations, and mutual influences between embedding and embedded narratives.[14]

Likewise, as Donovan's analysis demonstrates, the interaction between frame and inset material is a central characteristic of the framed-novelle genre in early modern fiction written by women. Donovan argues that women writers expanded and enriched the use of the framing narrative (well established by the early modern period) by having frame characters extensively debate and comment upon the stories they exchange. For instance, in Marguerite de Navarre's *Heptameron* (1549), each of the seventy-two inset novellas are followed by conversations within the narrative frame, whereby many of the novellas are seen to overtly illustrate participants' viewpoints; the frame thus becomes a "discussion-group forum in which the stories are interpreted and evaluated by the storytellers."[15]

In *Decameron* and *Canterbury Tales*, the narrators are particularized and described in detail, despite these literary portraitures' firm embedment in allegory and the genre of estates satire respectively. In both works, an extraordinary situation (an epidemic; a spiritual journey) as opposed to a socially routine one gives rise to an "alternative" community, within which regularly operative hierarchies (most prominently, gender roles in *Decameron* and social "stations" in *Canterbury Tales*) become suspended, challenged, and often overturned. Similarly, the cyclical narrative in early modern women's prose produces a purposeful discussion of feminist issues—enabled by the storytellers' diverse and often opposing viewpoints as expressed both discursively and through the stories they choose to relate—that would be unthinkable outside the framed-novelle format.[16]

The cycles of Gogol, Odoevsky, and Pushkin mentioned above, meanwhile, feature no such unifying linkages. The reader learns little, if anything, about the storytellers or whether, for that matter, they have ever met. There is no overt thematic coherency among the tales, nor any explicit rationale for their selection, number, and sequence.[17] In Pushkin's *Tales of Belkin*, the narrators are designated by rank and initials only: Titular Councilor A. G. N., Lieutenant Colonel I. L. P., Steward B. V., and "the maiden [*devitsa*] K. I. T."—and listed in a publisher's footnote.[18] In Odoevsky's *Motley Tales*, comprising eight stories, the narrators' names are not given at all.

In Gogol's *Dikan'ka Tales*, the narrators are described in an exceedingly elaborate yet, at the same time, seemingly random manner. With regard to the deacon Foma Grigor'evich, for instance, the reader learns, among other things, of his tobacco box and the handkerchief he uses to blow his nose. Stepan Ivanovich Kurochka is introduced as a "most kindly man," easily identifiable by his uniquely colorful pantaloons, his yellow frock coat, and his habit of swinging his arms while walking. Another storyteller is mentioned only by way of declaring his tales unfit for the cycle due to their horrific subject matter. The remaining narrators go unnamed, which omission is motivated by the fact that the reader "does not know them"[19] in any case. As for interaction among the storytellers, one of the more extensive exchanges concerns the proper method of fermenting apples (with or without the use of field daisies). The heated exchange of opinions on this subject, so far from illustrating or inspiring any story, results instead in the expulsion of one of the storytellers (a certain "gentleman from Poltava in a pea-green coat") from the gathering.

As distinct from the earlier western European tradition of cyclical narrative, the Russian cycle as it emerged and developed in the late 1820s and 1830s features no unified narrative situation, no explicit rationale for the selection of storytellers, and no readily observable thematic coherency among embedded tales. As against the "alternative communities" of storytellers prominently enacted in *Decameron*, *Canterbury Tales*, and women's framed-novelle, the communities (such as they are) of the Russian cycles seem strictly accidental. Similarly random are the tales' selection, number, and plots, which acquire coherence only through a post hoc critical gaze. In the Russian cycle, boundaries between and within embedding and embedded stories do not dissolve in anticipation of the "stitch-less" novelistic discourse as in Shklovsky's or Donovan's conception, but rather become more dense and impermeable. Given the dearth of explicit thematic and structural linkages that "piece together" and integrate earlier cyclical narratives into a generic entity, what, then, grants unity to the Russian prose cycle and serves as its organizing force?

Apparently, it is the figure of the tale collector—in Odoevsky's *Motley Tales*, for instance, Irinei Modestovich Gomozeiko, "Master of Philosophy and member of various learned societies." As the reader learns from the subtitle, the six tales that make up *Motely Tales* have all been "collected" [*sobrannye*] by Gomozeiko.[20] In the absence of any information on the narrators or the circumstances under which the stories were related, their having been collected by Gomozeiko is the single connecting link between the tales. In Pushkin's *Tales of Belkin*, the collector is deceased landowner Ivan Petrovich Belkin, said to have recorded five "mostly true stories heard from various people,"[21] the manuscript of which was found among his papers after his death. In Gogol's *Dikan'ka Tales*, the collector is village beekeeper Rudyi Pan'ko, who arranges storytelling sessions during evening gatherings at his house. Though the "evenings" provide an occasion for the exchange of stories, it is Pan'ko who writes the tales down[22] and determines the selection, sequence, and number of tales to be included in the cycle. As distinct from earlier cyclical narratives, in which an assemblage of tales provides an exhaustive and sequential account—albeit in Chaucer, an unfinished one—of the entire storytelling exchange as occurring, for instance, at a countryside refuge or during a pilgrimage, Pan'ko chooses at will from a number of stories told at his home by various people in the course of many "evenings."

In all three Russian cycles mentioned, otherwise accidental groupings of tellers and random assortments of tales acquire coherency *only* in the perspective of the collector. The Russian cycle annuls the situational motive for storytelling, constitutively featuring instead the persona of the tale collector, for whom storytelling is not contingent on external motivation; who, establishes, or rather embodies, such a motive. The collector, desirous of stories and actively seeking and soliciting them, bears within him/herself the motive for storytelling, thereby initiating and sustaining narration in the absence of external stimulus. This narrative persona, subsidiary in the earlier tradition of the cyclical narrative, now comes center stage, assuming the utmost literary-historical significance in the nascent tradition of original Russian fiction.[23]

Perhaps due to the collector's "low profile" in western European prose, this figure has received inadequate scholarly attention in both theoretical and historical approaches to narrative framing. On the one hand, despite the fact that, as William Nelles notes, "the study of the embedded narrative has become something of an academic boom industry,"[24] the tale collector is rarely if ever singled out in meticulous narratological classifications of personified fictional agents. The reason for this omission is that such classifications concern first and foremost narrators—homo- (hetero-, inter-, intra-) diegetic, overt and covert, reliable and unreliable, and so on—while the collector is, principally and significantly, *not* a narrator, but a compiler of *other* narrators' stories. This characteristic becomes particularly pronounced in the Russian cycle: another important distinction between the earlier cyclical tradition and Russian nineteenth-century cyclical narratives is the marked non-participation of the collector in a storytelling exchange. While, for instance, the collector of *Canterbury Tales*, "Chaucer the pilgrim," is one of the travelers who himself narrates two of the tales making up the cycle, Gogol's Pan'ko, having promised in his first preface to include a tale [*skazka*] of his own in the *Dikan'ka* cycle, ultimately declines to do so:

> I promised you, I remember, that this little book would have a story of mine as well. And really, I did mean to do that, but I saw that my story would need three such books at least. I thought of printing it separately, but I changed my mind. I know you, after all: you'd laugh at the old man. No, I don't want to![25]

In abandoning his initial determination to add his *skazka* to the *Dikan'ka Tales*, Pan'ko adheres faithfully to the status of collector, preserving the boundary between two principally distinct, for the Russian cycle, positions: narrator and collector of tales.

In literary-historical accounts of the extensive "found manuscript" tradition, meanwhile, the collector often remains overlooked. With its origins commonly traced to Cervantes's *Don Quixote*, the "found manuscript" device was prominent in early modern European prose,[26] and also became immensely popular in Russian fiction of the 1820s–30s. The device establishes a discontinuity between the creator of a fictional text and the persona of its "finder" (editor, publisher, or, in many cases, translator) who introduces the text to the reading public and relates the circumstances of its discovery. However, within the general format of the "found manuscript" device, the tale collector appears to be somewhat superfluous, coinciding neither with the "manuscript's" author or its "finder(s)." As discussed above, the collector is clearly not a narrator; neither is he or she the creator of a manuscript to be "found." In her analysis of Pushkin's *Tales of Belkin*, Ana Rodriguez Navas singles out Charles Augustin Sainte-Beuve's *Vie, poésies et pensées de Joseph Delorme* (1829) as that exemplar of the "found manuscript" tradition with which Pushkin engages most immediately and profoundly. At the same time, Navas points out a key distinction between Sainte-Beuve's poet Joseph Delorme and Pushkin's landowner Ivan Petrovich Belkin: the latter is a "compiler rather than a composer of tales."[27]

Of course, the "found manuscript" device, whether employed earnestly or parodied, can feature multiple participants; but all such participants fulfill the role either of the manuscript's creator or its "finder." Often the process of "discovery" is quite convoluted. Mander supplies an example of the device's employment (1736) by Charles de Fieux, Chevalier de Mouhy, which features, besides a laborer who has unearthed an oak casket with a manuscript from beneath the foundation of a house in Rome, also the laborer's wife, their neighbor, the neighbor's friend, a collector of antiquities, a burglar, the county clerk, an official with some knowledge of Italian and, finally, the translator and publisher, Mouhy himself. The Italian manuscript itself, however, has a single, albeit unknown, author. Within the "found manuscript" device, configured via a gap between two constituents, a manuscript's author and its finder(s)/translator(s)/publisher(s), the tale *collector* appears to present an excessive step, a sort of narrative loose end.

Neither does the collector coincide with the other constituent of the "found manuscript" device: the "finder" and publisher (editor, translator) of a manuscript. As distinct from the earlier cyclical tradition (*Decameron*, *Canterbury Tales*, the framed-novelle), wherein the compiler of tales is the same persona seeing to their publication and introduction to the reader, in the Russian cycle, the collector and publisher most typically appear as two distinct narrative agents. Both Odoevsky's *Motley Tales* and Pushkin's *Tales of Belkin* feature a publisher/editor (V. Bezglasnyi and A. P., respectively) whose prefaces accompany the tales.[28] In Mariia Zhukova's *Evenings on the Karpovka* (1837), the publisher is an anonymous "I" invited to the nightly gatherings (*evenings*) at the Petersburg dacha of the old lady [*starushka*] Natal'ia Dmitrievna Shemilova, and privy to the stories written and then read aloud by this hostess's close friends. It is the old lady herself who initiates the request for stories and who, consequently, fulfills the role of tale collector:

> No, it is sad to think that we [Russians] seem to pay no regard to literature; so few of us write, and those that do, do so with such reluctance, even as the Russian language is rich and Russian everyday life is not without poetry. I am certain that each of us, if only we were willing to search our memory, could find in it many things heard or seen; events in which we ourselves were dramatis personae or witnesses.[29]

The publisher of *Evenings on the Karpovka* confirms that the tales of the cycle "were written for the ailing old lady [*dlia bol'noi starushki*]." In Mikhail Zagoskin's *An Evening on the Khoper* (1834), the publisher is, once again, an anonymous "I," who visits his friend's uncle, Ivan Alekseevich Asanov, and listens to the stories of Asanov's guests. Asanov, the motive force behind the storytelling session taking place in his home, is de facto the collector of tales, while the publisher merely records them: "The stories and tales that I heard during the last evening I spent at Ivan Alekseevich's struck me as so curious that I wrote them down in my travel journal with the greatest precision."[30] These last two collectors, the "ailing old lady" and the recluse Asanov, make no effort whatsoever to write down the stories they hear, nor do they entertain any professional writerly or publishing ambitions, a fact rendering them collectors par excellence: their role within the cycle is "distilled" exclusively to the gathering of tales. In light of this "ideal" collector figure, we can discern a significant difference, perhaps even opposition, between the cyclical format of *evenings* and the "found manuscript" device. The latter implies the fortuitous, often sensational circumstances of the discovery of a text, whereas the hosts of *evenings*, to the contrary, do not just "happen" upon stories, oral or written; rather, they themselves solicit, request, and encourage storytelling by means of regularly and purposefully organized narrative sessions.

The debt of Russian cyclical narratives of the 1820s–30s to the western European "found manuscript" was readily recognized; contemporaries easily identified, moreover, the author most influential in Russian writers' embrace of this tradition: Sir Walter Scott, whose works were widely translated, imitated, and admired by readers, writers, and critics alike. In his article "Preface to the *Tales of Belkin* and the Narrative Devices of Sir Walter Scott," justly regardable as a seminal examination of the subject, Russian literary historian Dmitrii Iakubovich documents Scott's reception in Russia and, in particular, his influence on a host of fictitious authorial personae in 1820s–30s prose.[31] This influence was so pervasive that readers and critics of the time ridiculed Russian writers' attempts at literary disguise, deeming them derivative, predictable, and clumsy. The following excerpt from a review of Pushkin's *Tales of Belkin* neatly encapsulates this critical opinion:

> In France and England nowadays half the books are published without signed names, or with phony writers' names. They have started doing this in our country too: anonymous and pseudonymous works keep coming out, but what the English and French do out of an excess of strength is in our country an empty aping. . . . This I. P. Belkin, and this publisher of his works, who signs his name with the letters A. P. and who is spoken of in booksellers' advertise-

ments as our renowned poet—isn't this all like a child who covers his face with his hands and thinks you can't see him?[32]

The reviewer seems to blame the author of the *Tales of Belkin* for the inadequate concealment of his identity. Scholars later came to see this exposure as hardly resulting from any failure on Pushkin's part to deploy a proper textual masquerade. In her detailed examination of the parallels between Scott's and Pushkin's employment of authorial surrogacy, Sona Stephan Hoisington supplies ample evidence—the editor's "telltale initials"[33] (the name being, moreover, explicitly spelled out in the 1834 edition of the cycle); Pushkin's request that his name be "whisper[ed]" to booksellers such that they might in turn "whisper it to purchasers"[34]; and so on—that Pushkin was actually eager to be recognized as the author of the *Tales of Belkin*—in stark contrast to Scott who, his pure delight in elaborate literary mystifications notwithstanding, was genuinely intent upon hiding his authorship. Given the absence of any desire on Pushkin's part to deceive the public, his response to Scott can be understood either as, indeed, an "empty aping" of the devices of fictitious authorship (per the contemporaneous reviewer cited above); or, as Hoisington argues, a sophisticated parody thereof: "Whereas in Scott's prefaces everything is carefully motivated and our expectations fulfilled, in Pushkin's Preface things are made illogical for comic effect and are rendered absurd."[35]

However, Hoisington's own perceptive analysis, which further expands the parallels established by Iakubovich between Scott's *Tales of My Landlord, Collected and Arranged by Jedediah Cleishbotham* (1816–19) and Pushkin's *Tales of Belkin*, reveals a particular direction and focus in Pushkin's divergences from Scott which, I believe, propel them beyond mere "mockery of Belkin."[36] For instance, Hoisington notes that in contrast to the close collegial relationship between Scott's deceased manuscript author Peter Pattieson and the manuscript's inheritor and editor Jedediah Cleishbotham, in Pushkin's cycle, the late Ivan Petrovich Belkin and the editor A. P. are total strangers, and the reader never learns how A. P. came to acquire Belkin's manuscript.[37] Secondly, while the self-styled "antiquarian" Pattieson takes care to verify his accounts, and provides commentary in explanatory notes, Belkin makes no such effort.[38] Further, as Iakubovich notes, while Pattieson freely elaborates on the stories he has heard, at times even combining them for the sake of artistic effect,[39] Belkin is characterized by a "lack of imagination [*nedostatok voobrazhenia*]": his original input is confined to making up characters' names and using settings from his own neighborhood. Thus, as distinct from Pattieson, Belkin is interested neither in historiography nor creative (re)writing; he does not introduce, revise, or comment on his stories and, in general, remains "strangely silent."[40]

And yet there exists a light in which Belkin's deficiencies vis-à-vis Pattieson take on a positive valuation, namely, if we consider these two personae not merely as extra layers of narrative removal, but as, first and foremost, collectors of tales. Pushkin's departures from Scott, noted by Iakubovich and Hoisington, serve to clearly differentiate the tale collector from all other fictitious narrative personae within the configurations of the "found manuscript" device; his "revisions" of the Scottian precedent make a clean break between Belkin and the editor on the one hand (for these now stand, observes Hoisington, as two "separate entities") and, on the other, between Belkin and the storytellers (since Belkin neither corrects nor enhances their tales). Belkin's silence—as distinct from the editor's and the narrators' vocality—ceases to be "strange" if understood as the defining characteristic of his status as *solely* a collector. Pushkin neither imitates nor subverts Scott's narrative devices and strategies of fictitious authorship; rather, he accentuates and foregrounds a particular instance thereof: the figure of the tale collector.

Notably, in identifying Scott's own contribution to the "found manuscript" tradition (which had already been firmly established in western European prose), Iakubovich notes a narrative pattern he terms a "staircase" device, with the collector standing at its midpoint:

> Scott's system of devices consists of the following: the whole series of stories is entitled "Waverley Novels" and "Tales of My Landlord, first series," but, aside from the fictitious figure of the landlord, we are also given the fictitious figure of Peter Pattieson, the schoolteacher of the village of Gandercleugh who has collected these stories. Nor is that the end of it; still a third interpolated persona is introduced: the schoolmaster of the same school Jedediah Cleishbotham, who has published the stories. I call this a stepped device (a staircase):
>
> Narrator,
>   Tale collector,
>   Tale publisher
>
> in which each step is a step leading into a labyrinth of mystification away from the author.[41]

According to Iakubovich, despite the proliferation of numerous Scott-inspired agglomerates of fictitious personae in both European and Russian prose, this specific pattern of the "found manuscript" device (*priem nakhodki*)[42] is fully sustained only in Pushkin's *Tales of Belkin*:

> From 1824 on we have (as was also the case in Europe) a whole range of Russian books with prefaces à la W. Scott, with the device temporarily becoming

> clichéd, reduced to the level of parody. Portraits are also given of fictitious authors. But not *one* of the prefaces of this sort reproduces *the totality*, the whole system of W. Scott's devices.[43] (Emphasis in original.)

Iakubovich notes that with regard to fictitious authorship thus configured, the most direct correspondence exists between Belkin and Peter Pattieson, a deceased schoolteacher whose papers were left in the care of his patron and friend Jedediah Cleishbotham.[44] Both Pattieson and Belkin are "the late," the manuscripts of each being discovered and published posthumously—so far, the standard configuration of the "found manuscript" device. What is less typical, and distinctive for *Tales of My Landlord* and the *Tales of Belkin*, is that in both works, the "manuscript" represents not an original (or translated or recorded) tale of a single author/narrator, but an assemblage of tales the deceased heard from various people and wrote down. Pattieson and Belkin are neither authors/narrators nor publishers/editors/translators—elaborate successions of which were common in the "found manuscript" tradition—but collectors of tales. Scott's and Pushkin's "staircase devices" do not merely multiply layers of narrative removal, but feature a fictitious persona differing in principle from either creator or "finder."

Scott's four installments of *Tales of My Landlord* constitute a subset of the Waverley series, the other novels of which do not involve the collector, but present more straightforward (albeit often quite intricate) configurations of the "found manuscript" device. For instance, *The Monastery* (1820) is preceded by the "introductory epistle" of one Captain Clutterbuck, who relates how he has come into possession of a "genuine" Benedictine document and requests that the "author of *Waverley*" edit this work for publication. *Ivanhoe* (1820) opens with a "dedicatory epistle" by the fictitious writer Lawrence Templeton, addressed to the equally fictitious editor Dr. Dryasdust, in which the work is said to be based on an ancient document called the Wardour Manuscript.[45] For Scott, the collector was only one of the numerous fictitious authorial personae populating his historical novels.[46] It is not surprising that in a translation of *Tales of My Landlord* contemporaneous to Pushkin, Peter Pattieson was omitted altogether, with the tales attributed directly to the eponymous landlord: "The Russian translation of 1824 skipped the intermediary persona of the English text—the collector of the innkeeper's tales, the teacher Peter Pattieson (who corresponds most closely in his role to Belkin)."[47]

It is rather remarkable, then, that from the abundance, variety, and intricate network of fictitious participants in the creation and transmission of a text in Scott's novels, Pushkin singled out the tale collector and placed this figure at the heart of the narrative organization of his very first work in prose. As distinct from a number of writers who earnestly emulated, enhanced, or parodied Scott's narrative strategies on a scale Iakubovich terms "epidemic,"[48] Pushkin's engagement with the "found manuscript" tradition and, specifically, with Scott's literary mystifications underscored a narrative persona that remained peripheral within this tradition as it unfolded in the West: that of the tale collector.[49] Moreover, as the examples cited of Gogol's, Odoevsky's, Zhukova's, and Zagoskin's prose cycles demonstrate, Pushkin's response to Scott represents only one instance—a salient and well-studied one—of the tale collector's assumption of a key role in organizing narrative in Russian literature of the 1820s–30s. These writers' distinctly "selective" response to developments in western European prose in general and to Walter Scott's oeuvre in particular seems not so much an instance of borrowing (whether "straightforward" or creatively subversive); rather, it evinces the special significance of the collector figure not only for Pushkin, but for the evolving tradition of original Russian fiction generally. Elucidating this significance may shed light on the importance of the collector figure in Scott's own historical novels as well.

Hoisington notes a particular commonality of the literary careers of Scott and Pushkin: both were poets who at a certain point began to experiment with prose narrative, eventually turning their efforts largely in this direction:

> Like Scott, Pushkin was already a widely established poet when he published his first work in prose. One would suppose that he found it advantageous, as Scott did, to make his prose debut in disguise so that he could test the reaction of the public without endangering his literary reputation.[50]

As poets transitioning to prose, Scott and Pushkin found themselves in analogous circumstances, though a tradition of literary prose was well established in England by the time Scott published his first novel in 1814, whereas in Russia of the late 1820s it had yet to rise, requiring, in large part, Pushkin himself to launch it. In his brief yet suggestive essay "Pushkin's Path to Prose" ("Put' Pushkina k proze"), Eikhenbaum offers insight into the nature of this transition, ascribing to Scott's and Pushkin's reliance on fictitious authorship motives beyond the merely psychological or socioliterary.

Eikhenbaum demonstrates that in Russian literary practice and criticism of the late 1820s and early 1830s, it was felt to be urgent to move from poems—of which there were "too many" (*kotorykh slishkom mnogo*)—to prose.[51] The following excerpt from a literary review by Aleksandr Bestuzhev-Marlinsky neatly encapsulates this pining for prose:

> Poets, it is true, have not ceased their chirping on every corner, but no one wants to listen to verse now that everyone is writing it. A scattered grumbling has at last merged into a general cry: "Prose, prose! Water, plain water!"[52]

The "prosaic" quality of an artistic work was understood first and foremost as pertaining not so much to prose-like plots, themes, or ideas, but to narration itself; the task was to "create the very mechanism of prose discourse as literary material."[53] This mechanism was seen as fundamentally different from that of poetry; writers and critics alike considered Russian prose to be at an evolutionary standstill, shackled by the already highly developed language of verse. Pushkin, Russia's major poet, sensed this difficulty most acutely. Citing a number of Pushkin's essays, notes, and letters, Eikhenbaum asserts:

> Independent of the general theoretical question of the relationship between prose and poetry, we find here documentary evidence of the fact that for Pushkin these were utterly distinct forms of artistic discourse, such that the laws effective within one do not apply to the other.[54]

The "general theoretical question of the relationship between prose and poetry," set aside by Eikhenbaum in 1923, became central for Mikhail Bakhtin's seminal study "Discourse in the Novel," written in the 1930s.[55] In the second section of this work, titled "Discourse in Poetry and Discourse in the Novel," Bakhtin argues that a key distinction between poet and prose writer lies in their respective orientations toward the multifaceted discourses (social and historical heteroglossia) that at any given moment make up the apparent linguistic unity of a national language. Such orientation is not limited to verbal art, but is operative for any speaker who, in each and every utterance, seeks to resolve the conflict between, on the one hand, his or her own unique individual intention and, on the other, multiple contextualizations of the word encountered in other speakers' utterances:

> The word in language is half someone else's. It becomes "one's own" only when the speaker populates it with his own intention, his own accent, when he appropriates the word, adapting it to his own semantic and expressive intention. Prior to this moment of appropriation, the word does not exist in a neutral and impersonal language (it is not, after all, out of a dictionary that the speaker gets his words!) but rather it exists in other people's mouths, in other people's contexts, serving other people's intentions: it is from there that one must take the word, and make it one's own.[56]

In terms of their engagement with the words of others—words that are "half someone else's" or, as Bakhtin's *poluchuzhoe slovo* could also be rendered, "half-alien"—poetry and artistic prose are situated on opposite sides of "serious," real-world discourse. The poet strives to attain a singular language of his or her own; the generative force of the poet's interaction with the "alien" word is directed toward the definitive dislodgement (*vytesnenie*) of other speakers' intentions and accents in search of his or her own inimitable, self-sufficient verbal expression. For the prose writer, in contrast, the focal point of artistic representation is the infinite stratification of language, its "living heteroglossia."[57] Whereas in poetic genres, the word—first encountered as "half someone else's"—becomes the poet's "own," in artistic prose, conversely, it becomes fully "alien," owned entirely by "other people," suffused with their intentions. Consequently, for the prose writer, the activity of dislodgement (*vytesnenie*) is directed toward his or her *own* unique accent, voice, intention, such that at the apex of such dislodgement, *no* word is experienced as his or her own.

I would suggest that the persona of the tale collector as it emerged in the nineteenth-century Russian cycle embodies and sustains the orientation toward the stratifying forces of language that Bakhtin defined as fundamental for the prose writer. As discussed above, the cyclical narratives of the 1820s–30s feature, unlike earlier exemplars of the cycle tradition, no explicit thematic focus, no rationale behind the selection of tellers or assemblage of tales. This indifference toward the tales' sources and thematic coherency underscores the initiative of collecting itself, which activity, clearly separate from that of narrator or editor, is marked by the essential absence of communicative intention: collecting can be seen as the discursive mode most adequate for *non*-narrating, for conceptualizing the word as, in principle, "someone else's," as "reported" rather than uttered him or herself. Gogol's Pan'ko's ultimate decision to exclude his prospective tale from the *Dikan'ka* cycle palpably captures the moment of reflection upon the collector's lack of his or her own word: "I promised you, I remember, that this little book should have a story of mine as well. And really, I did mean to do that. . . . But I changed my mind. . . . No, I don't want to!"

The Russian scholar Sergei Bocharov, one of the most meticulous readers of Pushkin's prose, observes that as presented in the preface to the *Tales*, Belkin's character produces an "impression of absence" (*vpechatlenie otsutstviia*): it consists of traits either missing (e.g., lack of imagination or estate management experience) or qualitatively "neutral" ("Ivan Petrovich was of middling height, with gray eyes, lightish-brown hair, straight nose"; "Ivan Petrovich led a most temperate existence, avoiding any sort of excess"); or else these traits cancel each other out, for instance, his "great fondness for the female sex" and his "truly maidenly . . . modesty," which are not only mutually contradictory but also conflict with his supposed avoidance of excess.[58] This effaced, nonaccented character profile can be seen as a biographical projection of Belkin's discursive stance, that is, of his essential bereftness of communicative intention or voice, a quality that differentiates collectors from all other narrative personae—narrators, characters, and editors—and pushes them close to, or over the edge of, the temporal and spatial boundaries of the story world.[59]

In its extreme yet most adequate manifestation, this displacement is interpreted as the "death" of the tale collector. In his farewell to the reader (second preface), the collector of Gogol's *Dikan'ka Tales*, Rudyi Pan'ko, anticipates his approaching death, contemplating it in terms reminiscent of his fellow collector Belkin, who is "at peace" or "deceased" (*pokoinyi*) from the very beginning:

> And, indeed, it is high time *to rest* [*na pokoi*]. I expect you imagine, dear readers, that I am only pretending to be old. Pretend, indeed, when I have no teeth left in my mouth! . . . But then, it would not matter to you if I had never existed at all. One year will pass and then another—and none of you will remember or miss the old beekeeper Rudy Pan'ko.[60] (Emphasis mine)

Further examination of the collectors in Russian prose cycles of the 1820s–30s reveals their propensity for exclusion from earthly orders and categories, even when their death notices are not explicitly announced (as in the case of Belkin) or anticipated (as in that of Rudyi Pan'ko). For instance, Irinei Modestovich Gomozeiko, the collector of Odoevsky's cycle *Motley Tales*, is a scientist and philosopher who appears to stand apart from the rest of humanity by virtue of his possession of all possible knowledge:

> I number among the scholarly . . . that is, I know all manner of languages, living, dead, and half-dead; I know all the sciences taught and not taught in all the universities of Europe; I can argue about any subject known and unknown to me; and most of all I enjoy racking my brains over the origins of things and other unprofitable subjects.[61]

Gomozeiko's engagement with "unprofitable subjects" (*nekhlebnye predmety*) informs his status as outcast, his apartness from contemporaries; his role in society, it seems, can only be described apophatically:

> That said, you can imagine the pitiful role I play in high society. . . . I do not play cards, do not dance; I gamble neither for five nor fifty . . . am not adept at keeping an ear out for city news, nor even at speaking of these subjects . . . I cannot assist anyone in securing a position or a rank or even in discovering a chancery secret.[62]

Gomozeiko is doomed to this "pitiful role," but clearly wouldn't have it any other way; the wish "to be left in peace" is "written on his face":

> If somewhere you encounter, in the very corner of a drawing room, a small, thin, short little man in a black frock coat, who is very neat, whose hair is slicked back, and on whose face is written: "For God's sake, leave me *in peace*," and who, for this very reason . . . bows to everyone with the profoundest deference, and tries to strike up a conversation with this person or that . . . that is me, dear sir, me at your service.[63] (Emphasis mine)

The desire "to be left in peace" (*v pokoe*) affords Irinei Gomozeiko membership in the union of tale collectors alongside the eternally peaceful or late (*pokoinyi*) Ivan Petrovich Belkin and the aged Rudyi Pan'ko, who announces his retirement (*davno pora na pokoi*) in anticipation of his own impending death.[64]

The collector in Mariia Zhukova's *Evenings on the Karpovka* (1837), Natal'ia Dmitrievna, is quite ill, as the constant presence of the doctor at her side demonstrates. It is, moreover, the doctor who has advised Natal'ia Dmitrievna to establish permanent residence at her dacha, where the old woman's existence is one of peace and solitude:

> Having moved to the dacha on her doctor's advice, she nevertheless made little use of the so-called country air, due both to the foul season [the rainy summer of 1836] and to her frail health, and lived within a small circle of friends who gathered at her home every evening.[65]

The old woman's exclusion from the worldly bustle necessitates her "evenings" with friends and their storytelling pursuits. Natal'ia Dmitrievna's position at the margins of life, and at the margins of the big city, attests to her status as collector, situating this frail old lady right alongside her better-known male "contemporaries" Belkin, Pan'ko, and Gomozeiko.

Finally, we might consider the example of the collector of Mikhail Zagoskin's *An Evening on the Khoper*. Predictably, Asanov is a recluse who "never leaves [his] remote [estate]" (*zhivet bezvyezdno v glushi*) and is considered a suspicious outsider by the neighboring gentry:

> Some said he was a misanthrope and too proud; others called him crazy; there were even some kind people who claimed that he never went to services and that there was not a single icon in his house.[66]

However, Asanov's nephew has a different explanation for his uncle's seclusion: "He is an *old* man, who loves *peace* and quiet and moves with a terribly slow deliberation [emphases mine]."[67] Asanov's advanced age and desire for peace (*pokoi*) attest to his displacement from the temporal and spatial boundaries of the story-world; indeed, this displacement, typical of the tale collector, is cemented in the very first lines of *An Evening on the Khoper*: "The uncle of my friend Zarutsky, Ivan Alekseevich Asanov—may he rest *in peace* [literally, may God grant him the kingdom of heaven]—was a most kind old man [emphasis mine]."[68]

Thus Asanov, like Ivan Petrovich Belkin, is dead (*pokoinyi*) by the time the cycle is published.

These examples demonstrate a salient consistency in the narrative organization of Russian prose cycles of the 1820s–30s. Specifically, the tale collector, who is in one way or another "dead," emerges as a key constituent of the cycle's poetics. I would suggest that this "death" of the collector stems from his or her distinct narrative stance, namely, the essential absence of semantic and expressive intention, of any claim to his or her own word. In Gogol's *Dikan'ka Tales*, Rudyi Pan'ko's reflection upon his rapidly approaching feebleness coincides with his renunciation (in the same second preface) of the desire to include his own tale in the cycle. In his analysis of the *Dikan'ka Tales*, Viktor Vinogradov notes that the old beekeeper's aging in fact takes place *within* the narrative itself:

> In the introduction to his "other book" of *Evenings*, that is, upon a second literary encounter, [Pan'ko] already addresses the reader as an old acquaintance. The tone of the conversation becomes more senile, since old age is one of the topics of the introduction. . . . This process of the aging beekeeper's enfeeblement has occurred during the period of his acquaintance with the reader.[69]

Pan'ko's looming demise can thus be seen as a "physiological" consequence of his position as speaking subject, that is, of the withering and abandonment of his ambition to be an original author and his decisive resignation to the status of tale collector.[70]

Here I would stress that the collector's stance of resignation vis-à-vis his or her own word is not merely a condition of absence, but in fact has positive content: it constitutes an indispensable prerequisite for depth and acuity in perceiving the voices and accents of other speakers—that orientation toward language that, according to Bakhtin, defines the artistic experience of the prose writer. The collector's abdication of his or her own utterance can otherwise be described as his or her refusal to take words out of "other people's mouths" and fill them with his or her own intentions. This narrative stance vacates the word as it were for other speakers' semantic and expressive intentions and opens up a discursive space within which the potential of linguistic heteroglossia can be realized. In this light, the appearance of the tale collector in Scott's historical novels and the centrality of this figure in Pushkin's first prose work might stem from these two writers' shared need to accomplish a radical transition from the poet's pursuit of his or her own indisputable and self-sufficient verbal expression to the prose writer's heightened susceptibility to the diverse and infinite intentional possibilities of each and every word.

In "Discourse in the Novel," in a brief discussion of personified narrators as carriers of the "alien" word (*chuzhaia rech' na chuzhom iazyke*),[71] Bakhtin situates Belkin at the nexus between the poetic and prosaic domains in Pushkin's work. Specifically, Belkin represents the "prosaic" point of view on traditionally "poetic" plots, styles, and genres:

> Belkin was chosen (or, better, created) by Pushkin because of his particular "unpoetic" point of view on objects and plots that are traditionally poetic. . . . Belkin, who is on the same level with those narrators-at-third-remove out of whose mouths he has taken his stories, is a "prosaic" man, a man without a drop of poetic pathos. . . . The fruitfulness of the prosaic quality in Belkin's point of view consists in just this failure to understand poetic pathos.[72]

I believe these observations can be taken a step further in the direction of Bakhtin's own characterization of the poetic and prosaic narrative realms in "Discourse in the Novel." Despite his apparent biographical proximity to his "informants," Belkin's collector status radically differentiates him from any and all narrators. The "prosaic" quality of this status has to do not with a certain set of meanings, values, and stylistic tendencies which are thematically and stylistically opposed ("alien") to "poetic" ones (e.g., the purported pathos of the latter vs. the mundanity of the former; tragic end vs. happy resolution; etc.), but rather with the operative absence of *any* set of semantic or stylistic preferences on the part of the tale collector. This definitive absence, rather than certain "prosaic" characteristics, initiates the perception of the word as a meeting site for other speakers' infinite and infinitely diverse meanings, values, and intentions, and thereby enables the genesis of the "relativized . . . linguistic consciousness"[73] of the prose writer.

According to Bakhtin, this narrative stance, constituent to artistic prose, reaches its full potential in novelistic discourse. Rudyi Pan'ko's rationale for excluding his own work from the *Dikan'ka* cycle is notable in this regard: the beekeeper explains that his tale would not fit in a cyclical narrative because it is too long: "I saw that my story would need three such books at least." Pan'ko's description of his authorial ambitions and limitations closely resembles the literary profile of Pushkin's tale collector Ivan Petrovich Belkin. Asked by the publisher of the *Tales* (designated as A. P.) to provide information on the deceased, Belkin's friend and neighbor remarks that the late Ivan Petrovich was, in fact, a prolific writer who left a number of unpublished manuscripts, among which the *Tales* were his very first attempt at creative writing:

> In addition to the tales you were pleased to mention in your letter, Ivan Petrovich left a good many manuscripts behind, some of which are in my possession, though some have been put by his housekeeper to sundry domestic uses. For example, last winter all the windows in her wing of the house were sealed up with the first part of an unfinished novel of his. The tales mentioned above were his first efforts, I do believe.[74]

The status of Ivan Petrovich Belkin and Rudyi Pan'ko as writers is remarkably similar. Each aspires to author a narrative that is longer than a tale: Pan'ko has envisioned an opus requiring "three . . . books at least"; Belkin, for his part, has composed a work so voluminous that its first installment is sufficient to seal up the windows in his housekeeper's wing of the residence. But neither narrative is materialized in book form: Ivan Petrovich's untimely death has thwarted the completion of his project, and Pan'ko opts against committing his theoretically three-volume *skazka* to paper for fear of ridicule. Both Belkin and Pan'ko thus faithfully linger within the status of the collector, which coincides neither with the narrator of a tale nor with the author of a longer narrative. In relation to Belkin's unfinished work, this unattained longer narrative is explicitly identified as a novel: "Last winter all the windows in her wing of the house were sealed up with the first part of an unfinished novel of his." The collector's voice, "lost" within the cyclical narrative, is thereby marked as potentially capable of generating novelistic discourse.[75]

In its general outline, the collector's narrative stance as established in Russian prose of the 1820s–30s can be seen as yet another response to that unprecedented situation in the production and perception of the utterance that came to define nascent novelistic fictionality both in European and Russian prose. Chapter 1 defined this situation as that of the convergence of story and discourse: in the architectonics of discursive perspective thus configured, any textual action or "move" carries forward both events and their representation in such a way that no boundary can be drawn between the two. Certain prominent developments in early forms of the western European novel—the deliberate blurring of narrative levels in the "self-conscious" novel (Alter); and the opposite tendency, the disowning of narrative in the "factual" novel (Davis)—emerged as effects of the story-discourse convergence and, specifically, as textual "symptoms" of the impossibility of locating a "point of application" that would be strictly, exclusively authorial. In this light, the narrative position of the tale collector that institutes and sustains the principal absence of semantic and expressive intention can be seen as one more distinct realization of the same experience, this time, in the evolving tradition of Russian literary prose.

It is apparent that one's own communicative intention cannot, by any means, be suspended by a subject's conscious effort. The collector's lack of claim to his or her own word differentiates this persona not only from all other personified fictional agents in the cyclical narrative (narrators, editors, translators) but also from any real-world speaking subjects. This suspension of communicative intention, unavailable in "serious" discourse, accounted for the unique experience—uniquely aesthetic, properly speaking—of writers and readers of the 1820s–30s and, consequently, for the prose cycle's appeal and remarkable popularity in literary practice of the time.[76] Pushkin and other writers' distinct "path to prose" (Eikhenbaum), so intensely sought in their artistic and critical works, was discovered in the narrative potential of the "voiceless" collector of tales; this discovery, I believe, represents a key landmark in the history of original Russian prose. I would further suggest that the collector's perception of the word as fully and completely "alien," entirely given over to other speakers' intentions and voices, actualizes the narrative position befitting the author of a novel. In Russian fiction, this position takes form within the generic and compositional parameters of the prose cycle—that is, preemptively, *in advance* of the Russian novel itself.

Chapter Three

The Limits of Optic Power in the Society Tale

THE ESTABLISHED critical reputation of the society tale (*svetskaia povest'*)—a major novella subgenre of the 1830s already obsolete by the end of the following decade—can be described through an inversion of the metaphor of the dwarf standing on the shoulders of giants: while little of lasting value has been created within the generic confines of the society tale proper, its impact on the rise and advance of novelistic discourse in Russian fiction has been recognized as unmistakable and vital. The society tale appears as a literary-historical dwarf, scarcely discernible in the canonical trajectory of Russian prose, on whose shoulders the giant of the Russian novel somehow managed to anchor and balance itself.[1]

One emblematic example of the novel's indebtedness to the society tale is the fact that early drafts of *Anna Karenina*—the masterpiece of Russia's quintessential literary giant Leo Tolstoy—resemble the society tale more than any other prose form; moreover, as Tolstoy himself attests, his novel's conception was inspired by Pushkin's unfinished prose fragments written in the society tale genre.[2] On a more general level, scholars credit the society tale with providing the nascent novelistic discourse with such essential thematic and structural building blocks as plots of love intrigue, marriage, and adultery; the gender question; urban settings and topoi; and major character types, including ingénues, fallen women, predators, moral guardians, and social and financial seekers, among others.

In her pioneering study of the Russian society tale, Elizabeth Shepard sets aside the genre's thematic and ideological features, foregrounding instead its epistemology, namely, its discrimination between analysis and description, or "between the disclosure of internal events and underlying causes and the portrayal of external events and outerlying conditions."[3] Shepard provides ample evidence that Russian writers of the time were acutely aware of, and able to clearly articulate, their new aesthetic aspiration: to forgo the exoticism and eventfulness of historical and adventure narratives and reveal instead the secrets, intrigues, and dramas of domestic, private, and intimate life. In the lexicon of the time, the locus of the society tale's interest was also defined as the conflict between incident and character, or between observable events and the "*innermost* feelings and *inner* events . . . *secret, hidden, cloaked, masked*, and *varnished over*,"[4] that set these outcomes in motion.

In this chapter, drawing on Shepard's formulation of the genre's primary narrative impulse, I situate the society tale among prose forms of the 1830s, juxtaposing it specifically with another prominent genre of the time, the tale of the Caucasus, a quite different form at least in its thematic and ideological concerns. I show that both genres' distinguishing traits can be seen as textual effects of the exploration, in Russian fiction of the time, of the discrepancy between the subject's inner life and its outer manifestations: despite their obvious differences, both genres emerged and developed in the course of their writers' attempts to convincingly breach the gap between characters' observable behaviors and their underlying causes hidden within characters' hearts and minds.

At the same time, my examination of episodes—archetypal for both the society tale and the tale of the Caucasus—in which the novella narrator comes to interrogate observed events, attempting not merely to record, but interpret or decipher them, foregrounds the society tale's *failure* to account for characters' inner experiences. In these situations, the narrator's analytical exercises, however methodical, fall short of the aspiration declared and championed by writers and literary critics of the time: to penetrate the surface of characters' words, appearances, and behaviors and to access their inner thoughts and feelings.

To account for this failure, I suggest that the discrimination between character and incident—the core of the "innovative argument" informing the society tale's epistemology—occurred to Russian writers not, as Shepard claims, as a result of the French-inspired acknowledgment of the modernization of the subject and adoption of Balzac's analytical method of characterization but rather by way of the unprecedented situation of utterance formation and perception that, throughout this book, I define as the story-discourse convergence. The incongruity between inner experience and its external manifestations, revealed to the *speaking* subject within the boundaries of the artistic utterance, determined the subject's consequent recognition, in critical discussions of the time, as one whose deceptively impeccable appearance calls for artistic scrutiny of such societal, domestic, and intimate secrets as lie beneath.

Ultimately, the "innovative argument" proves incapable of realizing the society tale's generic aspiration, of bridging the gap between external behavior and its underlying causes in the human heart and mind. This chapter will show how in his transition from the unfinished *Princess Ligovskaia* to *A Hero of Our Time*, Mikhail Lermontov consummates the society tale's analytical method, exhausting it and demonstrating its inadequacy for the representation of the subject's interiority. In *A Hero of Our Time*, the subject emerges as fundamentally excessive with regard to any and all external manifestations, in the end defying understanding through observation and analysis—a perspective of character formation that is distinctly novelistic. I will argue that the establishment of this perspective, which sustains rather than resolves the incongruity between inner experience and its outer manifestations, can be seen as Lermontov's non-imitative response to Balzacian narrative, specifically, to Balzac's method of characterization. Moreover, Balzac's characterization itself will emerge as antithetical to the society tale's "innovative argument"—despite the pronouncements of 1830s writers and their commentators, both contemporaneous and subsequent, of Balzac as the Russian society tale's immediate literary predecessor.

I begin with two examples from the earlier works of Aleksandr Bestuzhev-Marlinsky, who would go on to be one of the most prominent practitioners of both the society tale and the tale of the Caucasus in nineteenth-century Russian fiction. In Bestuzhev's novella *A Night on a Ship* (1823), the narrator, a traveling Russian officer, strikes up a conversation with a British captain named Ronald, who then confides to the former the story of his tragic love. Before delegating the narrative voice to the captain, the narrator describes his "noble" appearance:

> There are eyes that, at first sight, express frankness and attest to friendliness; such was the noble face of Ronald. . . . His eyes sparkled rarely, but one could see that this was the glow of a former fire of passion.[5]

The narrator of *A Night on a Ship* asserts a direct correspondence—perceived "at first sight"—between the character's appearance and his thoughts, such that the sparkle in Ronald's eyes is a constituent of the same fire of passion burning within his soul. This correspondence established, Ronald's confession provides a reliable account of his experiences. By assuring the reader of the captain's unquestionable genuineness, the narrator of *A Night on a Ship* simply annuls the potential chasm between Ronald's feelings and his willingness and ability to express them, and spares himself any obligation to look beneath, interpret, or decode this character's face, words, or actions—the very obligation that comes to the fore in the society tale of the 1830s.

In another Bestuzhev novella, *The Red Veil* (*Krasnoe pokryvalo*, 1831), the narrator similarly rules out any incongruity between character feelings and their outward manifestations. The Muslim heroine's anguish at the loss of her beloved accounts for her otherwise unthinkable disregard for behavioral and cultural conventions:

> Her gaze was fixed on me, but her answer was barely audible, as if she were speaking with her own heart. . . . "I am already dead to the slander of my neighbors, to the vengeance of relations. Let them all see, let them all know. Before, you couldn't have wrested the secret of my love even by shedding my blood—now I am happy to tell anyone anywhere about it . . . I have nothing more to lose, nothing to fear."[6]

In *The Red Veil*, the heroine's confession is deemed trustworthy since it is presented as an unmediated, spontaneous expression of her inner suffering; her words come directly from her heart. In this regard, each of the Bestuzhev novellas just cited are representative of the 1820s: as discussed in chapter 1, prose narratives of the time typically relied on various forms of narrative embedding, with the framing narrator either an engaged and sympathetic listener of anecdotes/confessions, or else the fortunate "finder" of manuscripts, diaries, personal notes, or intimate letters. At the same time, the narrator's very need to preemptively highlight his characters' integrity both in *A Night on a Ship* and *The Red Veil* anticipates a discursive shift that is to occur in Russian fiction in the next decade.

Novellas of the 1830s feature a variety of situations in which the framing narrator, heretofore content to meticulously gather and record verbatim (*slovo v slovo*) the monologues of his or her interlocutors, now registers suspicion as to the credibility of his or her sources. Testimony, oral or written—the central constituent of the "found manuscript" device—is now perceived as problematic, dubious, insufficient. Is a fortuitously acquired "manuscript" authentic, or a work of fiction?[7] How honest is a witness or participant claiming his or her story to be "true to life"? When the framed narrator's trustworthiness is no longer taken for granted, and questions arise as to his or her motivations, the compositional forms of narrative embedding break down, as does the authenticity claim these forms had sustained. Narrative interest now shifts from story to story*teller*, that is, to the embedded narrator him or herself.

With the collapse of the "found manuscript" device and the framed narrator's morphing into a character under suspicion, the framing narrator also undergoes a crucial change: his or her capacity for compassionate listening and accurate recording proves inadequate to the society tale's central task of scrutinizing characters' words and behaviors in order to penetrate their inner life. The framing narrator, formerly approaching his character with all gentleness to kindheartedly solicit a confession (as in Bestuzhev's *A Night on a Ship*), now strives to erase himself from the character's field of vision, lying patiently in wait to catch his prey unawares. Incessant surveillance replaces sympathetic understanding as the means to access character interiority, with the society tale narrator frequently acting as face-reader, eavesdropper, and spy.

Shepard aptly formulates the significance of observation in the society tale's narrative organization: "The society tale . . . tends to record close observations of people who themselves are closely observing each other (or, to their misfortune, failing to do so), while they are observing, or appearing to observe, the proprieties [*nabliudat' prilichiia*]."[8] A number of the society tale's thematic and structural traits result from its narrator's need to scrutinize character appearance and behaviors: indoor settings ranging from the ballroom and drawing room down to the study and boudoir; gossip as a major force of plot development; and the prominent employment, both figurative and literal, of such optical instruments as microscopes, telescopes, mirrors, and opera glasses which, alongside writer/doctor and writer/scientist comparisons, become a central metaphor of intellectual and literary discourse in the 1830s.[9] These optical devices sharpen the observer's eyesight; more importantly, they allow for the viewing of events from a remote vantage point. The most advantageous position of observation is, of course, that of seeing without being seen. It is precisely this panoptical position that the society tale narrator strives to occupy by retiring to the margins and equipping him or herself with potent visual aids.

As a result, experiences foregrounding the incongruity between inner life and its outer manifestations come uppermost in the writerly imagination. The variety and peculiarity of subgenres in Russian fiction of the time can be seen as determined by authors' pursuit of narrative situations amenable to the exploration of the inner/outer dichotomy, particularly situations fraught with the discrepancy between the two. The society tale represents one of the novella subgenres that, in the 1830s, originate and develop in response to writers' interrogation of the boundary between external events and their inner-life causes. Polite society, with its constitutional principle of the "sense of propriety" (Pushkin's *chuvstvo prilichiia*),[10] presented a narrative site highly charged with the incongruity between its denizens' looks, words, and actions and their thoughts and feelings: the dweller of high society is, first and foremost, one capable of suppressing (indeed, obliged to suppress) his or her inner joy or pain, and to perform the utmost public politeness.

Another novella subgenre is the tale of the Caucasus, common in the 1830s alongside the society tale; and even as the former explored a markedly different social and geographical stratum than did the latter, the tale of the Caucasus can be seen as driven by the same search for incongruity between individual interiority and its outward expression. The exotic, far-flung settings of the Caucasus—like the all-too-familiar ballrooms and drawing rooms of the society tale—present Russian writers with another narrative site amenable to exploration of this discrepancy. In fiction of the time, the Caucasian emerges as one whose behavior is no less codified (hence no less opaque) than that of the high-society Russian; an equally heightened narrative effort is required to decipher and represent his or her inner experiences.

For instance, in Bestuzhev's *Ammalat-Bek* (1832), the military and personal authority of General Ermolov, commander-in-chief in the initial stage of the Caucasus war of 1817–64, is to a large degree determined by his adeptness at reading minds:

> One must admire how, on receiving days . . . he foils the Caucasians' plotting with a single comment (in vain do they try to hide their treacherous schemes in the innermost folds of their hearts—his gaze pursues them, rips them apart like worms; he guesses their thoughts and affairs twenty years in advance).[11]

Ermolov's ill-fated decision to forgive Ammalat-Bek his twice-committed disloyalty is, on the contrary, based on the latter's appearance, specifically the young man's "unusual handsomeness" (*neobyknovennaia krasota*), which clouds even the old general's penetrating gaze:

> Whoever has, like me, rubbed shoulders with the Caucasians, has certainly ceased trusting [Johann Kaspar] Lavater [the pioneer of physiognomy, to be discussed further below]; and puts no more stock in a beautiful face than in a letter of recommendation; but the eyes, the gait, and the bearing of this Ammalat made a remarkable impression on me—and I took pity on him.[12]

The decision proves disastrous: Ammalat-Bek, himself a victim of the treachery of one of the Russians' most inveterate enemies, kills his friend and benefactor Colonel Verkhovsky, who failed to heed Ermolov's warning upon Ammalat's release: "Just mark my words: if you want to take him in—don't trust him, don't warm a snake on your bosom."[13]

The animated and passionate Caucasian appears as secretive (*skrytnyi*) and prone to scheming (*kozni*) as the "lifeless" and "ice-cold" (Odoevsky)[14] high-society Russian who indulges in plots and destructive coercion. In his discussion of Lermontov's *A Hero of Our Time*, William Mills Todd notes that in this work, "deceit, theft, and violence are no less the dominant principles of the novel's polite society than they are of the Caucasian tribes. . . . The parallels between 'civilized' and 'uncivilized' society are clearly established by the novel's structural patterns."[15] With regard to Russian prose writers' exploration of the incongruity between a subject's external behavior and inner motivation, Lermontov's juxtaposition and conflation of the two ostensibly divergent sociocultural bodies can be considered an artistic consummation and conclusion.

At the same time, the lack of naturalness in both "civilized" and "uncivilized" societies—revealed in the course of the writers' search for correlation between motive and external performance—hardly signifies some special ideological deficiency on the part of these particular groups. After all, a "sense of propriety," to invoke again Pushkin's apt formulation, is an indispensable constituent of human behavior; as such it is no more or less conventional than any other social form of life. Denunciations of the extreme artificiality of high society in literary criticism of the time do not, I believe, reflect any special degeneracy on the part of Russian *grand monde* mores, but rather flow from the society tale practitioners' narrative struggle to access the interiority of the subject.

The writers' quest for a reliable path to inner experience results in the hardening of the very boundaries mediating the subject's thoughts and feelings. The more intensely the narrative gaze aspires to penetrate the ever-conventional forms by which these thoughts and feelings are expressed—aspires, that is, to catch sight of unique inner life—the more such conventional forms are discovered. Even manners formerly perceived as enabling self-expression seem increasingly stifling when examined by interiority-preoccupied prose writers of the 1830s. For instance, in her discussion of dueling in early nineteenth-century Russia, Irina Reyfman traces a distinct change in Bestuzhev's treatment of the institution of the duel over time. Reyfman remarks that, while Bestuzhev's attitude toward dueling had always been ambivalent, his historical tales more typically present the custom as a form of liberation from social constraints, an affirmation of individuality. But in his society tales, the duel appears itself a form of constraint, with the individual asserting his independence by (dignifiedly) avoiding it. Between the two genres, "Bestuzhev's society tales provide a far more complex and even contradictory view of the duel."[16]

Similarly, though Russian literary representation of the Caucasus has always been heavily laden with "complex and even contradictory" narrative and political impulses, prose fiction of the 1830s is marked by a distinct emphasis on purported Caucasian evasiveness and treachery, rather than, as in poetic discourse of the 1820s, genuineness and "savage" freedom. Certainly there are political and ideological reasons for this change.[17] But the shift in the representation of the Other in the tale of the Caucasus indicates, I believe, especially a *narrative* disillusionment in the possibility of connecting the subject's interiority with outward sociocultural forms, as witness the same shift when ethnic difference plays no role. The same disappointment, that is, informs the change in Bestuzhev's stance on dueling, and more generally fuels the society tale's critique of the Russian social elite's behavioral norms. This disappointment stems from the discovery of the fundamental lack of *any* forms adequate to the task of expressing the interiority of the subject, "civilized" or otherwise, Russian or Other.

To demonstrate this narrative failure to access inner life and examine its causes and consequences, I now turn to Mikhail Lermontov's unfinished prose work *Princess Ligovskaia* (1836), which, as Robert Reid remarks, "for all its imperfections and incompleteness has long been held up as exemplifying the society tale."[18] *Princess Ligovskaia* forcefully expands the society tale's generic potential, taking as far as it can go the narrative imperative, central to the poetics of 1830s prose, to bridge the subject's inner experience and outer performance.

The narrator of *Princess Ligovskaia* does not rely for his information on witnesses or solicited confessions; nor has he any need of magnifying optical devices, or any form of spying or eavesdropping. Instead, the narrator follows the characters ubiquitously, easily entering the most solitary places such as studies and boudoirs and inspecting them without any restraint. In his effort to become the most competent observer and analyst, the narrator of *Princess Ligovskaia* succeeds in occupying a position best described as invisible presence.[19]

A comparison with an episode from Bestuzhev's early novella *The Clock and the Mirror* (1831) underscores the freedom enjoyed by the narrator of *Princess Ligovskaia* in accessing characters' private spaces. In Bestuzhev's novella, the narrator's accidental visit to the heroine's study (*kabinet*) overcomes him with feelings so strong he is unable to convey them in his native Russian:

> It's a pity that we have no way of expressing the English word *awe*. This is neither fear, nor reverence, nor amazement, but something containing parts of all three. I was astonished not by what I saw, but by what I could conjecture or imagine. . . . With some sort of feeling of sweet terror I stepped into Sof'ia's room as if into a sanctuary.[20]

In *Princess Ligovskaia*, the study is similarly envisioned as that place in the house best enabling the fathoming of its dweller's inner life:

> Pechorin peered in curiously through the half-open ballroom door, attempting to deduce at least a faint trace of his hosts' family life from the room's decor; but alas! In the capital all ballrooms are as alike as all the smiles and all the greetings. Only the study can sometimes unveil domestic secrets; but the study is as impenetrable to outside visitors as the heart.[21]

In this episode, the family mysteries of the study remain inaccessible to the protagonist, Pechorin; the narrator, however, freely and matter-of-factly enters and examines these sacred domains: "The officer . . . went up the shiny staircase. . . . Now that he has taken off his snow-covered coat and entered his study, we can freely follow him and describe his appearance."[22]

Neither does the narrator bother to justify his access to characters' personal correspondence; instead, he simply observes him or her writing or reading a letter. In the following example, an anonymous letter found by Lizaveta Negurova in the privacy of her boudoir is presented to the reader verbatim:

> She impatiently threw her book on the table and suddenly noticed a letter addressed to her and stamped by the city post office. . . . The envelope is ripped open by trembling hands, the candle is moved closer, and her eyes eagerly scan the first lines. . . . The handwriting is noticeably distorted. . . . Instead of a signature, some sort of Egyptian squiggle is drawn at the bottom. . . . Here is the letter, from first word to last.[23]

Invisibility is the ideal vantage point for external observation. Being invisible, the narrator of *Princess Ligovskaia* emerges victorious in the crossfire of furtively inquisitive glances that his characters, equipped with assorted ocular devices, exchange at their various gatherings, social and otherwise. In addition, his supreme analytical skills allow the narrator to process information thus received: to decode the characters' appearances, words, and actions, and interpret them as outward expressions of their inner life. Endowed with the ability to "read very well the yearnings of the soul on faces" (*ia chitaiu ochen' khorosho pobuzhdeniia dushi na fizionomiiakh*),[24] the narrator engages consistently in such perusals, these truly "close" readings enabled especially by his state of unseenness.

In *Princess Ligovskaia*, invisibility functions as the logical extreme of the magnification of sight provided by microscopes, telescopes, and other optical devices, maximally amplifying the narrator's ability to observe and, consequently, to analyze. At the same time, this intensification of narratorial ability highlights a key defect in the means the society tale has at its disposal to connect exteriors with interiority. Despite his invisibility and great capacity for face-reading, the narrator of *Princess Ligovskaia* comes up against insurmountable barriers thwarting his representation of characters' inner life.

The narrator discovers, for instance, that different vantage points produce contradictory but equally plausible readings of one and the same character's personality. In the following description, Lizaveta Negurova's mother is presented from three points of view—that of her husband's colleagues, of other elderly ladies, and the opinion of young people in attendance at a ball—interpretive points not mutually complementary, but at odds with one another. Unable to choose only one, the narrator resorts to a mere assemblage of all existing opinions:

> Katerina Ivanovna was a clever lady according to the clerks who worked at her husband's office; a sly and crafty woman in the opinion of other old ladies;

> a kind and gullible mama according to the young people at the ball . . . I have not yet figured out her true nature; in describing her, I will try to combine and express together all three opinions mentioned above.[25]

The depiction of Pechorin, given as he enters his study, similarly comprises various conflicting viewpoints: that of high society, of the physiognomist-adherents of Lavater, and the opinion of the "crowd" (*tolpa*).[26]

A would-be face-reader must come up against one obvious limitation of physiognomy, namely, that changing expressions can radically alter a person's appearance. Vera Ligovskaia's facial illegibility is acknowledged by the character Pechorin—

> "It's strange," thought Pechorin, getting on the sleigh. "There was a time when I read all the movements of her thought on her face just as unmistakably as if reading my own manuscript, but now I don't understand her, I don't understand her at all."[27]

—and even by the expert physiognomist narrator, whose reading of Vera's face is suspended between dueling interpretations impossible to reconcile:

> Seeing her for the first time, you might say, if you are an experienced observer, that this is a woman who is strong, decisive, and cold . . . ready to sacrifice her happiness for the sake of rules, but not for the sake of rumors. But seeing her in a moment of passion and excitement, you would say something completely different—or, more likely, you wouldn't know what to say at all.[28]

The narrator discovers furthermore that different feelings can be manifested by the same external sign: there are tears of joy, for example, and tears of sorrow. Being invisible, the narrator can observe Vera crying behind closed doors; but when it comes to interpreting her tears, he is as helpless as the character herself:

> She closed the door behind her and threw herself into a broad armchair . . . tears appeared on her eyelashes and began steadily falling . . . and she cried, cried bitterly. . . . What was she crying about?—you might ask, and I would ask you, what don't women cry about. . . . They express frustration, joy, helpless hatred, and helpless love the same way: Vera Dmitrievna herself could not have accounted for which of these feelings was the main reason for her tears.[29]

The narrator's inability to represent inner experience becomes especially evident in episodes where a character, overcome with feeling, covers his or her face or turns it to the wall, as when Lizaveta Negurova receives an anonymous letter exposing what she had thought to be Pechorin's romantic interest in her as a cleverly orchestrated joke:

> Then she extinguished the candle and *turned her face to the wall*: she seemed to be crying, but so quietly, so quietly, that if you were standing at her bedside, you would have thought she was sleeping peacefully and serenely.[30] (Emphasis mine)

Thus is the narrator able, with his great powers of observation, to see that the heroine's apparently calm sleep conceals intense suffering; but unable to deduce specifically what is taking place in her heart.

Similarly, another character, Krasinsky, covers his face when Pechorin, having knocked him down with his carriage, refuses to take seriously the poor clerk's humiliation: "The clerk did not answer, he *covered his face with his hands*, his chest was heaving, and in his disconnected words one could discern despair; he seemed to be weeping [emphasis mine]."[31]

In one last example, Pechorin himself buries his face in his hands upon receiving word (via visiting card) that a woman he had once loved passionately has just arrived in St. Petersburg. Here the narrator closely follows Pechorin's every expression and gesture, but ultimately is forced to admit that his face-reading is futile, that his troubled character's train of thought is illegible:

> He turned pale and shuddered, his eyes flashed, and the visiting card flew into the fireplace. For about three minutes he paced back and forth about the room, making various strange gestures with his hands, and various exclamations, now smiling, now frowning; finally, he stopped, grabbed the fire-tongs, and hastened to pull the card from the fire: alas! half of it had turned to ashes, and the other was curled and blackened—one could only barely make out *Stepan Step*. . . .
>
> Pechorin put these mortal remains on the desk, sat once again in his armchair, and *covered his face with his hands* [emphasis mine]—and though I can read very well the yearnings of the soul on faces, it is precisely for this reason that I have no way of telling you his thoughts. He sat in this position for a quarter of an hour.[32]

From the standpoint of the impenetrable exterior/interiority barrier, Pechorin's covering of his face seems not to cause the narrator's inability to access his character's emotions; but rather to result from it. It is as if, unable to perform a reliable face-reading, the narrator, oblivious to the true cause of his failure—the fundamental disconnect between external and internal—

falls back on the "excuse" of a mere physical limitation, the burying of one's face in one's hands, in which pose the narrator keeps his character long enough to cover his own shortcomings.

Once again, a comparison with Bestuzhev's earlier novella *The Red Veil* underscores the narrative shift having occurred in the 1830s vis-à-vis representation of characters' inner life. As discussed above, in this novella, the intensity of the grief felt by the Muslim woman at her lover's graveside sufficiently accounts for the sincerity and spontaneity of her self-expression. Here the narrator is concerned primarily with justifying his ability to clearly observe the heroine's face, taking special care, accordingly, to emphasize that her customary Muslim veil does *not* conceal her face at the moment of their meeting:

> The red veil was thrown from her face—and how lovely, how expressive was the pallid face that she turned toward the sky! . . . The Turkish woman was startled but did not cover her face according to the general custom of Asian women: the sovereign power of melancholy had killed all her other cares.[33]

The difference between the two narrators' notions as to what constitutes reliable representation of their characters' inner life is apparent. In *The Red Veil*, the titular covering has to be removed, as it is all that stands between the narrator and the heroine's all-expressive, literally open, face. In *Princess Ligovskaia*, the narrator, being invisible, has no difficulty staring directly into his characters' faces; but having reached this privileged position of uninhibited observation, he recognizes that the face itself is never so expressive or open as to provide reliable access to the thoughts behind it. Here the face, along with gestures, words, actions, and other would-be signifiers of character interiority, become their own sort of "veil," obscuring feelings rather than revealing them. As an external observer, the narrator is incapable of removing this cover to read the heart directly. If Bestuzhev's narrator attempts to enhance his position of observation by ensuring a clear view of his character's face, the narrator in *Princess Ligovskaia* in effect blinds his all-seeing eye, "excusing" his inevitable interpretive failures via faces buried in hands or turned toward a wall.

In the course of this latter narrative, the fundamental incongruity between face-reading and mind-reading becomes apparent. The narrator's initial comparison of a private chamber with inner life—"the study is as impenetrable . . . as the heart" (*kabinet tak zhe nepronitsaem . . . kak serdtse)*[34]—proves inaccurate: the invisible narrator has no difficulty following a character into his study and thoroughly examining its interior; but the character's heart remains opaque even to this ubiquitous observer. The narrator has to acknowledge that in depicting his characters' psyches, he can only provide guesses—educated ones, via Lavater's physiognomy among other things, but guesses nonetheless:

> Of course, no faded beauty confided to me the thoughts and feelings stirring her bosom after a long ball or party. . . . But I can *surmise* that these musings must be painful, intolerable to the heart and pride. . . . In order to *make a better guess* as to what exactly Lizaveta Nikolaevna deigned to think, I must . . . tell you certain particulars of her life.[35] (Emphases mine)

Ultimately, the only reliable conclusion afforded by invisibility-panopticality—the vantage point so ardently sought by writers of society tales—is that when it comes to characters' inner thoughts and feelings, "only God knows":

> These conversations would be repeated, one way or another, every time the mother, father, and daughter were by themselves . . . the daughter kept quiet, but only God knows what was happening in her heart at these moments.[36]

When the narrator does attempt to account for a character's silent thoughts, he invariably presents even the most intimate emotions as connected with external circumstances. For instance, a character's daydreams can only be those shared with others of his socioeconomic class:

> Thus, a young clerk was walking along Voznesenskaia Street; he was coming from his office, weary from monotonous work and dreaming of his reward and a delicious dinner—*for all clerks are dreamers!*[37] (Emphasis mine)

Similarly, Pechorin's emotional lethargy on the eve of meeting his former love is explained as resulting from the influence of St. Petersburg's sky, which numbs the "vital organs" of those dwelling under it:

> Many inhabitants of Petersburg who spent their childhood in a different climate are subject to the influence of the sky here. Some kind of sad indifference, akin to that with which our northern sun turns away from the local ungrateful earth, creeps into the soul and numbs all vital organs. At this moment, the heart is incapable of enthusiasm, the mind unable to ponder. In such a disposition was Pechorin.[38]

Krasinsky's dreaminess proves as external a trait as the frock coat the government clerks of St. Petersburg are required to wear; and Pechorin's apathy appears no more interior than the city's climate. The external observer's effort to access character interiority via the reading of faces (or gestures, words, actions, boudoirs, studies, weather conditions, etc.) thus results in the total externalization of the given character's thoughts and feelings; such readings, taken to their extreme, render the boundary between internal and external meaningless.

Put another way, due to the architectonics of the narrator's gaze, the society tale character strives, but fails, to become a *hero*. Instead, characters in *Princess Ligovskaia* are catalogued into assortments of "collectives"—daydreaming government clerks; young people with time on their hands; emotionally cold women—that corroborate various rules or (socioeconomic, meteorological, physiognomic) principles.[39] The comparison of the fiction writer to the doctor/scientist performing an autopsy on the human heart, a trope employed with great expectations in the intellectual discourse of the 1830s,[40] backfires in the course of the society tale's search for the subject's interiority: as the hoped-for culmination of face-reading initiatives, the ultimate autopsy report would render *all* human hearts fully exposed (externalized) but at the same time indistinguishable from one another.[41] The narrator's solemn pronouncements on Pechorin's exceptionality and enigmatic complexity remain, within the generic confines of the society tale, strictly declarative; there is no narrative means by which to single him out or extract him from the general web of externalizations.[42] Under the inescapably externalizing gaze of its teller, the society tale renders inaccessible the particularity or uniqueness of the subject.

In the European-wide literary-historical context, the narrator's impulse to take stock of the external manifestations and behaviors in the first place can be connected to Edmund Heier's view of Lermontov as Russian prose's first practitioner of nuanced and sophisticated "predictive physiognomy."[43] Having located the primary sources of the psychophysiological method of characterization in the theories of Lavater and Gall—widely popular in Europe and Russia—Heier also identifies a most powerful and immediate literary influence in Lermontov's artistic appropriation of physiognomy: French fiction of the 1830s, specifically, the *Comédie humaine* of Honoré de Balzac.

> Like Balzac, and before him, Lavater, Lermontov seems to have embraced the concept of constant interaction between the physical and the spiritual, between the outer and the inner. Thus the world of matter surrounding the personality, from the hand to the decoration of one's room, constitutes part of the total unity of a character.[44]

The method of predictive physiognomy is, of course, in full accord with the premises of the "innovative argument," that discrimination between incident and character which, according to Shepard, lies at the core of the society tale's epistemology. So it is not surprising that, in tracing the sources of Russian writers' fascination with the philosophical and artistic potential of the "innovative argument," Shepard, too, stresses the influence of Balzac, thereby concurring with 1830s writers' and critics' own recognition of the French novelist as their literary predecessor, evidenced for instance in Aleksandr Turgenev's description of Balzac as a "physiologist and anatomist of the soul" and Apollon Grigor'ev's pronouncement that the society tale appeared in Russia "no later and no sooner than Balzac."[45]

Princess Ligovskaia employs predictive physiognomy with subtlety and sophistication; but as the analysis above has shown, it also unambiguously attests to this method's inadequacy in representing interiority, a failure acknowledged by Lermontov himself, who eventually abandoned the project. Rather than exemplifying the triumph of predictive physiognomy, *Princess Ligovskaia* brings the "innovative argument" to an impasse, revealing the principal discrepancy between the inner life of the subject and its outward manifestations, a gap unbridgeable by the analysis, however meticulous, of faces, hands, room decor, or any other external (biographical, sociological, professional, etc.) attributes. The inadequacy of the panoptical view to access interiority evinced in *Princess Ligovskaia*, wherein, as noted, observational freedom and ubiquity are taken to an extreme, is emblematic of the society tale's essential inability to represent consciousness. A character's covering of his or her face or turning it to the wall, then, can be seen as the narrator's desperate attempt to salvage, or make a case for, the subject's excess in relation to any and all external manifestations and behaviors.

Noteworthy in this regard is that some of the most incisive studies of Balzac's novels also underscore in his method of characterization a certain excess, one that cannot be accounted for by positing Balzac as progenitor of sociohistorical and psychological typification (the core of the "innovative argument"). Perhaps the most prominent example of this observation is Fredric Jameson's chapter on Balzac in his seminal work *The Political Unconscious*, which presents a detailed reading of two of Balzac's novels while simultaneously elaborating Jameson's own critical method of literary analysis. Jameson brilliantly demonstrates that in both novels, each character's traits and behaviors emerge as either mutually exclusive or else strangely redundant. For instance, in *The Old Girl* (*La vieille fille*), the two main participants in the matrimonial contest that is the focus of the plot exhibit attributes hardly coalescing into coherent portraits; rather, each set of attributes evinces a stark incongruity in terms of, on the one hand, sexual potency, and on the other, class affiliation:

> The combination of semes that make up [Chevalier's] portrait can be shown to be contradictory, and the reading mind must on some level worry the question: how is it possible for the graceful, effeminate, elderly Chevalier to be more "potent" than the rough-and-ready bourgeois speculator Du Bousquier? Meanwhile, the latter offers no less of a paradox.[46]

In the other novel, *The Black Sheep* (*La rabouilleuse*), two clashing interpretive paradigms, one sociohistorical and the other psychological, are shown by Jameson as operative simultaneously in the characterization of the protagonists (two rival brothers) and their conflict (the struggle for an inheritance):

> *La Rabouilleuse* makes use of two distinct diagnoses, two independent and mutually exclusive explanatory systems or "psychologies," to account, in a curiously superimposed and overdetermined fashion, for one set of character traits; and with this curious reduplication—of an essentially objective or sociological diagnosis with an essentially subjective or protopsychoanalytic one—we are at the heart of the novel and the place from which its twin registers can be distinguished.[47]

According to Jameson, these contradictions and superimpositions acquire coherence only if Balzac's characters are understood not as unified subjects, whose outward behaviors can be elucidated through analysis of underlying sociohistorical and psychological causalities, but rather as textual effects, or "anthropomorphic combinations"[48] generated by the only subjectivity truly at work in the Balzacian narrative: that of the author himself. It is the twofold—in relation to both history and biography—*authorial* excess that, according to Jameson, establishes and fuels characterization patterns, narrative tactics, and plot developments that otherwise appear either contradictory or redundant.

Jameson defines this excess in terms of a wish-fulfillment fantasy that seeks to resolve a set of intolerable contradictions in empirical history, both social and familial. For Balzac, the two major aspects of this fantasy are the "dream of landed establishment" and the "fantasy of ultimate reinstatement in the mother's eyes and ultimate triumph over the unworthy sibling rival."[49] The key constituents of the Balzacian text are determined by the impossible desire—personal and political—to transform the apparently immutable yet unbearable givens of sociohistorical and familial situations, to open up a narrative space within which some satisfaction of desire is possible.[50]

Jameson further argues that whether the wish-fulfilling mechanism rises to the level of genuine literary and cultural production depends on the workings of the reality principle, or censorship within the daydreaming process. This principle constitutes a central mediating link between desire and history, compelling the desiring subject to conjure up and thoroughly enumerate all possible objections thwarting the fulfillment of his or her fantasy. The reality principle also plays a decisive role in Jameson's solution to the "fundamental problem for aesthetic creation" posited by Freud in his "Creative Writers and Day-Dreaming":[51] it is precisely the engagement of the reality principle that separates artistic creations from private daydreams or, in the Lacanian terminology employed by Jameson, "Symbolic" texts from "Imaginary" ones:

> "Symbolic texts" entertain a far more difficult and implacable conception of the fully realized fantasy: one which is not to be satisfied by the easy solutions of an "unrealistic" omnipotence or the immediacy of a gratification that then needs no narrative trajectory in the first place, but which on the contrary seeks to endow itself with the utmost representable density and to posit the most elaborate and systematic difficulties and obstacles in order the more surely to overcome them, just as a philosopher imagines in advance the objections his triumphant argumentation will be summoned up to confute.[52]

Consequently, Balzac's superb physiognomic skills, his nuanced understanding of sociohistorical and psychological tensions, and his method of characterization, acclaimed as "analytical" and "scientific" by Russian writers of the 1830s and their contemporaneous and subsequent commentators, all stem from the earnest workings—earnest in the sense of braked by the built-in reality principle—of the wish-fulfilling mechanism, from the desiring subject's "incorrigible fantasy."[53] This fantasy cannot in principle be satisfied by any textual configurations that it generates, hence cannot be deduced from these configurations or subjected to sociohistorical or psychological analysis. On the contrary, impossible desire precedes, conceptually and chronologically, the alignment and unfolding of the narrative's representational strategies—including methods of characterization—which emerge as discursive trajectories of the social and personal fantasy's unrelenting yet ultimately futile struggle for fulfillment.

I am in complete agreement with Jameson's claim that the essential features of Balzac's novels should not be viewed as representations, however perceptive, of contemporaneous sociohistorical reality (e.g., the private life of high society or the "capitalization" of the spirit[54] in nineteenth-century Europe); let the emphasis be, rather, on the utterance's producer, or author, whose definitive excess in relation to this reality generates textual effects on the levels of both story and discourse, effects whose meaning and configuration cannot be derived from any characteristics of the world outside the text. At the same time, Jameson's conceptualization of this excess in terms of desire applies in equal measure to both artist and daydreamer: the difference between the two lies solely in the weightiness and density of obstacles conjured by their fantasy-driven imaginations—not unlike, to cite Jameson's analogy, the difference between a philosopher who seeks to preemptively refute all potential objections to his theory, and one who doesn't bother.

For Jameson, the transition from "Imaginary" to "Symbolic" involves no change in the subject him or herself: the difference between private daydreams and artistic creations lies exclusively in the efficacy of the reality principle within the wish-fulfilling mechanism. In the former, desire is easily satisfied; in the latter, it "comes to grief"[55]—but it is the *same consciousness*, that of the desiring subject, the "wish-fulfilling mind,"[56] that conceives of and carries out both daydream and artistic utterance. On the contrary, I would insist that the perspective of utterance formation and perception actualized in novelistic utterance—namely, that of story-discourse convergence—enables a subjective activity fundamentally different from that of the desiring subject, actuating a narrative dynamic radically divergent from daydreaming or wish-fulfillment fantasy.

This qualitative difference comes to the fore if one posits as a prerequisite to any desire the experience of privation, or absence of a particular object or state. The desiring subject, no matter the content of his or her desire (landed estate, maternal approval, etc.) is thus constituted by the discrepancy between here-and-now, wherein the desired object or state is absent, and there-and-then—projected either into the past or future—where and when the desired object may be attained. The axiological heterogeneity of time and space thereby presents the prime "obstacle" for wish fulfillment: even the most instantaneous of gratifications, the most immediate and omnipotent of solutions generated by fantasy (a genie snapping his fingers, say), has to surmount the "instant" (spatial and temporal) between here-and-now and there-and-then.

The workings of fantasy, attempting to compensate for the subject's immanent temporal and spatial deficiency (manifest in the experience of privation), are catalyzed by the discrepancy between present and nonpresent (the latter situated either in the past or future), and so are fully conditioned by temporal and spatial categories. The wish-fulfilling mechanism thus sustains and reinforces the subject's dependence on the constraints of time and space. In other words, the narrative trajectories of desire correlate with the desiring subject's inability to implement a choice, that is, to carry out subjectivity itself. Balzac's *The Wild Ass's Skin* (*La peau de chagrin*), part of the *Études philosophiques* series, offers a dramatization of this assertion: in this novel, the workings of the wish-fulfillment fantasy, gratifying instantly via the magic skin, result in the hero's death—the ultimate manifestation of the subject's spatiotemporal deficiency.

A decisive change in the subject's dual experience of privation and desire occurs only in the situation of the production and perception of fictional narrative. Throughout this book, I define this situation as that of the story-discourse simultaneity or convergence: both producer and perceiver of artistic utterance find themselves in a position from which narrated events and the event of narration concur in time and space; events do not precede their representation but rather arise and develop with and within it. This unique—aesthetic proper—perspective of utterance formation came to define novelistic fictionality in both Europe and Russia, radically distinguishing novelistic discourse not only from preceding genres of literary prose, but from any and all nonfictional narratives, including, I would now add, those born of daydreaming or wish-fulfilling mechanisms, wherein the "event"—in this case, the imaginary gratification of a personal or political desire—launches the workings of these mechanisms and drives them forward.

In the architectonics of the novelistic discursive perspective, any textual action or "move" carries forward both events and their representation in such a way that no boundary can be drawn between the two; narrated events and the event of narration, story and discourse, completely and utterly converge in time and space. The subject (whether producer or perceiver of an artistic utterance) thereby experiences the simultaneous unfolding of multiple temporal and spatial trajectories, and has no grounds on which to prioritize or privilege one spatiotemporal context over another. In aesthetic activity, the axiological heterogeneity of time and space, which as argued preconditions and sets in motion the daydreaming or wish-fulfilling mechanism, is annulled; consequently, this mechanism itself comes to a stall. A consciousness engaged in aesthetic activity is liberated from temporal and spatial heterogeneity, and contains all possible "objects" within itself; it has nothing to feel bereft of and nothing to wish for—a condition that cannot be anchored to any real-life state of mind, whether conscious or unconscious.

The excess in relation to the analytical method of characterization, superbly demonstrated in Jameson's reading of Balzac's novels, stems, I believe, from the establishment of the aesthetic proper perspective of utterance formation and the concomitant change in the narrating subject's state of consciousness; and not from this or that specific content of this consciousness. In this light, some of the major properties of Balzacian characterization appear not as results of the earnest exertions of the wish-fulfilling mind, but rather as consequences of the suspension of the daydreaming mechanism within the artistic utterance. Scholars consistently single out Balzac's two major modes of conduct as ambition and mania; in my view these modes are not amplified forms of desire, but two mutually complementary character-effects of the annulment of the space-time heterogeneity within the novelistic utterance, and of the resulting cessation of the wish-fulfilling mechanism.

In his discussion of the dynamics of disillusionment in Balzac's *Lost Illusions* (*Illusions perdues*), D. A. Miller observes that "in the very novel that is often considered the supreme representation of this experience, no disillusionment really occurs."[57] Instead, in a pattern that is repeated throughout the novel, the protagonist Lucien de Rubempré's every illusion is no sooner lost than replaced by another. Miller traces this "economy of illusion"[58] not to the psyche or sociological makeup of Balzac's characters, but to the underlying principle of the Balzacian text, which he defines as "narrative functionality":[59]

> The Balzacian *ambitieux* regularly encounters a stinging dispossession: of his lover, his success, his writing, etc. But unlike many of its readers, Balzac's fiction never hypostatizes this aspect of disillusionment (as evidence of a critical consciousness), but places it within a more inclusive process which quickly reappropriates it.[60]

According to this principle, desire is divested from particular objects—whether "money, women, roles, stories,"[61] seen as more or less fungible—and is committed only to the processes of exchange, or circulation. A peculiarity of ambition as evinced by Balzac's social climbers is that they do not really climb *up*—a trajectory befitting the sociopsychological profile of an *ambitieux*—but rather perpetually "cycle" through equally privileged objects and social stations. I see this distinctive unfolding of ambition as a character-effect of the annulment of spatial heterogeneity: consistent indifference to specific objects of possession, to these objects' actual attributes, attests to Balzac's social climbers' insusceptibility to spatial diversity, their detachment from the hierarchy of spatial contexts. As distinct from Miller, who posits the characters' indifference to particular objects as evidence of the Balzacian narration's subscription to the "basic principles of nineteenth-century social order,"[62] I consider this consistent noncommitment to ostensible goals in Balzac's novels to be a form of *resistance* to spatial constraints, a kind of implementation of choice with regard to spatial limits.

The other mode of figural conduct in Balzac—that of obsession or mania—appears to stand in exact opposition to that of ambition, since a maniac exhibits *excessive* attachment to a particular object, person, idea, or social status. In an earlier work devoted to Balzac, Jameson argues that the driving force of Balzacian narrative is desire for an object or, in Balzac's own terminology, *volonté*:

> The novelistic creation of Balzac rests in general on the premise that human existence is at all times motivated by *appetency*, that is, by a clear desire that always poses a precise object before itself. . . . The individual consciousness in Balzac is at all moments impelled by the desire to have something: a woman, a certain kind of house or situation. . . . This is to say that the universe of Balzac, although difficult for its characters, is never *problematical*.[63] (Emphasis in original)

Frustration of maniacal desire does not lead to the displacement of one object and its immediate substitution with another à la Miller's principle of circulation; this mania is configured rather as monomania, that is, exclusive commitment to one irreplaceable object (person, state, idea, etc.). Jameson depicts the fate of Balzacian maniacs in the aftermath of frustrated desire thus: "Frequently they fail to reach the objects of their desire, and then they retreat into its dialectical opposite, into a mortification of the will, into solitude, or the convent."[64]

In order to account for ambition and mania as two *simultaneously* present and irreducible modes of conduct in Balzac's novels, I suggest viewing them as mutually complementary character-effects of the annulment, within the artistic utterance, of the heterogeneity of space and time. Just as ambition registers the annulment of spatial heterogeneity, obsession or mania banishes the heterogeneity of time. In this light, unwavering commitment (i.e., unaffected by the flow of time) to a specific object seems not, as in Jameson's interpretation, an alienated form of sexual desire,[65] but rather as evidence of Balzacian maniacs' insusceptibility to temporal constraints, to the diversity and hierarchy of temporal contexts. A maniac's excessive preference for a specific object is a form of resistance to temporal constraints, a kind of implementation of choice with regard to temporal limits.

Patterns of ambition and mania in the Balzacian narrative, then, signal no effacement or dissolution of the subject, whether via the societal logic of perpetual exchange or the universal forces of sexual energy. Instead, these character-effects manifest the subjective activity (that of the artistic utterance's producer, or author) that actualizes the possibility of choice with regard to temporal and spatial limits; and thus enact subjectivity itself, insofar as subjectivity can only be carried out through the execution of choice. The character-effects of ambition and mania in the Balzacian text have a distinctly aesthetic foundation: they are determined by the suspension, within the artistic utterance, of temporal and spatial heterogeneity, by the abolition of that provisional spatiotemporal otherness which is presumed and perpetuated by the faculties of the wish-fulfilling mind.

In light of this alternative reading of the Balzacian narrative, Russian writers' engagement with it deserves a fresh examination. Authors of the 1830s and their contemporaneous and subsequent commentators declared Balzac the progenitor of keen-eyed inquiry into the hidden motivations of societal and personal behavior (Shepard's "innovative argument"). However, as my discussion of characterization in Balzac shows, the "innovative argument" that is at the core of the society tale's narrative epistemology is, in crucial aspects, directly opposed to Balzac's method. The society tale's generic imperative to reveal the underlying conditions of human behavior construes character as fully determined by sociohistorical and psychological causalities, hence fundamentally incapable—however nuanced these causalities may be—of implementing choice. By contrast, the primary Balzacian character-forms, mania and ambition, actualize the subject's excess in relation to external determinants, temporal and spatial respectively. The society tale writers' meticulously performed analytical exercises appear in this light a superficial, strictly imitative response to Balzac's novelistic narration, not unlike 1820s writers' enthusiastic adoption and "epidemic" (Iakubovich) mimicry of Sir Walter Scott's strategies of fictitious authorship and "found manuscript" devices.

I propose as a Russian text that fully engages with Balzac's method of characterization, presenting a congenial rather than imitative response to the French novelist's artistic vision, *A Hero of Our Time*, the prose work Lermontov wrote upon abandoning *Princess Ligovskaia* and, as Eikhenbaum observes, "instead" of it: "The large form [attempted in *Princess Ligovskaia*] does not succeed. From the solid novel [*sploshoi roman*] Lermontov transitions to a 'chain of tales' (as he himself says in 'Maksim Maksimych') united by the figure of Pechorin."[66] This rejection of the prospective novelistic "large form" and adoption of cyclical narrative, ostensibly a compositional setback, in reality marks a decisive shift from the society tale's generic parameters—its "innovative" analytical method and strategies of "predictive physiognomy" (Heier)—to distinctly novelistic characterization.

The name of the protagonist of *A Hero of Our Time* is also Grigorii Pechorin; but I would emphasize that this "second" Pechorin resembles not the main character of *Princess Ligovskaia* but rather its narrator, the consummate observer and prognosticator. The Pechorin of *A Hero* excels at deducing other characters' thoughts and fates by reading their appearances and behaviors. His calculations range from predicting a woman's inevitable infatuation with him ("Princess Mary") to divining the signs of impending death on a person's face ("The Fatalist"). This supreme capacity for face-reading (an essential feature of the society tale narrator) allows Pechorin to successfully manipulate the lives of other characters, casting them as dramatis personae in his own scripts. In theatrical terms, effectively employed in critical discussions of *A Hero of Our Time*, Pechorin not only "acts" superior to other characters but also aspires to "direct" the entire performance, including his own acting.[67]

In the society tale, consistent application of the analytical method that deduces characters' inner life from external circumstances leads, as seen, to these characters' distribution into particular groups (daydreaming government clerks, climate-affected Petersburgers, emotionally cold women, etc.) depending on the factors conditioning their actions. The position emergent as exclusive or unique in these interpretive exercises is that of the narrator him or herself—the only persona of the society tale to escape categorization. Crucial to Lermontov's transition from society tale to *A Hero of Our Time* is the shift between narrative levels: the all-seeing and invisible narrator of *Princess Ligovskaia* is personified in a character in the later work. As a result, the analytical method—the essence of characterization in the society tale—becomes the protagonist's character trait.

In *A Hero of Our Time*, Lermontov vacates the narrative position of the panoptical observer and keen analyst consolidated in *Princess Ligovskaia* (and in the 1830s society tale generally) and reverts to the devices and strategies of narrative embedding and the "found manuscript" tradition prominent in Russian prose a decade earlier: a framing traveling narrator; an eyewitness framed narrator; and a fortuitously obtained personal diary. At the same time, as evinced in Eikhenbaum's cautious generic designation of *A Hero* as a "chain of tales" (*tsep' povestei*), generations of critics have emphasized the distinct singularity of the narrative organization of this celebrated work, at the center of which is a disjuncture between discourse and story: the order in which events are narrated does not correspond to the order of their occurrence.

Contemplating this double chronology, William Mills Todd observes: "One salient effect is surely to keep the reader moving back and forth between sections, evaluating Pechorin's actions and statements in terms of what was learned earlier but may have happened later."[68] Such evaluation, however, remains inconclusive; as Todd notes, Lermontov scholars continue, even after however many *re*readings and comparative diagrams, to disagree on the positioning of two of the five tales, "Bela" and "The Fatalist."[69] The frustration of efforts to "unscramble" narrated events and situate "earlier" and "later" moments on a temporal axis informs readerly activity in *A Hero of Our Time*, especially with regard to the reader's perception of Pechorin. According to Todd, Lermontov's work "impels the reader to question the possibility of character development" and "renders attempts to create a biography for its hero ultimately fruitless."[70] In the terms employed in this chapter, the narrative organization of *A Hero of Our Time* enables a state of consciousness—that of the reader of the artistic utterance—within which temporal heterogeneity, a prerequisite to any biographical or developmental construction, becomes irrelevant.

An analogous effect, in this case with regard to the diversity of spatial contexts, is produced by the other distinctive feature of this work's narrative organization: the shift from the external to internal perspective on the hero. Ever since Belinsky's 1840 review of *A Hero of Our Time*, critics have envisioned this shift as providing the reader an ever more intimate and revealing view of Pechorin; but it has also been noted that the movement from outer to inner perspective generates no coherent psychological or sociohistorical portrait, exposing, rather, a series of gaps and contradictions. As Melissa Frazier observes, the transitions from talking about the hero to encountering him and finally to his own confessional account do not uncover the "real" Pechorin; instead "Pechorin's diary reveals our hero to be a contradictory, inconsistent, and even untrustworthy narrator of his own thoughts . . . the 'real' Pechorin never entirely coincides with himself."[71]

The turn from the ubiquitous, invisible-panoptical narrator of *Princess Ligovskaia* to the localized, flesh-and-blood narrators of *A Hero of Our Time* marks Lermontov's rejection of the pursuit of external/internal correspondences central to the society tale's narrative epistemology. *A Hero of Our Time* offers both external and internal perspectives on Pechorin, simultaneously withholding any opportunity for their reconciliation. The hero's "blank" interiority is contained within its various outward expressions (including self-expressions), securely protected from even the most expert would-be face-reading. This absence of a privileged point of view on Pechorin is an annulment of spatial heterogeneity: no point in space is privileged over any other, all of them being equally removed from the hero, and equally inadequate for insight into him.

Perception of Pechorin, in other words, is carried out by a readerly consciousness within which the heterogeneity of time and space, or the discrepancy between here-and-now and there-and-then, is rendered irrelevant. I believe that the architectonics of perception thus configured not only indicate Lermontov's decisive departure from the generic path of the society tale, but also his artistic response to Balzacian narrative, wherein, as discussed above, modes of ambition and mania represent the character-effects of the annulment of spatiotemporal heterogeneity. While in Balzac's *Comédie humaine* the consequences of this annulment are most prominently observed on the level of story, namely in the coexistence of the mutually complementary character-forms of the *ambitieux* and the maniac, in *A Hero of Our Time* the annulment occurs on the level of discourse: the heterogeneity of space is rendered irrelevant through a multiplicity of equally unprivileged points of view on the hero; the heterogeneity of time, through the irrecoverable chronology of events. Whereas in Balzac, the subjective activity of a character is configured as excessive in relation to either spatial (for the *ambitieux*) or temporal (for the maniac) determinants, it is the *reader's* release from *both* temporal and spatial diversity—which diversities constitute unavoidable premises of the activity of perception—that is actualized in *A Hero of Our Time*.[72]

The character in Lermontov's work—the object of readerly perception thus configured—emerges as excessive in relation to any and all external (spatiotemporal) parameters of characterization. This excess, which sets Pechorin apart from his unwarrantedly enigmatic namesake in *Princess Ligovskaia*, and from other society tale characters, invariably boxed as they are into classes and categories, is engendered not by Pechorin's particular character traits or actions, but by the state of the perceiving (readerly) consciousness liberated from the condition of space-time heterogeneity. In this light, Pechorin's incapacity for enduring connections whether of friendship or love, and the resulting "boredom" that ultimately destroys him,[73] emerges not as some emotional stuntedness or psycho- or even pathological deficiency of the hero (sociohistorically justified, perhaps, by "our time"), but rather as an allegiance to this excess, or (to attempt the maximum psychological interpretation of Pechorin allowable in this view) as his inkling of the fact that attachment to any concrete, spatiotemporally specific object presents a limitation and, therefore, a distortion of love and friendship—experiences fundamentally excessive in relation to their objects' properties.

This attitude toward objects of desire differentiates Pechorin from both Balzacian character-forms of excess: the maniac's excessive attachment to a specific object and the *ambitieux's* excessive indifference to it. Notably, the only explicit mention of Balzac in Lermontov's work occurs in the following description, in which Pechorin's physical and emotional frame seems stretched almost to the breaking point, as if only thus can his unbearable excess be sustained:

> When [Pechorin] lowered himself onto the bench, his erect build sagged as if he had not a single bone in his back; his whole posture now portrayed some sort of nervous weakness. He sat as would a Balzacian thirty-year-old coquette in a down-cushioned armchair after an exhausting ball.[74]

Pechorin is commonly termed a "superfluous man" (*lishnii chelovek*), a definition that gained critical currency with the appearance of Turgenev's *The Diary of a Superfluous Man* (*Dnevnik lishnego cheloveka*, 1850); but I would argue that this label is best applicable for aesthetic rather than the more typical sociohistorical or psychological reasons. In *A Hero of Our Time*, the character is configured as excessive, *lishnii*, in relation to any and all of his temporal and spatial manifestations—a perspective of character formation that is distinctly novelistic.[75] Notably, the novelistic hero in Lermontov's work emerges within the compositional parameters of cyclical organization—not unlike how, as seen in the previous chapter, the tale collector's essentially novelistic bereftness of communicative intention or voice is actualized in the prose cycle of the 1830s, that is, before the advent proper of the compositionally unified novelistic discourse.

Having abandoned *Princess Ligovskaia*, Lermontov foregoes the society tale's generic aspiration to account for the subject's inner experiences through observation and analysis. The exhaustion of the narrative potential of the position of external observation, the discovery of its inadequacy for representing the subject's interiority, can be viewed as the society tale's major contribution to the genesis of the novelistic form in Russian fiction of the 1830s. The distinctive organization of *A Hero of Our Time*, which sustains rather than resolves the incongruity between internal events and their external expressions (including self-expressions), renders the "found manuscript" device and the society tale's narratorial panopticality equally deficient, and simultaneously opens up a qualitatively new position of narration. In this light, Pechorin's demand for love—"if everyone loved me, I'd find in myself endless wellsprings of love [*esli b vse menia liubili, ia v sebe nashel by beskonechnye istochniki liubvi*]"[76]—which appears unwarranted in a story-world wherein it is Pechorin who consistently rejects other characters' affection, can be seen not as an egotistical whim but rather as the hero's "call" for an author whose narrative perspective would surpass his own supreme aptitude for observation and analysis.

The anticipated response to this call is not a surplus of knowledge, that is, an even greater ability to observe and analyze; it is instead the capacity to engender and sustain the correlation between the hero's inner life and its outer manifestations as arbitrary, hence unique. This capacity emerges as the sole prerogative of the producer of artistic utterance, setting the author of fictional narrative apart from doctors, scientists, sociologists, historians, and other expert researchers, analysts, and face-readers. With the demand for this qualitatively new narrative stance, exclusive in its temporal and spatial organization, the emergent novelistic author is released from the need to justify his or her account with reference to knowledgeable informants or authoritative sources—be they historical documents, sociological observations, or Lavater's physiognomic principles—and comes out from behind his anonymous, mock-, and pseudo-subsidiaries as an independent narrative agent, self-sufficient and therefore fully *reliable*.

Chapter Four

Types, Doubles, and the Fantastical Sources of Narrative Realism

IN THE VIEW of literary critics both contemporaneous and subsequent, the two major currents in Russian prose of the 1830s–40s, romanticism and naturalism, typically flow in a sequential opposition. The stability of this opposition is owed largely to the fact that, when consolidating as a literary movement, adherents of the "natural school" used romanticism as a foil to formulate their own agenda. Advocates of the new movement, most prominently Vissarion Belinsky in "A Look at Russian Literature of 1847" ("Vzgliad na russkuiu literaturu 1847-go goda," published in the *Contemporary*), proclaimed the transition from romanticism to naturalism an encouraging sign of Russian fiction's laudable maturation. In literary practice of the 1840s, the gradual but steady loss of "romantic" aspirations, increasingly marked as "youthful," became a driving force of plot and character development, a prominent example being Ivan Goncharov's *A Common Story* (1847), to which Belinsky devoted a large portion of his programmatic survey.[1]

Modern scholarship acknowledges the richness and complexity of 1830s–40s literary-cultural history, but this period in the development of Russian prose continues to be understood as, at its root, a transition from romanticism to naturalism—with the latter viewed as a precursor to realism.[2] In contrast to this established view on the relationship between the two major currents of 1830s–40s literature, this chapter will argue that, despite their manifestly different thematic, ideological, and stylistic concerns, their sequential arrival on the Russian literary scene, and their reciprocal (and quite explicit) hostility, romantic and naturalist poetics appear as correlative and mutually complementary when viewed from the standpoint of the positions of narration discovered and secured within the two discourses.

This approach does not discard the literary-historical rivalry between romanticism and naturalism in the Russian tradition, but rather seeks to demonstrate that the opposing characteristics of romantic and naturalist discourses stem from a *single* source. The chapter juxtaposes two major genres of romanticism and naturalism in the 1830s–40s—the fantastic novella and the physiological sketch, respectively—to show that the positions of narration established therein not only diverge and collide, but also supplement and amplify one another. In the course of this side-by-side reading, the two discourses evince an unexpected congruity, exemplified particularly by an affinity between the "doubles" inhabiting romantic novellas and the "types" populating naturalist sketches. This affinity emerges when "doubles" and "types" are considered not merely as aspects of characterization, engendered by their authors' ideological or sociological concerns, but also, or primarily, as discursive effects of the temporal and spatial organization of the positions of narration actualized within romantic and naturalist discourses.[3]

The chapter further considers the development of realism in Russian fiction, understood, again, as first and foremost the emergence of the authorial position that engenders and sustains the realist novel's discourse. The study of the novel is indebted to Ian Watt, not only for his still-influential "rise of the novel" paradigm, but also for his offering of one of the first comprehensive critical treatments of the elusive notion of realism. In his classic study, taking care to emphasize that realism, like any other literary mode, is a discursive convention, "a set of narrative procedures" (hence his qualification of "*formal* realism"), Watt singles out its defining characteristics: the particularization of time, place, and person; a natural and lifelike sequence of actions; and a literary style that restricts itself almost entirely to the descriptive and denotative use of language. Watt famously compares the realist novel's mode of representation to that of a jury in a court of law: both the jury and the novelistic reader "want to know 'all the particulars' of the given case—the time and place of the occurrence; both must be satisfied as to the identities of the parties concerned, and will refuse to accept evidence about anyone called Sir Toby Belch or Mr. Badman . . . and they also expect the witnesses to tell the story 'in their own words.'"[4]

While Watt's approach to the novel's origins (confining these to eighteenth-century Britain) has been substantially modified or outright rejected by subsequent historians of the genre, the conceptual core of his notion of "formal realism" has by and large retained its validity in contemporary novel theory. Temporal, spatial, and linguistic particularity remain at the heart of post-Watt definitions, whether these construe the realist aesthetic as an aspect of ideology, rhetoric, or Barthes's "reality effect." Moreover, scholars who dissociate the "rise of the novel" from the sociohistorical context of eighteenth-century Britain (or from Europe, or from "modernity" itself) continue to use the very parameters of realism outlined by Watt to prove their expansions of the novel's genealogy. The consequences of this interpretive tactic are twofold: on the one hand, realism becomes a ubiquitous literary phenomenon, as does the genre of the realist novel; on the other, Watt's "formal realism" is streamlined, delimited to such features as detailed characterization[5] or adherence to rationally explicable causality; or even reductively categorized as the literature of social critique.

In a recent study of the nineteenth-century novel, Geoffrey Baker provides an incisive overview of conceptions of realist aesthetics that emerged in the wake of critiques (and even caricatures) of realism's mimetic claims by modernist and postmodernist critics. Complex and nuanced, these conceptions foreground "energies or epistemologies irreducible to the historiographical and empirical allegiances of realism as most critics—and most realist novels themselves—have understood and constructed it."[6] In his own analyses of Balzac, Trollope, and Fontane, Baker demonstrates that these "canonically realist authors regularly amplify their texts' own claims to empiricism and secularism while simultaneously—and often explicitly and self-consciously—troubling those very claims."[7] The sources of these "counterweight"[8] epistemologies and energies are located elsewhere: most prominently, in supposedly outdated idealism, enchantment, and romance, in the premodern "longing for magic and providential mystery" (Jameson).[9] The realist narrative thereby becomes a site of struggle, or contest, echoed in the title of Baker's study, between the "warring core concepts of empiricism and enchantment."[10]

As I argued in the introduction, a key deficiency of the standard mimetic conceptualization of narrative realism is its inability to account for a literary-historical and theoretical hallmark of the realist novel: representation of figural consciousness. Transparency of minds cannot be understood as a product of "naiveté," or as some constructed mimetic project, for this transparency is absolutely unavailable in real life. Representation of consciousness reveals a key shortcoming of Watt's otherwise fruitful comparison of realist representation to a jury in a court of law. However sincere and articulate (or insincere and inarticulate) the witnesses interrogated before the "jury" may be, a crucial distinction remains: the reader of a realist novel—unlike even the most conscientious real-life juror—is granted direct access to a character's heart and mind, and can thereby "judge" accordingly.[11]

Representation of character consciousness as a key constituent of realist aesthetics most immediately challenges the conception of realist epistemology as empirical, historiographical, or scientific. Yet, as distinct from the energies of enchantment identified by Baker and other scholars, this challenge cannot be seen as some holdover from romanticism, as it is precisely in the realist novel that figural minds attain transparency for the first time in the history of literary prose. This is not a matter, then, of alternative modes of narration, borrowed from wherever, complicating or challenging the realist novel's ostensibly "default" (empirical, etc.) narrative strategies.

Positing representation of consciousness as the hallmark of realist discourse calls for the pinpointing of realism's *own* resources for decidedly nonempirical and nonscientific representation; narrative realism should be redefined such that its theoretical framework substantiates represented consciousness as a constitutive trait of the realist novel. This framework would thereby elucidate the chronological coincidence between the emergence of realism in literary prose on the one hand, and the unlocking of character consciousness on the other—a correlation Cohn posits as central for understanding realist aesthetics, yet herself deems paradoxical, and thus far inexplicable.[12]

Attempting to establish such a framework, this chapter provisionally suspends associations between narrative realism and mimesis (whatever the analytical remove at which we situate the notion of "reality"), and argues that realism emerges not from the aspiration to produce more conscientious, multifaceted representations of reality (or to fashion such representations in the service of a "reality effect"), but rather as the result of a qualitatively new—new in its temporal and spatial organization—position of fictional narration. According to my central premise, the distinct discursive status of the artistic utterance's producer and perceiver was enabled by the perspective (a standpoint, properly speaking, aesthetic) of the utterance's formation and perception—namely, the perspective of the story-discourse convergence. In this (again, aesthetic proper) communicative situation, the utterance's producer or author is privy to at least two discourses—one being represented, the other performing the representing—that completely and utterly converge in time and space. Despite the fact that, at any given moment, the author operates (makes a "move") within only one narrative level, his or her activity advances multiple discourses simultaneously, existing, so to speak, "in between." The producer of the artistic utterance cannot be situated, then, within a single spatiotemporal context, cannot be localized in time and space. In my discussion of Russian literary prose of the 1820s–40s, I have traced the textual consequences of the status of the speaking subject thus configured, including the narrator-character conversion in the frame novella (chapter 1); the tale collector's bereftness of communicative intent in the prose cycle (chapter 2); and the society tale's discovery of the character's excess in relation to any and all of his or her external manifestations (chapter 3).

My emphasis on the unique (spatiotemporally delocalized) discursive status of the producer of the artistic utterance resonates with a number of analytical models that attempt to substantiate, one way or another, the nonreferential status of the narrative agent in fictional texts. Some of the most pertinent and effective solutions to the authorial stance in fictional narrative have been to account for its source in apophatic terms. Thus Käte Hamburger builds a narrator-*less* model for third-person fiction, while Ann Banfield refers to the "unspeakable sentences" of free indirect discourse—those not occurring in spoken language, and therefore unattributable to any speaking subject—that came into being with the advent of the novel.[13] At the same time, as Cohn acknowledges in *The Distinction of Fiction*, while the need to dissociate the authorial voice in fictional narrative from any participants in real-life discourse stands as a postulate of contemporary literary theory, the application of this principle to literary analysis remains a challenge.[14] It is fair to say that the consequences of fictional non-referentiality have not yet been adequately explored in critical practice, and that more radical steps in this direction are in order.

A crucial theoretical resource for investigating the authorial stance in fictional narration, I believe, can be found in Mikhail Bakhtin's phenomenology of aesthetic experience, specifically, in his key concept of "outsideness" (*vnenakhodimost'*), also translated as "being-beyond," "extopy," and "extralocation." Bakhtin defines "outsideness" as the authorial exemption from the temporal and spatial—as well as the ethical and cognitive—constraints of the narrated world: "The author's fundamental, aesthetically productive relationship to the hero . . . is a relationship in which the author occupies an intently maintained position outside the hero with respect to every constituent feature of the hero— . . . space, time, value, and meaning."[15] In other words, the authorial position that engenders and sustains novelistic experience can be described as unmindfulness of temporal, spatial, cognitive, and ethical constraints. This definition makes a decisive break with any analytical configuration of authorial "omniscience," which implies supreme cognitive and ethical aptitude, and concomitantly implies a relative rather than absolute polarity (the author's knowledge in full vs. the hero's knowledge in part). According to Bakhtin, aesthetic activity consists in establishing and maintaining a boundary between two interdependent and mutually conditional activities, the author's and hero's; the boundary is of an absolute nature. This starkness distinguishes Bakhtin's understanding of the author-hero relationship in fictional discourse from the currently dominant methodologies, which conceive the authorial position as one or another form of surplus or privilege (temporal, spatial, cognitive, ethical) in relation to the hero.

Drawing on Bakhtin's phenomenology of the author-hero relationship, this chapter suggests that in Russian fiction of the 1830s–40s, naturalist and romantic discourses actualize mutually complementary authorial exemptions from the constraints of space (naturalism) and time (romanticism). Furthermore, the positions of narration established within the two discourses, and specifically in the genres of physiological sketch and fantastic novella, correlate with *excessive* implementation of spatial and temporal boundaries respectively on the level of narrated events. This excessive spatial and temporal localization manifests itself in specific character-forms: naturalist "types" and romantic "doubles." I also propose that in the ensuing realist novel, the hero likewise presents a form of excess, namely, his or her excessive mindfulness of temporal and spatial constraints, which has its counterpart in the authorial unmindfulness of these constraints—the aesthetic proper narrative stance that Bakhtin describes through the notion of "outsideness." I will argue here that the temporal and spatial specificity of narrated events and the representation of figural consciousness can be seen as correlative discursive effects of the architectonics of the authorial position actualized in literary prose with the rise and advance of the realist novel's discourse.

Central to the passionate polemics accompanying the establishment of the "natural school" in Russian fiction in the 1840s was the topos of "corners" (*ugly*), with the new literary movement's advocates and opponents alike immediately recognizing the portrayal thereof as a crucial constituent of naturalist poetics. "Corners" were understood both metaphorically, as the socioeconomically disadvantaged peripheries of society, as well as literally, as the precise designation of the living quarters of the urban poor who, unable to pay for a whole room (let alone an apartment), would rent just a corner of it.

The naturalist preoccupation with "corners" is seen, for instance, in Dmitrii Grigorovich's sketch "Petersburg Organ-Grinders" ("Peterburgskie sharmanshchiki," 1845). Here the process of narrative perspective is one of relentless narrowing: having wandered throughout Europe, Italian organ-grinders settle in a shabby Petersburg building in the corner of a dark yard. Their world contracts even further when it transpires that their apartment is situated at the very end of a staircase: one must stoop down in order to enter it. In Nikolai Nekrasov's "Petersburg Corners" ("Peterburgskie ugly"), the protagonist, in search of a "corner" to rent, plumbs the lower depths of urban life in an ever-tightening descent:

> The building whose yard I entered was extraordinarily huge, run down, and cluttered. . . . The corner for rent was in the back of the yard: I had to pass through another gate. I entered and saw another yard, somewhat smaller than the first, but a thousand times more cluttered. . . . Having taken twenty paces . . . I came to a door leading to a basement; I slipped and went flying . . . or, more precisely, went sliding—downward, of course.[16]

In Iakov Butkov's collection of sketches *Petersburg Heights* (*Peterburgskie vershiny*, 1846) space contracts, instead, as one ascends (hence the title), foregrounding the uppermost "corners" of urban life: the top floors—fourth, fifth, and sixth—and garrets of Petersburg apartment buildings, also the abodes of the poorest tenants.[17]

In the following passage from Butkov's *Petersburg Heights*, even the colossal expansion of urban space is tantamount to its simultaneous (and "infinite") fragmentation:

> On the islands between the Ligovka and Nevka rivers, buildings are growing in height and width, buildings that at the time of Petersburg's conception were little more than tiny huts . . . that with their many floors have since hurled themselves into the clouds, into a free space now seized by stuffy and cold cells under the human name of rooms, partitioned into infinite corners under the German name *kvartira* and the Russian *khvatera*.[18]

When the Nekrasov-edited collection of sketches *Physiology of Petersburg* (*Fiziologiia Peterburga*) was published as a manifesto of the "natural school" in 1845, the title of Nekrasov's above-cited contribution "Petersburg Corners" quickly became the byword of the movement. One of naturalism's most zealous adversaries, Faddei Bulgarin, who himself coined "the natural school"[19] as a derogatory term, cited as the new writers' sole source of inspiration the "dark corners and back alleys of life" (*temnye ugly i zakoulki zhizni*):[20]

> These are all geniuses who accept nothing from the past . . . they are creating a new world, a new world with *corners* at that [*da pritom s uglami*], and in these corners they are laying up the treasures of their minds and taste in order to fertilize the soil of a new Russian literature![21] (Emphasis mine)

Belinsky, who as the movement's most zealous proponent proclaimed the 1840s the decade of the "natural school" in Russian literature, also singled out the representation of "corners" as a distinctive trait of naturalist discourse:

> Muzhiks in bast shoes and heavy kaftans who often smell of bad homemade vodka; the woman a sort of centaur, a creature whose gender you couldn't tell right away by her clothes; *corners* [*ugly*] as the refuges of poverty, despair, and depravity you have to cross a courtyard knee-high in mud to get to.[22] (Emphasis in original)

Over a century later, Aleksandr Tseitlin, a leading scholar of the Russian "natural school," referenced Belinsky when defining heated 1840s debates around naturalism as essentially an argument about "corners": "The question of the natural school was first and foremost a question of the literature of 'Petersburg corners'. . . . Does literature have the right to portray these 'refuges of poverty, despair, and depravity' populated by people in rags?"[23] Largely concurring with nineteenth-century critics, Tseitlin ties the naturalist preoccupation with "corners" to modern urbanization and its concomitant conflicts and themes, fascination with which was fueled moreover by Western, especially French, "physiologies," published in Russia both in French and translation, and by avid discussions of these in the Russian press of the time.[24]

Such evaluations of the sociological and literary genealogy of the Russian "natural school" are well established. I would propose, however, that naturalist writers' preoccupation with the "corners" of life stems not only from the aspiration to uncover Paris-worthy urban mysteries in St. Petersburg[25] or pay tribute to the lower classes hitherto ignored by men of letters. Preeminent in this outlook, rather—indeed, *a priori* enabling the practice of such sociological vision—is the excessive implementation of spatial boundaries on the level of narrated events, a phenomenon in turn engendered by the architectonics of the authorial position established and exercised in naturalist discourse. Authorial unmindfulness of spatial constraints in naturalist discourse, that is, brought previously obscure, hard-to-reach places into the author's field of vision for the first time; exemption from the constraints of space encouraged authorly forays into dark corners, slums, and seedy back alleys.

Representation of "corners" is one instance of the excessive implementation of spatial boundaries on the level of narrated events in the physiological sketch. Another example, perhaps the most prominent, is seen on the level of characterization. According to Viktor Vinogradov's classic study of Russian naturalism, the central unifying feature of the "natural school" was an "epidemic craving for types, a striving to select marionettes as symbols of a particular class, profession, or psychological stratifications within these groups, sometimes even as symbols of this or that personified passion."[26] Iurii Mann pinpoints three major criteria by which characters are typified in physiological sketches of the 1840s: a particular attribute, most often social or professional; location, for instance theater, market, dance class, and so on; and such occasions as weddings, tea-ceremonies, and so on.[27] Alongside representation of the "corners" of urban life, typification became a defining generic trait of naturalist discourse.

All-encompassing categorization in the physiological sketch operates both inwardly and outwardly; its inward development, for instance, results in the continuous division of types into subtypes. Pavel Efebovsky's sketch "Petersburg Peddlers" ("Peterburgskie raznoschiki," 1846) begins with the narrator's rumination over the various possible ways to classify urban peddlers: by the season in which they work, the goods they offer, and the phrases they cry as they hawk their wares. Each type is then subdivided; the group of peddlers defined as "sellers of food" is said to include seventeen different categories, each then described in detail, often with further subdivisions: thus, sellers of oranges are categorized by the clothes they wear.

Moreover, even having provided these extensive classifications, the narrator admits that the "shades" of peddlers "are endless" (*ottenki beskonechny*), and that an exhaustive account, while theoretically possible, would in practice require innumerable volumes.[28] Another detailed yet partial taxonomy, in this case of the various kinds of braggarts, is found in a sketch by Evgenii Grebenka:

> Oh my goodness! There are still so many different kinds of braggarts: those who brag of their family happiness, their health, how much they can drink, their wives, their dogs, their friends, their hairstyles, the way they pronounce the letter *r*, the color of their noses, the shine of their boots—in short, there is no subject regarding which a person cannot brag.[29]

The obsession evinced in these passages with elaborately classifying human "types" is commonly seen as informed by the naturalist writers' sociohistorical or scientific concerns. But some features of the typification process as it unfolds in naturalist discourse can hardly be seen as stemming from such concerns; nor do they readily fit the ideological agenda, routinely ascribed to the Russian "natural school," of popularizing or ameliorating the plight of the lower classes. I would stress, rather, that the types portrayed in physiological sketches of the 1840s often challenge and infringe upon the frontiers of human space, both personal and societal, blurring major categorical distinctions. Vladimir Dal's sketches present a rather radical example of this generic feature, his typologies repeatedly traversing the border between the animal and human worlds. In 1844 the *Literary Gazette* (*Literaturnaia gazeta*) announced Dal's forthcoming publication of a collection of sketches entitled *The Menagerie* (*Zverinets*), devoted to the physiology and psychology of animals.[30] Of this prospective cycle, five sketches—"The Bear" ("Medved'"), "The Wolf" ("Volk"), "The Fox" ("Lisa"), "The Camel" ("Verbliud"), and "On Domesticated Animals" ("O domashnikh zhivotnykh")—were published in the *Literary Gazette*.

In Dal's sketch "An Officer's Valet" ("Denshchik"), the narrator professes to believe that for the purposes of "physiological" description, animals and humans should be categorized in different ways, the appearances and behaviors of the latter being considerably more complex. However, the difference between man and beast in relation to the titular character turns out to be merely quantitative, given his resemblance to not one but five different animals—camel, wolf, dog, hamster, and beaver: "I would draw the officer's valet Iakov Tortsegolovyi as an unprecedented, hitherto unseen monster comprising five animals; one would not suffice, because Iakov's merits are too diverse."[31] Dal's portrayal of the valet results in a representation that is "monstrous"—encompassing, that is, more than one category. In the physiological sketch in general, the distinction between animal and human, and even animate and inanimate, is never established for certain. Vinogradov deems the "symbolism of animals and things" (*zverinaia i veshchnaia simvolika*) an essential feature of naturalist poetics. In a study of Nekrasov's unfinished 1840s novel *The Life and Adventures of Tikhon Trosnikov* (*Zhizn' i pokhozhdeniia Tikhona Trosnikova*), the scholar of Russian naturalism Galina Shpilevaia makes a similar observation: "People are compared to animals and insects in numerous similes. . . . People, like spiders, crows, owls, and pigs, do not have any stable feelings toward one another, and the nature of their relationships is instantaneous and involuntary."[32]

"Monstrosity" in a character's appearance often corresponds to his or her uncategorizable societal status: characters in the physiological sketch are at times pushed not only to the margins of society, but even beyond. According to Mann, in naturalist discourse "society becomes an enormous 'body' and is divided into parts and cells that one can scrutinize and investigate."[33] Like the modern city with its formerly hidden "corners," the "organism" of contemporary society appears to the naturalist writer as systematically divided into infinitesimal "cellular" parts. Societal "monsters," then, are characters not fitting any cells or categories—much as corporeal "monsters" transgress the confines of the human body.

In Nekrasov's "Petersburg Corners," the two kinds of "monstrosity," corporeal and societal, appear simultaneously. One of the sketch's characters, who is never named, but identified only as "the green gentleman" (*zelenyi gospodin*) by virtue of the color of his frayed overcoat, has a striking, "monstrous" appearance: he is half-man and half-object, "a half-shtof [*polushtoff*, half a shtof, an old measure of liquid] stopped up with a human head instead of a cork."[34] This character—a seminary graduate dismissed from his former position as gymnasium teacher for alcoholism—is humiliated by the craftsmen who inhabit the destitute "corners" of a huge Petersburg apartment building:

> The yard servant poured a glass of wine, called the green gentleman over, and pulled a cruel new farce: he brought the glass to the green gentleman's lips and suddenly, when the latter had stretched out his lips and was entirely prepared to drink, snatched away the glass and drank it down himself. But the green gentleman was not even angry: his sense of dignity, utterly conquered by the smell of homemade spirits having reached his nose, kept silent. He started to humbly ask the yard servant "not to joke."
>
> "Dance a little, and I'll let you have it . . ."
>
> And the green gentleman began, no ifs or buts, to dance.[35]

The "green gentleman" does not fit any societal niche, not even the most obscure or marginal "corners"; the narrator concludes: "There are some unfortunates who have no place even in garrets and basements."[36]

This infringement upon the confines of human and societal "bodies" can be seen as an ultimate consequence of naturalist discourse's excessive implementation of spatial boundaries. In their "epidemic craving for types" (Vinogradov), authors of "physiologies" are determined to exhaust every human category possible, including those populating society's tiniest "cells," the city's remotest "corners." In the course of this process, communal margins, and the outlines of the human body itself (the elementary unit of human space), loosen, bulge, and burst their seams, producing "monsters" that defy social classification and blur the boundary between animal and human. Bodily and societal "monsters," frequent apparitions in physiological sketches of the 1840s, stem from the excessive implementation—pushing the very limits of personal and collective topography—of spatial boundaries within the narrated world. This excessive spatial localization on the level of narrated events has its source in the authorial unmindfulness of spatial constraints established in naturalist discourse via what Bakhtin describes as a life-and-death struggle for the position of "outsideness."

The prime compositional format of the 1840s "natural school" is the succession of sketches or essays. As Tseitlin observes, naturalist prose typically featured allusion to upcoming pieces and assurances of "to be continued":

> The "physiologists" emphatically refer their readers to the next issue of their work in progress, "promising" to address it next time, and so on. "However, this question is huge; I will discuss it next time," says Grebenka in his sketch "A Provincial in Petersburg." "In a future article, we will develop a psychological view of the sales clerk," promises A. Likhachev in his sketch "Sales Clerks."[37]

The naturalists' choice of serial format—a continuous adding-up of texts that are complete in and of themselves—can be understood as another discursive effect of naturalist discourse's excessive implementation of spatial boundaries, in this case, on the generic and compositional levels.

Here I would propose that in romanticism, a correlation between authorial position and narrated events can be observed, one that is complementary to the correlation in naturalist discourse just described. In romantic discourse, that is, authorial unmindfulness of temporal constraints has its counterpart in excessive implementation of temporal boundaries on the level of narrated events. The supernatural tale, a key genre of romantic prose, most vividly exemplifies this correlation. In the discussion below, I examine the supernatural tale of the 1820s–30s, focusing especially on "The Fair at Sorochintsy" ("Sorochinskaia iarmarka"), the opening tale of Gogol's *Dikan'ka* cycle. I show that, according to Tzvetan Todorov's classic definition, the Russian supernatural tale of the late 1820s and 1830s belongs to the "fantastic" (as opposed to the "marvelous" or "uncanny") mode of presenting and interpreting supernatural elements; I then consider this "fantastic" perception as an aspect of temporality actualized in the discourse of romanticism.

In Todorov's classification, the central component of the "fantastic" is that the text "must oblige the reader . . . [or character] to hesitate between a natural or supernatural explanation of the events described. . . . At the same time the hesitation is represented, it becomes one of the themes of the work."[38] In the "fantastic" proper, hesitation is maintained throughout the story, the natural or supernatural question going unresolved, which differentiates this category from, on the one hand, the "uncanny," with its resolution via natural explanation, and on the other, the "marvelous," wherein the supernatural is accepted.

Chapter 1 has cited several examples of supernatural tales that fulfill Todorov's criteria for the fantastic.[39] In Odoevsky's *The Apparition*, the rational explanation for the seeming appearance of ghosts in a certain castle, offered by a diehard positivist inveighing against naive belief in the supernatural, is thoroughly undermined by another character with a "cold, convincing voice"; in the end, however, the framing narrator refuses to reconcile the two interpretations, depriving characters and reader alike of any conclusive answer regarding the meaning of events in the castle. Another novella of the same author, *The Sylph*, subtitled *From the Notes of a Reasonable Man*, maintains throughout the text two conflicting perspectives on one and the same series of events: the protagonist's experiments with mysticism are undercut by his doctor, who interprets the patient's exalted visions as symptoms of a mental disorder. In the end the doctor's treatment is successful, but does not in fact resolve the tension between the two perspectives in favor of rationalism, instead merely preventing the "cured" protagonist, now a "man like any other" (*chelovek kak drugie*), from experiencing visions interpretable as mystic.

Having closely examined the two editions of Gogol's novella *The Portrait* (*Portret*)—one published in 1835 in *Arabesques* (*Arabeski*), the other significantly reworked for the publication of *Arabesques* in Gogol's collected works of 1842—Ann Marie Basom convincingly demonstrates that the latter version exemplifies Todorov's fantastic, sustaining to the end as it does the "hesitation," by both protagonist and reader, between natural (psychological, sociological) and supernatural (demonic) interpretation of events. In the second version of *The Portrait*, "the two readings vie for prominence"[40]—in contrast to the first, wherein the marvelous mode of representing the supernatural clearly prevails.[41]

Basom's emphasis on the ultimate indeterminacy of the presence of the supernatural in the second version of *The Portrait* sets her study apart from the tendency, discernible in contemporary Gogol scholarship, to expand the presence of the demonic into writings of Gogol formerly thought innocent thereof.[42] Critical reappraisal of "The Fair at Sorochintsy" (1831) exemplifies this incremental expansion. Ever since Dmitrii Merezhkovsky's *Gogol and the Devil* (*Gogol' i chert*, 1906), the presence of the demonic in Gogol's oeuvre has remained a provocative and fruitful topic of investigation; but "The Fair at Sorochintsy" had long been viewed by scholars as the most innocuous of all Gogol's writings. For instance, Vasilii Gippius, having defined the overarching theme of the *Dikan'ka* cycle as "the intrusion [*vtorzhenie*] of the demonic into human life, and man's struggle with it,"[43] counts this tale as an exception: "No other tale [of Gogol's] contained such merriment as did 'The Fair at Sorochintsy'; no other tale was so close to the comic tradition already established in Ukrainian literature."[44] For Gippius, this joyous mode is called into question only in the tale's finale, when an evil force, manifesting itself in the macabre dance of old women, creeps in.[45]

Following Merezhkovsky's and Gippius's foundational inquiries into Gogolian demonology, a number of readings of "The Fair at Sorochintsy" have traced the ways in which the narrator's concluding meditations subvert the overall festive and comic mode of the tale.[46] In the course of these scholarly analyses, demons have gradually spread their encroachment from the tale's conclusion to its entirety. Attributes of the demonic have been discovered first in the tale's antagonist Khivria, who is explicitly compared to the devil by other characters; next in the Gypsies who aid Grits'ko in winning Paraska's hand, and ultimately even in the young lovers Paraska and Grits'ko themselves.[47] Early readings of "The Fair at Sorochintsy" as the story of a maiden's rescue via trickery from her abusive stepmother, then, have given way to the demonically charged (or overcharged) account of the devilish Grits'ko who, with the aid of devilish accomplices, abducts the devilish Paraska from her devilish possessor. In Todorov's terminology, scholars who insist on the workings of the demonic in "The Fair at Sorochintsy" argue against filing the tale under the uncanny (the supernatural explained rationally, in this case, as trickery) and see it as a covert—hence in need of critical elucidation—example of the marvelous.

Notably, these persistent attempts to locate the devil within the tale coincide with the major concern of the tale's *characters*, themselves utterly preoccupied with the devil's secret presence at the "accursed place" that is the Sorochintsy fair:

> The old woman who sold pretzels thought she saw the devil in the shape of a pig, bending over the wagons as though looking for something. The news soon flew to every corner of the resting camp, and *everyone would have*

thought it a crime to disbelieve it, in spite of the fact that the pretzel seller, whose stall was next to the drinking booth, had been staggering about all day and could not walk straight.[48] (Emphasis mine)

Despite all evidence to the contrary, and common sense itself, rumors that the *red jacket* (*svitka*, emphasis in original) appearing among the goods on offer belongs to the devil fully determine the characters' actions and reactions. One of the devil's best-known attributes is his association with pigs; thus, anything porcine fills the characters with horror:

At that moment an indistinct sound not unlike the grunt of a pig was audible; everyone turned pale. Drops of sweat stood out on Tsibulya's face.

"What was it?" cried the panic-stricken Cherevik.

"Nothing," answered Tsibulya, trembling all over.

"Eh?" responded one of the guests.

"Did you speak?"

"No!"

"Who was it grunted [or oinked]?"

"God knows why we are so flustered! It's nothing!"

They all turned about fearfully and began rummaging in the corners.[49]

Not unlike the characters of "The Fair at Sorochintsy," students of Gogol's demonology also insist that the devil is hidden somewhere within the tale, and that his attributes will reveal him, so long as these are properly identified. Christopher Putney, for instance, disputes James Holquist's assessment that in the *Dikan'ka* tales, diabolic figures are easily recognized, invariably appearing in "full regalia";[50] Putney adduces instead a set of complex and subtle attributes of the demonic from "a variety of influences, including Orthodox theology and the traditional representation of the devil in the medieval literary record."[51] For example, Khivria's link to the diabolic is supported, according to Putney, by her "savage" physical appearance, her status as a stepmother, and her strong sex drive. These less readily discernible attributes should enable the reader and critic to recognize the devil's more treacherous disguises. While differing in the parameters of their search, interpreters of "The Fair" share with its characters a fascination with detecting and unmasking latent evil.[52]

However, reliance on attributes hardly results in conclusive incrimination of the devil. For instance, in one of the most thorough investigations of the demonic in Gogol, Mikhail Epshtein assigns to this category the sound of ringing: "In 'A Terrible Vengeance' the light itself rings; in 'The Portrait' it is the gold that rings; in *Dead Souls*, finally, the little bell (*kolokol'chik*) emits a ringing sound."[53] Bells also ring, Epshtein notes, in "Vii"—and more than once. This observation of the prevalence and importance of bell-ringing in Gogol's works is convincing; but it remains undetermined that this sound necessarily manifests the demonic. Against this conclusion may be cited the fact that, as noted in a recent study of the sound code in Slavic folk cultures, a little bell may have an opposite significance: "According to Slavic materials, the little bell is a ritual object and its tolling was used to ward off all supernatural forces. . . . It was believed that the sound of the bell wards off all sorts of evil, witches, the unquiet dead, hail, storms, wild animals . . . and so on."[54] To be sure, the degree of ethnographic accuracy in Gogol's early writings has been debated since the very appearance of the first volume of the *Dikan'ka* tales, and the folklorist's data does not establish that bell-ringing in Gogol's works casts out rather than manifests the demonic; for that matter, the existence of a guard against the supernatural could be taken as a signal that this presence indeed lurks. Still, the discrepancy between the folklorist's and the literary critic's interpretations of bells underscores the problematic nature of relying on attributes in discerning the demonic, given that the same sound (or sign) can be interpreted in different, even diametrically opposed ways.

Indeed, however forewarned are the characters of "The Fair at Sorochintsy" regarding unmistakable (from their point of view) signs of the demonic, they can never certify its presence or absence with absolute confidence: they assure themselves that "it's nothing," but still fearfully "rummage through corners." Likewise, readers of the tale inevitably vacillate between two possible explanations of narrated events, never fully committing to either. It is precisely this vacillation that manifests itself in the spectrum of analyses of the tale. On the one hand, Gogol scholars have long since abandoned the "naive" reading of "The Fair" as a mere series of slapstick episodes; but on the other, to espy the incarnation of evil forces—even in the likeliest character-candidate, the abusive stepmother Khivria—is to take a good joke perhaps too seriously:

> "Stop! There is something lying here! Show a light this way!"
>
> Here they were joined by several others.
>
> "What's lying there, Vlas?"
>
> "Why, it looks like two men: one on top, the other under. Which of them is the devil I can't make out yet!"
>
> "Why, who is on top?"
>
> "A woman [*baba*]!"
>
> "Oh, well, then that's the devil!"
>
> A general shout of laughter roused almost the whole street.[55]

Is Khivria a mere *baba*, or a "devil"? All that can positively be asserted regarding the diabolic contamination of events in "The Fair at Sorochintsy" is that the tale's narrative perspective invites characters and readers alike to engage in a never-ending game of hide-and-seek with the devil, sniffing out clues in appearance, clothing (several scholars, for example, compare the devilish red jacket to Khivria's rosy complexion, and to the red color on Paraska's mirror), and other attributes (e.g., the Gypsies' foreignness, or Khivria's lust).[56] The indeterminacy of the devil's presence is an essential constituent of the reader's perception of the tale, rendering it a perfect example of the fantastic in Todorov's definition.

Critics' attempts to attribute the tale to the marvelous, moreover, are immediately undermined by another aspect of "The Fair at Sorochinsty," namely, its possession of a clearly identified narrator; it is told, as we learn at the beginning of the tale following it in the cycle, by the "young gentleman in the pea-green coat" (*panich v gorokhovom kaftane*) from Poltava who is eventually expelled from the storytelling gatherings following a heated dispute on the proper method of fermenting apples. In other words, "The Fair at Sorochintsy" is a frame narrative—a status it shares with all the romantic supernatural tales already mentioned in this chapter. Indeed, the Russian supernatural tale of the 1820s–30s—a quite popular type[57]—may consistently be seen to feature, like "The Fair," a correlation between an emphatically mundane source of narration on the one hand and, on the other, manifestly improbable narrated events (in the case of "The Fair," implied devilry). In Konstantin Aksakov's novella *Walter Eizenberg: Life in a Dream* (*Val'ter Eizenberg: Zhizn' v mechte*, 1836), for instance, the story of a painting come to life is told and then retold by two students:

> I will most likely not be believed when I say that this is a true story and that it happened not so very long ago; but I myself knew Karl, who was recently in Moscow and told me much about his friend. A few days before dying, Walter confided in him.[58]

In Mikhail Zagoskin's *An Evening on the Khoper* (1838), the narrator, a district police officer, solemnly attests to his own veracity: "I will tell you not a fairy tale, but a true event. Perhaps you will not believe me, but I swear to you on my honor that it is the truth."[59] In Valer'ian Olin's novella *A Strange Ball* (*Strannyi bal*, 1838), the description of a demonic sabbath is framed as the account of an old general handed down to the traveler-narrator:

> "And is this indeed a true story?" asked Savva Trofimovich.
>
> "Subject to not the slightest doubt," answered the traveler. "I heard it from the general himself, who had just recovered from *delirium tremens*."[60] (Emphasis in original)

As evinced in these examples, the incongruity between narrated events and the source of narration is explicitly recognized and entertained in a variety of ways within the tales: narrators who swear to the credibility of their mind-boggling stories are doubted, questioned, and teased by embedded interlocutors (or by "reality" itself, as with the added detail of *delirium tremens*). Nevertheless, the discrepancy itself remains a distinct characteristic of the Russian supernatural tale of the 1820s–30s. In Bestuzhev-Marlinsky's three successive *Evenings* (*Evening on a Bivouac*, 1823; *A Second Evening on a Bivouac*, 1823; and *Evening at the Caucasian Waters in 1824*, 1830), the activity of storytelling advances from the participants' sharing of everyday incidents to an exchange of increasingly bizarre and terrifying ghost stories. The progression of Bestuzhev's *Evenings* demonstrates that the persona of the framed narrator compellingly attracts, or draws in, supernatural material, creating and sustaining a discrepancy between time and place-specific ("realistic") storytelling and the overtly improbable content of the stories.[61]

I would suggest that this discrepancy enables the fantastic mode of the reader's perception of narrated events even in works in which, in Holquist's words, the supernatural appears in "full regalia"—as, for instance, in the other tales of the *Dikan'ka* cycle ("A Terrible Revenge" ["Strashnaia mest'"], "The Night before Christmas" ["Noch' pered rozhdestvom"]) that would seem unambiguously to belong to the marvelous.[62] Regardless of the presentation of supernatural elements in the embedded narratives, the very attribution of a story to a single, time and place-specific narrative voice inevitably activates the mechanism, crucial to the fantastic, of "hesitation." The workings of this mechanism are rendered explicit when, as in the examples cited above, embedded listeners express their disbelief, which however hardly dampens their eagerness to hear the stories. In this perspective, *Dikan'ka's* storytellers stand as guardians against readerly acceptance of the devil's supernatural power, their narrative voices heard as "little bells" (*kolokol'chiki*) by readers making their way through the "demonic" landscape of "The Fair at Sorochintsy" and other supernatural tales of the 1820s–30s.

The fantastic mode of perception in the Russian supernatural tale of the 1820s–30s may also be described as susceptibility—on the part of character and/or reader—to the fraughtness of *anything* with something completely different (e.g., a *baba* contains, and may return in the guise of, the devil; a flower may shape-shift into a sylph). The "hesitating" perceiver can be said to seek out the boundaries *within* a given object, in other words, to differentiate an object from itself—a process of *temporal* differentiation, as opposed to differentiation in *space*, that is, of one object from another. For the character and/or reader of the fantastic, temporal differentiation is excessive, since more than one "content" lays claim to the same spatial outlines (e.g., those of a *baba* or flower).

Fantastic perception can extend to the character-perceiver him or herself, in which case it takes the form of excessive *self*-differentiation, producing that archetypal figure of romantic prose, the double. One example of the romantic double (of the many citable) fully matching Todorov's criteria for the fantastic is found in another frame narrative of the time, Antonii Pogorel'sky's novella *The Double, or My Evenings in Little Russia* (1828). Here the protagonist, a provincial landowner named Antonii P., is paid a visit at his remote estate by an eponymous character, his exact replica:

> At this moment I took a closer look at the stranger and suddenly I was covered in cold sweat from head to toe. I became convinced that he resembled me in every particular. I don't know why, but this terrified me.[63]

The double fully reproduces the hero's body, thereby precluding spatial differentiation—of oneself from another. At the same time, the "contents" occupying this selfsame body are quite different from, indeed diametrically opposed to, that of the protagonist. Antonii the landowner is a dreamer with a vivid imagination:

> Passing imperceptibly from one memory to another, from one thought to another, I embarked, in my imagination, on that favorite pastime of mine when I am alone and without any occupation . . . namely I began to build castles in the air. . . . I can hardly complain of the idleness of my imagination, and thus the castles rose with incredible speed, each more beautiful and more splendid than its predecessor.[64]

In contrast, the sober Mr. Double (*gospodin Dvoinik*) is a staunch advocate of rationalism who, throughout the novella, consistently demolishes the hero's "castles in the air":

> The briefest of reflections will assure you that the most important, the most useful, and the most indispensable kind of intellect is common sense. Its relations to other kinds is as the relation between diamonds and all the rest of precious stones. . . . All the other kinds of intellect are nothing without common sense.[65]

Doubles represent a most overt example of the excessive temporal differentiation actualized in romantic discourse, with the stark differentiation of one from oneself (i.e., the meeting of one's copy) typically resulting in madness. Descent into insanity in romantic prose[66] is analogous to corporeal and societal monstrosity in naturalist discourse: much as characters of supernatural tales go out of their minds, naturalist characters "go out of" their bodies, both physical and collective, as a result of the excessive spatial differentiation, of oneself from another, actualized in naturalist discourse.

Some of the most important examinations of Russian romanticism view romantic subjectivity as marked by instability, fragmentariness, and intense self-consciousness. Monika Greenleaf's study of Pushkin brings together the notion of romantic irony and the genre of the fragment as aspects of the construction of the self; the romantic poets, most prominently Byron and Pushkin, "never give up their right not to coincide with themselves, to create a sincere new identity with every utterance—a series of 'stills' of a subjectivity in constant motion."[67] The romantic poet's intense and ongoing process of self-fashioning results in the juxtaposition of utterly divergent elements within one and the same narrative, in the "suturing of stylistically and perspectivally clashing fragments"[68] within a single artistic work. Melissa Frazier sees the ultimate expression of the romantic self in the persona of the "chameleon-like figure of the writer as editor, plagiarist, and/or critic."[69] In Frazier's analysis, the omnipotence of the critic emerges as a central constituent of the romantic aesthetic: "Romanticism . . . never loses sight of the fact that the critic is that strange creature, a reader who is also a writer and so potentially contains intersubjectivity within him- or herself alone."[70]

Both the phenomena just described—the romantic poet's continuous assumption of diverse ideological and stylistic identities demonstrated by Greenleaf; and the activity of the "all-encompassing critical consciousness"[71] that, as Frazier argues, contains the subjectivities of writer and reader within itself—can be said to consist in intense and infinite self-differentiation or, in the terminology adopted here, temporal differentiation. The major constituents of the romantic aesthetics identified by Greenleaf and Frazier (irony, fragment, critical omnipotence) can thus be viewed as aspects of romantic temporality. As I argued above, it is the authorial unmindfulness of temporal constraints (exemption therefrom, or temporal "outsideness," in Bakhtin's terminology) actualized in romantic discourse that generates excessive temporal differentiation in the "participants" (writer, character, reader, and critic) of the romantic utterance; this unmindfulness also manifests itself on the generic and compositional level, evinced in Pushkin's romantic fragment as conceptualized by Greenleaf, in Frazier's interpretation of the all-encompassing "library" as literary genre,[72] or in Todorov's fantastic.

In this light, the character-effect of "doubling" in the romantic supernatural tale can be seen as the spatial analogue of this same process, its planar unfolding so to speak, like the self-sketches in the margins of Pushkin's manuscripts, "always in medallion-like profile but in a variety of expressive styles,"[73] that Greenleaf analyzes in concluding her study. Greenleaf's discussion of autobiography vs. autoportraiture can be read as elucidating the difference between "regular" temporal differentiation and the excessive variety: in the latter, one's differentiation from oneself, enabled by the authorial exemption from temporal constraints, occurs independently from the flow of narrated time, and winds up bursting into *space*, producing a "kaleidoscopic dispersion of the self in an 'infinite' series of representations."[74] In order for an entity to be differentiated within itself (like *baba*/devil), its regular temporal development (growth, aging, etc.) must be suspended. The following passage from Pogorel'sky's *The Double* makes explicit the connection between the arrest of narrated time and the "doubling" effect in the supernatural tale. In the novella, the hero's habitual state is "boredom"—an experience of temporal homogeneity:

> I have almost confessed already that . . . I was bored at times. This often happened in the evening, when the peasants enjoyed their rest after a day's work and the street near my house became empty. At such moments I was wont to sit down by the open window and pensively listen to the dejected song of the young peasant girls, reveling at their parties till late at night.[75]

"Boredom" here signals the arrest of narrated time, a precondition for the excessive temporal self-differentiation carried out in Pogorel'sky's novella through the hero's meeting with his double. Notably, Mr. Double's own perception of time is similarly amorphous:

> "God forbid," retorted Mr. Double, "That [timekeeping] is again an example of one of the strongest of human superstitions. For us, all hours of the day and night are the same. The custom of dividing the day into a certain number of parts is quite unnecessary for spirits. I assure you that we know neither Breguets nor Ellicotts [renowned eighteenth-century watchmakers]. I am leaving you now only because it's time to sleep."[76]

Keeping with the premise that romanticism and naturalism exhibit mutual complementariness, I would propose that—much as, in this Pogorel'sky example, excessive temporal differentiation spills over into space—in naturalism, excessive spatial differentiation (of oneself from another) necessitates an unfolding in *time*, which is manifested in seemingly endless urban forays unconstrained by any schedule and in the discovery of ever more "types" and "subtypes," and which, on the generic and compositional levels, mandates the sketch's invariable status of "to be continued."

Thus, despite their manifest differences and "school" rivalry, romanticism and naturalism can be envisioned as mutually complementary from the standpoint of the writers' singular quest for authorial "outsideness." In romanticism, the author occupies a position of "outsideness" in relation to narrated *time*, whereas the naturalist physiological sketch entails authorial exemption from the constraints of *space*. The excessive implementation of *temporal* boundaries on the level of narrated events in the supernatural tale, which ensures its attribution to the fantastic (Todorov) mode of (self-)perception, has its correlate and immediate source in the authorial unmindfulness of temporal constraints in romantic discourse. Similarly, the physiological sketch's excessive *spatial* localization, incessantly revealing the literal and sociological "corners" of urban life, and proliferating types on an "epidemic" (Vinogradov) scale, stems from the authorial exemption from the constraints of space in naturalism.

Romantic and naturalist discourses stand at opposite extremes vis-à-vis supernatural intrusion in narrated events. Whereas the excessive implementation of temporal boundaries generates the fantastic plots of romanticism, the excessive implementation of spatial boundaries in naturalist discourse results, by contrast, in the utter eradication of perceptual ambiguity: the physiological sketch often slips into scientific (e.g., socioeconomic) commentary, ruling out by definition anything unexplainable or supernatural. The fantastic is thus an essential constituent of both romantic and naturalist poetics, despite being of "negative value" within the latter.

In the emerging Russian novel, the fantastic seems to disappear. There is a definite—albeit inverse—correspondence: as the credulity-straining plots of romantic prose recede (along with naturalist writers' objections thereto), temporal and spatial specificity comes to the fore in the realist novel. This inverse correspondence can be traced, I believe, to the transformation of the relationship between the source of narration and narrated events, that is, to the *reversal* of the relationship between story and discourse. The emergent realist novel did not *exile* the fantastic (with the author, according to the common understanding of realism, now ostensibly eschewing the implausible); rather, the nascent realist narrative *displaced* the supernatural element onto the authorial position itself. In the realist novel, the spatiotemporal specificity of narrated events stems from the authorial unmindfulness of both temporal and spatial constraints—a *fantastic* position, not in the sense of Todorov's typology, but as it were really fantastic. *Fantastically*, the realist novelist engenders spatiotemporal specificity of narrated events—in inverse congruence to the "realistic" framing (heard from a reliable friend, etc.) of implausible stories in romantic prose.[77]

Authorial exemption from temporal and spatial constraints is thus crucial to the emergence of the temporal and spatial particularity that is, whether "naive" or self-consciously construed, commonly placed at the center of realist aesthetics. In the realist novel, the specific nature of narrated events space- and time-wise—novelistic "exactness" or "verisimilitude"—has its counterpart in the author's independence from any possible space-time configuration. Indeed, it is precisely the absence of such constraints that deprive the supernatural element any purchase within the realist story. The supernatural, in all its manifestations, is fully conditioned by temporal and spatial categories, deviations therefrom being essential for the classification of events as either plausible or wondrous. The author of the realist novel gains his or her independence from narrated time and space; and in their essential absence, the supernatural has no "material" over which to triumph, no grounds for occurrence within the narrated world. The novelistic author's exemption from space-time requires that narrated events themselves be "realistic," that is, space- and time-bound (in Watt's terminology, "particular"). From this perspective, the emergence of realism stands as an event *within* the bounds of the artistic utterance, or an *intraverbal* event consisting in the establishment of a qualitatively new—new in its temporal and spatial organization—position of narration.

I would further suggest that the temporal and spatial specificity of narrated events, enabled by authorial unmindfulness of temporal and spatial constraints, determines the form of figural excess actualized in the realist novel. In romantic and naturalist discourses, excessive implementation of boundaries, temporal and spatial respectively, generates character-forms that are driven by infinite differentiation either in time (self-differentiation, epitomized in romantic "doubles") or space (differentiation of oneself from another, performed through naturalist "types"). In realist discourse, the spatiotemporal parameters of the narrated world have become "particular," falling into place so to speak, and figural excess takes the only form available, that of the perception of these boundaries as emerging from the character's own conscious choice.

The realist novelist's spatiotemporal unmindfulness has its counterpart in the hero's *excessive* mindfulness of such constraints. This perception has no external manifestations or signifiers; temporal and spatial parameters are themselves configured as aspects of an event in the life of a character, as pertaining to this character's consciousness. Representation of this event thus coincides with representation of figural consciousness—the only adequate mode within which this event can be narrated. Temporal and spatial specificity of narrated events and the representation of consciousness—which latter endeavor Cohn deems "uniquely privileged and entirely unreal," insofar as no position in time and space could make such representation possible—thereby emerge as two *correlative* constituents of the emergent novelistic discourse.

A character's mind thus becomes transparent due to the architectonics of the authorial position established in realist discourse. The realist novelist finds ways to represent consciousness not because of his or her emergent interest, whether sociohistorically or psychologically motivated, in the workings of human hearts and minds, but rather due to the attainment of an authorial position that has at long last enabled such representation. That is, rather than considering it paradoxical, as does Cohn, that realist aesthetics is bound up with the "unreal" representation of figural consciousness, I propose the interdependence of these phenomena as two major discursive effects of the realist novelist's exemption from narrated space-time. The next chapter will explore further implications of these conclusions, examining two novellas of Turgenev that especially illuminate the narrative circumstances in which the character's mind becomes transparent for the emergent author of the realist novel.

Chapter Five

No Need for Dogs or Women: Transparent Minds in Turgenev

DORRIT COHN'S typology of the narrative modes for presenting consciousness in fiction has long served as a starting point for any critical inquiry into fictional minds. At the same time, Cohn's insights into the historical dynamics of novelistic characterization have received far less scholarly attention. Concerns of literary history fall largely outside the scope of *Transparent Minds*, but in the introduction to this fundamental study Cohn insists that "historical continuity underlies [her] typological approach to the presentation of consciousness in fiction."[1] Specifically, Cohn's vision of the history of the novel is driven by an intuition of a decisive *dis*continuity in the novelistic presentation of fictional minds: according to Cohn, the novel develops from its early avoidance of the presentation of inner life to this category's Joycean "full Bloom in the stream-of-consciousness novel and beyond,"[2] a process she describes, moreover, as the "gradual unfolding of the genre's most distinctive potential."[3]

Cohn's view on the novel's historical development implies that access to character consciousness, post hoc taken for granted by novels' writers, readers, and critics, should be acknowledged and conceptualized as a major *event* in the history of literary prose in general and novelistic discourse in particular.[4] As discussed in the previous chapter, Cohn takes this event's coinciding with the establishment of realist aesthetics as a thing worthy of genuine wonder, accounting it all "the more surprising . . . that the novelists most concerned with the exact representation of life are also those who place at the live centers of their works this invented entity whose verisimilitude is impossible to verify."[5] Cohn's is a wonder that not only marks the boundaries of her distinctly synchronic and typological study, but also calls for further inquiry into the shifts and turning points in the history of consciousness presentation in fictional narrative.

Cohn observes that eighteenth- and many nineteenth-century novels are marked by a distinct "refusal to look inside,"[6] with characters rarely afforded any opportunity for silent self-communion, exhibiting instead a tendency toward the performative dramatic speech:

> While prolonged inside views were largely restricted to first-person forms, third-person novels dwelt on manifest behavior, with the characters' inner selves revealed only indirectly through spoken language and telling gesture. . . . In most works by Dickens, Turgenev, Fontane, and other masters of the novel of manners, character portrayal is far more contextual than "intrinsic."[7]

Citing works by these and other novelists, including Thackeray, Fielding, and Goethe, Cohn notes that their characters' self-reflecting monologues, when such do occur, are conducted in an "audibly soliloquizing voice," with "the volume . . . turned up quite as high as in drama,"[8] and are accompanied by reporting phrases and extensive introductions by the narrator. With the novel's further development, the formerly distinct voice of monologizing characters becomes muted: "In Stendhal's time . . . exclamation (or even muttering) in solitary moments is no longer the rule, and becomes increasingly associated with a strange 'habit,' or with moments of extreme agitation."[9] Finally, in the realist novel, the inaudibility of the character's inner voice becomes a discursive default for both writer and reader. "Silence is now implied regardless of whether thinking or saying verbs are used."[10]

Cohn's observations on the history of consciousness presentation in European prose lead her to formulate what she calls the "seesawing relationship between authorial and figural minds,"[11] that is, the inverse correspondence between the narrator's explicit presence and the clarity or sustainedness of the view into characters' minds. Whereas in earlier novels, the avoidance of representation of consciousness is accompanied by the narrator's own obtrusive audibility, in later forms,

> with the growing interest in the problems of individual psychology, the audible narrator disappears from the fictional world . . . [and] a fully developed figural consciousness siphons away the emotional and intellectual energy formerly lodged in the expansive narrator. . . . It is no coincidence that those writers who first insisted on the removal of vociferous narrators from fiction—notably Flaubert and Henry James—were also the creators of fictional minds with previously unparalleled depth and complexity.[12]

Taking Cohn's formulation one step further—for my own, diachronically oriented inquiry into the presentation of fictional consciousness, a crucial step—I would propose that in earlier forms of the novel, what precludes authorial access to characters' inner life is not the writers' dearth of psychological concerns, but rather their narrative position itself, their external vantage point, whose domain is the hearing of character soliloquies and the observing of their "telling gestures." Chapter 3 has shown how the Russian novella of the first half of the nineteenth century discovered an unbridgeable gap between the subject's inner life and its every outward manifestation, a gap rendering the position of external observation ineffective for accessing character interiority. In Lermontov's unfinished society tale *Princess Ligovskaia*, this discovery is made explicit when the narrator, ubiquitous and discerning as he is, realizes among other things that a woman's tears can convey virtually any emotion from joy to despair, and has finally to admit that where the character's heart and mind are concerned, only "God knows." Lermontov's decision to abandon *Princess Ligovskaia* indicates the discordancy between his undertaking a novel (*Princess Ligovskaia* being subtitled with that generic designation) and the position of external observation he adopted thereupon. In this chapter, I provide readings of two works by Ivan Turgenev, the novella *Mumu* (1852) and the tale "The End of Chertopkhanov" (1874), in which the position of external observation, problematized in *Princess Ligovskaia*, is not only brought to its narrative dead end—albeit under two distinct sets of literary-historical circumstances—but also surmounted, thereby enabling unmediated presentation of figural consciousness.

In the past twenty years, interest in the presentation of consciousness in fiction has intensified in the wake of literary scholars' increased engagement with the findings of cognitive sciences. Cognitive approaches to the presentation of consciousness in fiction posit an analogy between knowledge and comprehension as experienced by real-world minds and the writerly and readerly work of constructing fictional minds in the literary text; thus insights of social and evolutionary psychology, neuroscience, philosophy of mind, psycholinguistics, and other disciplines are drawn upon to create analytical frameworks for examining the fictional presentation of consciousness. Succinctly explicating this method, Lisa Zunshine states that her book "makes a case for admitting the recent findings of cognitive psychologists into literary studies by showing how their research into the ability to explain behavior in terms of the underlying states of mind—or *mind-reading* ability—can furnish us with a series of surprising insights into our interaction with literary texts."[13] Zunshine hastens to clarify that, as used by cognitive psychologists, mind-reading "has nothing to do with plain old telepathy";[14] on the contrary, this concept implies the process of interpreting people's mental states (thoughts, feelings, desires, etc.) on the basis of their words or observable actions or behaviors—a process both intrinsic to human cognition and, at the same time, fraught with nuance and uncertainty.[15]

From Zunshine's elucidation of the tenets of cognitive approaches, it is clear that if the findings of real-mind disciplines are to be meaningfully applied to fictional characterization, the emphasis must be on the complex and often subtle ways in which the workings of the figural mind, and readerly comprehension and construction thereof, are manifest in physical and social context. Cognitive literary theorists are bound to occupy, to use Alan Palmer's terminology, an "externalist" rather than "internalist" perspective in their examinations of fictional mentation:

> The two perspectives form more of a continuum than an either/or dichotomy, but the distinction is, in general, a valid one:
>
> –An internalist perspective on the mind stresses those aspects that are inner, introspective, private, solitary, individual, psychological, mysterious, and detached.
>
> –An externalist perspective on the mind stresses those aspects that are outer, active, public, social, behavioral, evident, embodied, and engaged.[16]

Palmer does not dispute the fictional narrative's exclusive prerogative to provide its reader unmediated access to a consciousness not his or her own—an opportunity that comes as a "relief from the business of real life, much of which requires the ability to decode accurately the behavior of others."[17] But his focus is decidedly the externalist examination of fictional consciousness; cognitive theory is applicable to fictional minds only insofar as these are revealed through the subtleties of characters' manifest behaviors:

> In one sense, . . . we are invisible to each other. But in another sense, the workings of our minds are perfectly visible to others in our actions, and the workings of fictional minds are perfectly visible to readers from characters' actions. Most novels contain a wide variety of material or evidence on which readers base their conjectures, hypotheses, and opinions about fictional minds.[18]

Palmer's views have become the focus of exciting polemics on the relevance of cognitive approaches to literature and the parameters of their applicability in narrative theory.[19] My own examination of the historical dynamics surrounding the presentation of consciousness in nineteenth-century Russian fiction is not meant to undermine the potential and heuristic value of concepts inspired by the real-mind disciplines for literary criticism; but it does lay bare one particular limitation of cognitive approaches to fictional narrative. Namely, such approaches deal first and foremost with externalized thought, with mental activity as manifest in speech, gesture, and behavior, and have no analytical grounds from which to theorize the unique *event* of attaining direct access to fictional minds, an event standing as a key moment in the history of the novel, and inaugurating the "unfolding of the genre's most distinctive potential" (Cohn).[20]

The diachronic perspective on forms of presented consciousness in nineteenth-century Russian fiction assumed in this chapter corroborates Cohn's intuition that in the history of prose narrative, and specifically within the period of the rise and advance of the realist novel, the externalist and internalist presentations of fictional minds are not complementary—that is, they do not form, as Palmer maintains, a "continuum"—but rather are incompatible and antagonistic. In Turgenev's novella *Mumu*, written on the very eve of Russian literature's breakthrough to the novelistic form, the position of external observation is thoroughly undermined, as its protagonist, the serf Gerasim, is deaf, mute, facially inexpressive, and as was typical for the Russian peasantry of the mid-nineteenth century, illiterate, all of which renders the externalist perspective largely ineffectual for providing insight into the character's inner life.

A hero offering precious little material for inferring his mental state is unamenable to narrative strategies of observation and analysis operative in the presentation of the inner experiences of a "typical"—speaking, hearing, facially expressive, perhaps even letter- or diary-writing—character. Turgenev's novella consummates the tendency, already observed in Lermontov's *Princess Ligovskaia*, of delimiting the characterological potential of external observation. Apparently, this decisive undermining of the external vantage point in the history of Russian prose cannot be theorized via analytic frameworks developed within the real-mind disciplines, since cognitive approaches, examining ways in which interiority is inferred rather then directly accessed, themselves operate within the externalist perspective.

Notably, Cohn as cited above numbers Turgenev (along with Fontane and Dickens) among novelists who eschew inside views, relying instead on direct speech and outward behavior as major modes of characterization, and whose works thus lie "outside the central compass of [her] study" of fiction's "transparent minds."[21] For my own, diachronically oriented, examination, concerned with the historical *event* of characters' minds becoming transparent, Turgenev's oeuvre presents, on the contrary, the most advantageous material: it was largely with Turgenev that the genre of the realist novel was first established in original Russian fiction, and with it the realist novel's repertoire of consciousness-presenting techniques. As mentioned in the introduction, Turgenev "struggled with the longer narrative" (Costlow) early in his literary career, destroying his first attempt at the novel (*Two Generations*), and turning to the narrative organization of the prose cycle with *A Sportsman's Sketches* (1852), the work that brought him immediate recognition.

In terms of its approach to figural interiority, *A Sportsman's Sketches* continues, in many ways crowning, Russia's prose-cycle tradition of the first half of the nineteenth century. In this collection of tales, the narrator's mobility, determined by his hunting pursuits, his capacity for sympathetic listening and faithful recording, as well as his aptitude for falling asleep at the right place and then waking up at the right time to overhear confessions (as happens, for instance, in the tales "Ermolai and the Miller's Wife" ["Ermolai i mel'nichikha"] and "The Office" ["Kontora"]) consolidate the position of external observation that is at the core of the cycle's poetics.[22]

Yet only four years separate Turgenev's first novel *Rudin* (1856) from *A Sportsman's Sketches*, and from the novella *Mumu* as well. This chapter will show how in the course of narration in *Mumu*, an authorial position qualitatively different from that of external observation is established. Also definable as a transitional narrative in Turgenev's corpus is "The End of Chertopkhanov"; but this is a rare case of "backward" transition, that is, from novel to novella, this work having been written and incorporated into *A Sportsman's Sketches* more than twenty years after most of the other stories in the cycle, during which interval Turgenev had produced his major novels. I will demonstrate that the narration of "The End of Chertopkhanov," otherwise sustaining the position of external observation in accordance with the rest of the cycle's stories, in one particular instance "lets slip," as it were, its author's capacity for novelistic presentation of character interiority. This peculiar moment provides an exceptional opportunity to explore the discursive circumstances in which the fictional mind attains novelistic transparency.

Toward the end of Turgenev's *Mumu* (written 1852, published 1854), the deaf and mute serf Gerasim drowns his beloved dog Mumu to placate his despotic mistress, whose Moscow estate he quits shortly thereafter to return to his home village. By leaving without his "owner's" permission, Gerasim commits one of the most gravely punishable offenses in the institution of Russian serfdom. Turgenev scholars commenting on *Mumu* tend to reconcile the incongruity of these two successive acts by assigning primary significance to only one or the other. Critics' attention is focused either on the main character's killing of his dog as the ultimate manifestation of his enslavement, or on his escape. Accordingly, Gerasim appears either servile, resigned to his fate; or a defiant rebel.

For instance, in one of the few works devoted solely to a thorough examination of *Mumu*, Edgar Frost interprets Gerasim's flight from Moscow as a spontaneous reaction to his own deed rather than the carrying out of a deliberate plan: "Disturbed enough to leave Moscow, Gerasim is still submissive enough to kill the thing he loves."[23] According to Frost, Gerasim's return to his home village does not liberate him at all, but rather finalizes the hero's loss of humanity: "The stress in the last paragraph of the story is on the apparent sameness of circumstances surrounding the hero [as he continues to perform "the work of four men as before"]. . . . It seems clear that the reason for this sameness is to set up a distinct contrast between it and the one aspect that is not the same: the protagonist's opportunity to love and to be loved. Without this opportunity, Gerasim remains less than a man, which is exactly Turgenev's point."[24]

Interestingly, much the same conclusion is reached in scholarly works examining *Mumu* from an entirely different theoretical standpoint. In post-Soviet Russian literary criticism, Turgenev's story—hitherto discussed exclusively in terms of an ideologically approved denunciation of serfdom—has rather unexpectedly become the focus of meticulous psychoanalytic analyses, with critics thus oriented proclaiming, like Frost, the ultimate defeat of Turgenev's hero at the hands of the powers that be. Thus, for example, sums up Sergei Zimovets: "The bull-bear Gerasim returns to the bosom of Mother Nature; he is once again an animal. . . . But now a castrated animal."[25] Despite their obvious differences in theoretical stance, both Frost and Zimovets offer remarkably similar formulations regarding the essence of Gerasim's degradation from human being to "less than a man."

But such conclusions on the hero's ultimate submission do not take into account, first of all, the way in which Gerasim's flight to his home village is presented in Turgenev's story. On his grueling, all-night trek into the countryside, Gerasim appears neither degraded nor defeated but, on the contrary, very much aware of himself and what he is doing, and, indeed, liberated:

> He was hurrying on without looking back; hurrying homewards, to his own village, to his own country. . . . He walked along . . . with a sort of invincible purpose, a desperate and at the same time joyous determination. . . . Gerasim . . . smelt the familiar scent of the ripening rye, which was wafted from the dark fields; he felt the wind, flying to meet him—the wind from home—beat caressingly upon his face and played with his hair and his beard. He saw before him the . . . road homewards [showing white and] straight as an arrow. He saw in the sky stars innumerable, lighting up his way, and stepped out, strong and bold as a lion.[26]

As for the animal symbolism evoked by Zimovets, Turgenev's comparison of Gerasim here at the end to the king of all cats enhances rather than demeans his status; the escapee seems to have regained the noble wildness described early in the story as lost when, as a "strong young bull," he had been dragged from his home village—domesticated, as it were—to work at the Moscow estate as a porter:

> When he was transported to the town, he could not understand what was being done with him; he was miserable and stupefied, with the stupefaction of some strong young bull, taken straight from the meadow, where the rich grass stood up to his belly, taken and put in the truck of a railway train, and there,

> while smoke and sparks and gusts of steam puff out upon the sturdy beast, he is whirled onwards, whirled along with loud roar and whistle, whither—God knows![27]

Furthermore, in postulating the "absence of love" as the hero's irrevocable destiny, Frost fails to notice that Gerasim's rushing through the night is directed precisely toward what the hero perceives to be the call of the so to speak original (i.e., maternal) love: "He hastened as though his old mother were waiting for him at home, as though she were calling him to her after long wanderings in strange parts, among strangers."[28] And it is also notable—or perhaps, in this case, symptomatic—that psychoanalytic examinations of *Mumu* totally ignore Gerasim's sudden recognition of a maternal presence in his life after Mumu's death.

Further militating against the interpretation of Gerasim as ultimately defeated is the story's divergence from the actual incident on which Turgenev's novella is based. A serf of Turgenev's mother named Andrei had killed his beloved dog on her order, but then faithfully resumed his service to this "owner."[29] Turgenev changes the serf's dutiful compliance into his hero's flight from Moscow, thus appearing to transform the oppressed slave into a rebel.

However, the view of Gerasim as in revolt has its own shortcomings, perhaps best revealed if one considers the "naive" issues raised by readers of Turgenev's story who are literally childlike. *Mumu* is routinely taught in Russian elementary schools, and teachers report that its ending invariably provokes their pupils' resentment at such a plot development.[30] That is, faced with the interpretation of the hero as a rebel (the one favored, naturally, by Soviet scholarship, and still predominant in Russian literature textbooks), children spot the inconsistency in Gerasim's protest: if he is going to break from his mistress's tyranny anyway, why does he kill Mumu at all, rather than just take her along with him to his home village?

In a pedagogical experiment conducted in one Russian school, students were asked to rewrite the ending of *Mumu*, and consistently had Gerasim take the dog along in his flight from the Moscow estate. What's more, the children, eager to spare Mumu her undeserved death, provide exceptionally close readings, detecting textual details that might escape a more "sophisticated" audience. They note, for instance, that no one at the mistress's estate can know for certain whether Gerasim in fact kills Mumu; the drowning takes place in the middle of a river, at some distance, and out of sight of any potential witnesses. Thus if Gerasim were really determined to escape his mistress, he should have had no difficulty defying her terrible demand.[31]

The "naively realistic" scenarios unfolding in the children's compositions are in full agreement with the reading of Gerasim as rebel[32]—as fully as the serf Andrei's loyalty to Varvara Petrovna Turgeneva corresponds to the conduct of a slave. However, the character's behavior does not easily fit one mold or the other; he acts neither like his real-life prototype, nor like the hero the children would have unambiguously take a stand against serfdom and animal cruelty. Instead, Gerasim follows *both* realistically comprehensible patterns of behavior: he destroys the love of his life, thereby demonstrating servile submission, the thoroughness of his being "owned"; but in running away, he rebels against this iniquity.

The only plausible way to account for the incongruity between the hero's two actions without minimizing the significance of either, it seems, is to envision his flight from Moscow as directly informed by the killing of his beloved dog. It is only *after* drowning Mumu that Gerasim's capacity to break free from serfdom (which system had completely conditioned his life to this point) finally manifests itself. In other words, on his way to the fatal river, Gerasim does not yet know that he will later quit his mistress's estate; it is only after he drowns Mumu that this previously unthinkable flight becomes possible. One textual detail attests to this version: from the conversation of other serfs, the reader learns that after drowning Mumu, Gerasim had returned to his garret to collect his belongings (briefly witnessed by one of the other serfs), only afterward leaving for good. This piece of information, in other respects insignificant, confirms that the hero did not intend to leave his mistress until after he had killed his dog on her order.[33]

Thus Gerasim undergoes a remarkable change after Mumu's death: this change, however, hardly seems either an ultimate defeat at the hands of serfdom or a conscious revolt against it. And here I would stress that Gerasim's muteness is crucial to understanding the essence of his transformation. Scholarly readings of *Mumu* have typically considered the hero's muteness as simply intensifying either his humility or his protest, depending on where the interpretation comes down on that score. But I propose examining the hero's lack of speech not as an idiosyncratic physical trait ("borrowed" from real life and/or symbolically charged), but rather as a narrative circumstance that provides a unique resolution to the issue of the presentation of character consciousness in Russian fiction of the time.

The only sound Gerasim is able to produce is not human but animal—specifically, bovine, denoted as "mooing" (*mychanie*). With a mute hero, his inner life lacking *any* means of being articulated, the long-problematic discrepancy between consciousness and its outward manifestation reaches its maximum tension.[34] Neither is Gerasim's face any more expressive, which fact is ascribed to his being deaf and mute:

> The next morning Gerasim came out of his garret and went about his work. He came in to his dinner, ate it, and went out again, without a greeting to any

> one. His face, which had always been lifeless, as with all deaf-mutes, seemed now to be turned to stone.[35]

Accordingly, the narrator can hardly rely on nonverbal clues to the character's inner life when observing the mute hero's "lifeless" face.

From their standpoint of external observation, novella narrators of the 1830s–50s present characters' inner life by construing a network of "signifiers" (words, actions, gestures) most pertinent to the "signified." With a hero like Gerasim, for whom "mooing" is the *only* possible signifier, the futility of this narrative strategy becomes apparent. In *Mumu*, the character Antipka performs the function, archetypal for novella narration, of spying; but spying on Gerasim (to assess the consequences of a plot to trick the porter out of a courtship potentially disruptive to the household), he can make no sense of his observations:

> For the next twenty-four hours, [Gerasim] did not come out. . . . The postilion Antipka said afterwards that he saw Gerasim through a crack in the wall, sitting on his bedstead, his face in his hand. From time to time he uttered soft regular sounds [or "mooed"]; he was wailing a dirge, that is, swaying backwards and forwards with his eyes shut, and shaking his head as drivers or bargemen do when they chant their melancholy songs. Antipka could not bear it, and he came away from the crack. When Gerasim came out of the garret next day, no particular change could be observed in him. He only seemed, as it were, more morose, and took not the slightest notice of Tatiana or Kapiton.[36]

Secret surveillance proves as useless as open observation: neither provides a clue as to the mute hero's inner experience. The narrator of the novella finds himself in the same situation as the inquisitive Antipka: even when the narrator can safely intrude upon Gerasim, or follow as some other character does so, the inner life of the observed remains arcane.

Gerasim's muteness foregrounds a fundamental discrepancy between character interiority and its outer manifestations in speech, gesture, and behavior—a discrepancy at the very heart of the novella narrator's struggle to represent inner life. Taken to its logical conclusion, this discrepancy means that any sound (gesture, action) can correspond to any meaning, any aspect of inner experience whatsoever, and is therefore, with respect to this meaning, nothing but "mooing." Turgenev's unusual hero thus models the dilemma the narrator of a novella encounters in approaching the inner life of *any* character, however sincere, expressive, or articulate.

Being inaccessible to external observation, the deaf, mute, and illiterate hero thwarts the reliance on speech, gesture, and behavior as a window to inner life; the novella narrator accustomed to such methods is, in effect, at a dead end. But I propose that in *Mumu* this situation, rather than standing as a narrative impasse, engenders a unique resolution. That is: the search for adequate signifiers proving hopeless, physically ruled out in this case, the essence of this search—the very discrepancy between signified and signifier, inner life and its outer manifestations—comes uppermost in the narrator's view. Instead of engaging in the infinite pursuit of congruencies between interiority and its "evidence," which activity defined the presentation of consciousness in the Russian novella of the first half of the nineteenth century, the narrator is now uniquely positioned to confront the discrepancy itself. A "mooing" hero having laid bare the definitive shakiness of such congruences, the narrator must look for ways to *forgo* words in order to access his character's inner life. I suggest that in *Mumu*, this deliverance from words comes about because these previously evidentiary words—words, that is, plural—have become, in Turgenev's novella, literally a single word: Mumu.

Gerasim's muteness sets him apart from the rest of the servants: "He was a splendid peasant, and, were it not for his affliction, any girl would have been glad to marry him."[37] Falling in love with Tatiana and entertaining thoughts of marrying her, Gerasim attempts—and fails—to bridge the gap between himself and his fellow humans. Muteness renders him both an intimidating figure to Tatiana herself, and a victim of the other servants' plot to trick him into believing that she is a drunk in order to scuttle his courtship of her.

Frost notes the striking similarities (emotions, physical traits described) between Gerasim's connections to Tatiana and to Mumu, and that the "ascendancy of the Mumu-Gerasim relationship"[38] plays a significant role in structuring Turgenev's story: "No sooner has the cart bearing her [Tatiana, leaving the estate forever with the husband the mistress has in effect picked for her] lurched out of his view than Gerasim turns off along the river and notices the as-yet-unnamed Mumu wriggling helplessly in the mud there, trying to extract herself."[39] At the same time, there is a crucial difference between the hero's relationship with the woman he loves and his relationship with the dog. This difference is established at the very moment just described, when Gerasim first finds the dog as a puppy, rescuing her from the same Moscow river in which he will later drown her: "He had even given her a name—the [mute] know that their inarticulate noises [or "mooing"] call the attention of others. He called her Mumu."[40] The homodiegetic motivation for this name is Gerasim's physical deficiency: "moo" is the only sound he is able to produce. In scholarly interpretations, meanwhile, Mumu's name is charged, or overcharged, with symbolism. For instance, in his psychoanalytic reading of Turgenev's story, Vadim Kolotaev not only connects the word "Mumu" with other of the story's associations of Gerasim with bovinity, but also grounds both the word and such imagery in Mumu's maternal status in the hero's life: "Gerasim resembles an infant who has pronounced his first word, a word that denotes mother. Mumu and mama, Mumunia and mamania—these words sound alike and are related. Moo-moo is the sound made by a cow, the mother-nurse who nourishes her child with her milk."[41]

Kolotaev's point that in effect Gerasim is a child uttering his first word is well taken. But, the possible associations evoked by "Mumu" aside, quite glaring in this situation is that in naming the dog, the otherwise mute Gerasim acquires the ability to pronounce a *word*; the animal sound he is able to produce becomes a human word. Gerasim's long-standing "moo-moo," it turns out, has a real-world application—it is the name of this particular dog; and when calling it, Gerasim, for the first time in his life, makes sense.[42]

The authenticity of Gerasim's word is confirmed by its recognition and acceptance by the dog as its "addressee," and by the community at large: "All the servants in the house liked her, and called her Mumu, too."[43] Gerasim's muteness-fueled alienation from the human world thus ceases at the very instant when he first calls to his dog. This radical change in the hero's status is particularly stark against the background of his divergent relationships with the two objects of his love: Tatiana and Mumu. In courting the former, Gerasim appears helpless; however tender his feelings for the girl (and indeed, when later they finally part, she cries as if beweeping a lost chance at true love), he is physically unable to convey them:

> One day she was stealing across the yard, with a starched dressing-jacket of her mistress's carefully poised on her outspread fingers . . . someone suddenly grabbed her vigorously by the elbow; she turned round and fairly screamed; behind her stood Gerasim. With a foolish smile, making inarticulate caressing grunts [or "sweetly mooing"], he held out to her a gingerbread cock with gold tinsel on his tail and wings. She was about to refuse it, but he thrust it forcibly into her hand, shook his head, walked away, and turning round, once more grunted [or "mooed"] something very affectionately to her. From that day forward he gave her no peace. . . . The poor girl simply did not know how to behave or what to do.[44]

When addressed to Mumu, however, the inadequacy of Gerasim's mooing (*mychanie*) evaporates. The very same sound coincides with the human word capable of expressing his feelings, for instance, his anguish upon his dog's temporary loss when, unbeknownst to him, the footman Stepan tries to appease the mistress's wrath by selling Mumu at a nearby market:

> He stood still opposite the windows of the mistress's house, took a searching look at the steps where a group of house-serfs were crowded together,

> turned away, and uttered once more his inarticulate "Mumu." [Significantly, also translatable as simply "turned away, and mooed once more: 'Mumu!'"] Mumu did not answer. He went away. Every one looked after him, but no one smiled or said a word.[45]

Thus, by naming his dog Mumu, the only name he is capable of giving, Gerasim acquires speech, even if his language consists only of this one word.

With the death of Mumu, this language is lost. *Mumu* is thus a story not only of a serf's unjust loss of his pet but also, somewhat paradoxically, of this deaf and mute hero's loss of speech; which is not the same thing, I would stress, as falling back into muteness—a conclusion that would support the reading of the novella's end, albeit in a manner other than that usually proposed, as Gerasim's final defeat. It would be more accurate to suggest that although Gerasim loses his capacity for articulate speech with Mumu's death, he does not so much relapse into muteness as *fall silent*. With Mumu gone, Gerasim literally has nothing more to say, is liberated from the very need to speak. Muteness strives to be resolved into words and, therefore, precedes speech; but silence comes after it, standing as the volitional transformation of muteness, the human choice, that is, not to make a sound.

I would further suggest that Mumu's death also has crucial consequences for the presentation of her master's inner life. The naming of this dog has granted articulateness not only to the name-giver Gerasim, but also to the novella's narrator, who is finally able to "catch" his mute hero in this singular moment of reliable expression. "Mumu" is not just Gerasim's sole pronounceable word, it is also the only word of his that the narrator can break down into signifier and signified. Thus when Gerasim names his dog, gaining the power of speech, the narrator gains something as well: liberation from merely "mooing" about his mute character's inner life.

When Mumu is drowned, this single reliable word is spoken one final time, then lost forever. Like his character, the narrator no longer needs to speak (to narrate), certain as he is that he will have no more words at his disposal to provide him access to his mute hero's inner life. The narrator thus also falls silent, that is, opts not to narrate, in doing so willingly coinciding with the intrinsic limits of novella narration—limits he had attempted to circumvent by searching for reliable signifiers of consciousness. Confronted with a hero who has finished speaking his only word, this search has finally proved inadequate for the task of representing this character's inner life. I would stress, however, that in *Mumu*, the narrator realizes this inadequacy, but it does not stand as some "professional" failure on his part. Much like Gerasim, who unexpectedly for himself breaks free of the law hitherto binding him unconditionally to the Moscow estate, the novella narrator, having agreed to accept the limits of his genre, now finds the possibility of escaping them. Gerasim heads back home. Where is the narrator's "flight" headed?

As mentioned above, the strongest textual evidence that Gerasim experiences some sort of conversion or personal liberation after Mumu's death comes in the description of his journey from the Moscow estate back to his home village. His night trek is presented as a flight not from but rather *toward* something; specifically, Gerasim hears "the call of his mother" and hurries to meet it.

> He was hurrying on without looking round; hurrying homewards, to his own village, to his own country. . . . He walked, his shoulders thrown back and his chest expanded; his eyes were fixed greedily straight before him. He hastened as though his old mother were waiting for him at home, as though she were calling him to her after long wanderings in strange parts, among strangers.[46]

But what is so striking here is not just the sudden manifestation of a familial presence, a maternal call, in the hero's life; it is that this deaf hero seems suddenly able to respond to it. At the beginning of the novella, Gerasim is characterized by deafness and muteness as ever-present physical conditions; but now that his muteness has become silence, his deafness is transformed as well, and he can perceive his mother's voice. He has gained, that is, the ability to listen—which, indeed, one cannot do without first falling silent as Gerasim has done; and which ability differs from hearing just as silence differs from muteness.

The narrator of Turgenev's novella, I would emphasize, undergoes a similar transformation, his opting not to narrate engendering an analogous capacity to *listen* to his unspeaking character, that is, to comprehend him without reliance on some audibly authenticated word. This choice exempts the narrator from narrated events, simultaneously granting the author access to the character's inner life. In the course of the narration of Turgenev's novella, an authorial position qualitatively different from that of external observation is discovered. Exemption from the temporal and spatial constraints of the narrated world and the unmediated presentation of figural consciousness appear as two interrelated and mutually conditional constituents of this newly emergent discursive stance. Essentially, this is the position of the author of the realist novel, who renders his characters' hearts and minds transparent—a position soon to be established and explored in Turgenev's subsequent prose and in the ensuing Russian novel of the second half of the nineteenth century.

At the end of the novella, Gerasim lives in his hut all by himself, and has no interaction with either humans or animals:

> And Gerasim is living still, a lonely man in his lonely hut; he is strong and healthy as before, and does the work of four men as before, and as before is serious and steady. But his neighbors have observed that ever since his return from Moscow he has quite given up the society of women; he will not even look at them, and does not keep even a single dog. "It's his good luck, though," the peasants reason, "that he can get on without female folk; and as for a dog—what need has he of a dog? You wouldn't get a thief to go into his yard for any money!" Such is the fame of the [mute] man's Titanic strength.[47]

Gerasim is not deprived of dogs or women, but rather has no need for them. His freedom from the need to speak informs his lack of need for animals or humans, sounds or meanings.[48] In this voluntary exemption from the narrated world—the world of speaking and hearing—Gerasim's life at the end of the novella resembles neither the seclusion of a defeated pariah nor the lying-in-wait of some undercover rebel. Instead, the hero's disinterested, time- and space-unbound existence ("And Gerasim is living still") finds its closest counterpart in the authorial exemption from temporal and spatial constraints—a position discovered in *Mumu* in the course of narration. Within the narrated world, this authorial stance finds its nearest correspondence in the phenomenon of unconditionally accepting maternal love, and it is toward this manifested presence that Gerasim rushes through the night.

"The End of Chertopkhanov" stands out among the tales in Turgenev's first successful literary work, the prose cycle *A Sportsman's Sketches*. As mentioned earlier in this chapter, the tales in *Sketches* conform to that narrative organization of Russian novellas of the 1820s–50s by which the external narrator presents characters' thoughts and feelings either by employing such "documentary" materials as confessional stories, diaries, personal notes, and intimate letters (especially prevalent in the frame narrative of the 1820s), or else by attempting to "catch" the character unawares in a moment of spontaneous self-expression (a method especially resorted to in the society tale of the 1830s). In Turgenev's *Sketches*, characters' inner experiences are portrayed entirely from the position of external observation: the tales' narrator is an itinerant nobleman hunter whose need to wander the countryside in search of game, as well as his keen eye, equanimity, and somewhat detached compassion, render him a perfect candidate for observing the lives of widely diverse characters, from fellow landowners to serfs. The only tale in the cycle not fully hewing to the principle of external observation is "The End of Chertopkhanov."

Exceptional, first of all, is that in all the other tales, the sportsman-narrator is explicitly present to witness and faithfully record narrated events, and to appeal to various intermediaries for additional information as needed. This convention holds true for the tale that immediately precedes "The End of Chertopkhanov" in the cycle's compositional layout, "Chertopkhanov and Nedopiuskin." During one of his hunting sessions, the sportsman meets the destitute yet willfully proud landlord Pantelei Chertopkhanov and his devoted friend, the kindly but hapless Tikhon Nedopiuskin; later on, the sportsman also becomes acquainted with the Gypsy girl Masha, who is "not exactly [Chertopkhanov's] wife but as good as one."[49] An account of these meetings, accompanied by the sportsman's dutiful research on the characters' backgrounds, makes up the story of "Chertopkhanov and Nedopiuskin."

"The End of Chertopkhanov" which follows, describing events of the two subsequent years in these characters' lives, is the only tale in *Sketches* in which the sportsman-narrator does not appear in person. Calamities[50] befalling Pantelei Chertopkhanov in quick succession in this period—the departure of Masha, the death of Nedopiuskin, and the loss of the horse Malek-Adel—and culminating in the "end" to which the title refers, are described without reference to conversations of the sportsman with any of the characters, or to his having sought other sources of information.

This distinction can easily pass unnoticed by readers of *A Sportsman's Sketches*; "The End of Chertopkhanov" appears a mere sequel to "Chertopkhanov and Nedopiuskin," a follow-up prompted by the narrator's diligence. It is indeed possible to picture the sportsman behind the narration in "The End of Chertopkhanov" acting entirely in the same capacity of "gatherer of information"[51] as in other tales of the cycle, when describing, for instance, a character's childhood he himself could not possibly have witnessed. There are even, as the sportsman readily admits, some lacunae in his account, which further reinforce the impression of a personified—hence investigatively limited—storyteller. For example, the report on Masha's decision to leave Chertopkhanov is accompanied by the following speculation:

> What induced her to forsake his roof, where she seemed to be so thoroughly at home, it is hard to say. Chertopkhanov to the end of his days clung to the conviction that a certain young neighbor . . . named Yaff was at the root of Masha's desertion . . . but one must suppose that the vagrant gypsy blood in Masha's veins had more to do with it. However that may have been, one fine summer evening Masha tied up a few odds and ends in a small bundle and walked out of Chertopkhanov's house.[52]

As discussed in chapter 1, such gaps in knowledge are often employed in novellas of the 1820s–50s in order to strengthen their claim to authenticity, one of the major characteristics of the period's prose; within the "found manuscript" tradition, such omissions are often attributed to the document's damaged condition (as from ink stains, for instance, in Vel'tman's 1839 novella *Radoi*). An assemblage of diverse, often contradictory, opinions on a character's personality or motivation (such as the rivaling explanations offered for Masha's departure) is also a common textual effect in prose of the time, one that marks the external narrator's limits in accessing figural interiority. Chapter 3 cited an analogous example from Lermontov's *Princess Ligovskaia* in which the "composite" portrayal of the novella's protagonist Pechorin is undertaken from several conflicting viewpoints: that of high society, of Lavater-inspired face-readers, and the "crowd."

At the same time, the most decisive events in "The End of Chertopkhanov"—all directly related to the nadirs of the hero's three "calamities"—take place under circumstances that should have been difficult, if not impossible, to observe. The final parting of Chertopkhanov and Masha occurs late in the evening, two versts away from the village, on the high road leading to the district town. The spot appears quiet and desolate, with no one intruding upon their thirty-minute confrontation, during which Chertopkhanov "came close to her, he fell back, he shook his fists at her, he bowed down before her, he wept, he scolded";[53] nor do there appear to be any witnesses as, desperate to convince Masha to stay with him, Chertopkhanov repeatedly throws himself on the ground and even discharges his pistol.

Similarly, there is no one to see Nedopiuskin's dying moments, to hear his last words, other than Chertopkhanov—certainly not the doctor, who arrives too late:

> He did not lose his memory at once: he still knew Chertopkhanov, and to his friend's cry of despair, "How can you desert me, Tikhon, without my consent, just as Masha did?" he even responded with faltering, uncertain tongue, "O . . . Pant-lei . . . E-e-ich, am . . . al-always . . . glad . . . to o-bey you." This did not, however, prevent him from dying the same day, without waiting for the district doctor, who (on seeing the hardly cold body) found nothing left for him to do but, with a melancholy recognition of the instability of all things mortal, to ask for "a drop of vodka and a snack of fish."[54]

Finally, it is even harder to locate a possible witness for Chertopkhanov's killing of the "imposter" Malek-Adel (on which more below); indeed, the reader is explicitly informed that there is none, at least among the ranks of the human:

> But his own voice terrified him—it sounded so wild and strange under the cover of dark branches in the close, decaying dampness of the forest ravine! Moreover, in response to his exclamation, some great bird suddenly fluttered in a tree-top above his head. . . . Chertopkhanov shuddered. He had, as it

> were, roused a witness to his act—and where? In that silent place where he should have met no living creature.[55]

At the same time, in each of these episodes it is possible to conceive of a *virtual* witness, since events are presented as entirely audible and visible; as are expressions of the characters' inner experiences. Here I would cite a few examples that readily call to mind Cohn's observation on the "audibl[e] soliloquizing," "exclamation[s]," and "muttering"[56] of characters in early forms of the novel, whose authors, avoiding peeking into figural minds, provided drama-like externalizations of speech.

In the first example, when Chertopkhanov decides that it is Capt. Yaff who is to blame for Masha's betrayal, and rushes to confront him—but is told by this fellow's valet that he has left for Moscow—Chertopkhanov speaks aloud, despite addressing not Yaff himself, but his portrait on a wall:

> "Then it is so!" *cried* Chertopkhanov furiously; "there was an arrangement between them; she has run away with him . . . but wait a bit!"
>
> He broke into the young cavalry captain's room in spite of the resistance of the valet. In the room there was hanging over the sofa a portrait in oils of the master, in the Uhlan uniform. "Ah, here you are, you tailless ape!" *thundered* Chertopkhanov; he jumped on to the sofa and with a blow of his fist burst a big hole in the taut canvas.[57] (Emphases mine)

Then there is Nedopiuskin's reaction to Masha's departure, which crushes this kindly soul even harder than Chertopkhanov himself:

> "She has torn the heart out of me," *he would murmur to himself* as he sat on his favorite sofa and twisted his fingers. Even when Chertopkhanov had got over it, he, Nedopyuskin, did not recover, and still felt that "*there was a void within him.*" "Here," *he would say*, pointing to the middle of his breast above his stomach.[58] (Emphases mine)

Finally, in the remote forest where he has come to do away with the "false" Malek-Adel, Chertopkhanov speaks to the horse aloud:

> Not far from the forest to which he was leading his horse there stretched a small ravine, half overgrown with young oak bushes. Chertopkhanov went down into it. Malek-Adel stumbled and almost fell on him.
>
> "So you would crush me, would you, you damned brute!" *shouted* Chertopkhanov. . . . "Away with you, devil, to the four winds of heaven!" he *muttered* . . . .

> Suddenly something poked him behind between his shoulder-blades. He looked round. Malek-Adel was standing in the middle of the road.
>
> "Ah!" *shouted* Chertopkhanov, "of yourself, of yourself you have come to your death! So, there!"[59] (Emphases mine)

In one notable moment, a mental view is attempted but then quickly withdrawn, substituted with the character's audible remark, as if the author has caught himself peeking into interiority and changed his mind, or censored his own such move. The moment occurs during Chertopkhanov's farewell meeting with Masha: walking away, the latter begins to sing, and it is only now that Chertopkhanov fully comprehends the finality of their breakup: "'She does it to spite me,' *thought* Chertopkhanov; but *at once he moaned*, 'oh, no! it's her last farewell to me for ever'—and he burst into floods of tears [emphases mine]."[60]

Thus, despite the absence of a personified narrator/observer, "The End of Chertopkhanov" fully conforms to the approach to figural consciousness actualized throughout Turgenev's *Sketches*, as well as, in general, in Russian fiction of the first half of the nineteenth century, wherein characters' inner experiences are not accessed directly, but rather presented through their external manifestations in speech, gesture, and behavior. However, the tale includes one solitary, hence quite striking instance in which this otherwise ironclad principle of external observation breaks down, and does so spectacularly.

The circumstances leading to this moment in the course of narrated events unfold as follows. Having lost both Masha and Nedopiuskin, Chertopkhanov finds his ultimate object of affection in Malek-Adel; his infatuation with the horse combines and surpasses his feelings for both previous attachments:

> From that very day the chief interest, the chief occupation, the chief pleasure in the life of Chertopkhanov, was Malek-Adel. He loved him as he had not loved even Masha; he became more attached to him than even to Nedopyuskin.[61]

When Malek-Adel is stolen in the middle of the night, Chertopkhanov undertakes a search, finally finding him, it would seem, a year later at a horse fair, and recovering him for a large sum of money. However, doubt plagues Chertopkhanov, who cannot let go of the suspicion that he has misidentified Malek-Adel and brought home a different horse, one only outwardly resembling the original. This initially vague fear soon proves justified: the village deacon points out to Chertopkhanov that the gray-colored

Malek-Adel would have whitened during the year of his absence, while the horse bought at the fair is still gray. Stricken by the undeniable proof of his mistake, Chertopkhanov rushes home and locks himself in his room. It is at this moment that the narrator abandons his heretofore-unswerving position of external observation. Chertopkhanov's inner turmoil is presented in the clearly identified and intensely sustained narrative mode of free indirect discourse—the single example of unmediated presentation of consciousness not only in "The End of Chertopkhanov," but in the entire cycle of *A Sportsman's Sketches*:

> That this worthless jade was not Malek-Adel; that between him and Malek-Adel there was not the smallest resemblance; that any man of the slightest sense would have seen this from the first minute; that he, Chertopkhanov, had been taken in the vulgarest way—no! That he purposely, of set intent, tricked himself, blinded his own eyes—of all this he had not now the faintest doubt! . . . His vanity suffered intolerably; but he was not only tortured by the sting of wounded vanity; he was overwhelmed by despair, stifled by rage, and burning with the thirst for revenge. But rage against whom? On whom was he to be revenged? On the Jew, Yaff, Masha, the deacon, the Cossack-thief, all his neighbors, the whole world, himself? His brain was giving way. The last card was trumped! (That simile gratified him.)[62]

This glaring breach in the narrative technique typically goes unremarked in scholarly discussions of *A Sportsman's Sketches*. Critics commenting on "The End of Chertopkhanov" tend to minimize the differences between this tale and the rest of the cycle. For instance, Dale Peterson refers to "The End of Chertopkhanov" as a conclusion to "Chertopkhanov and Nedopiuskin," which naturally "falls into its assigned place."[63] Consolata Delaney observes that this "remarkable story" contains "several small dramatic scenes from which the narrator simply stands back."[64] Likewise, Leonid Grossman, who terms this tale "undoubtedly one of [Turgenev's] masterpieces"—noting that it is "not recognized as such even now, however"[65]—defines the generic surplus of "The End of Chertopkhanov" vis-à-vis the rest of the cycle in terms of drama, asserting that the dynamism and complexity of plot development in "The End of Chertopkhanov" "creates in the dimensions of the short story the conflicts of genuine tragedy."[66]

However, the presentation of Chertopkhanov's anguish as his misidentification of the horse sinks in is technically not "dramatic," but markedly novelistic: the hero's inner state is not mediated either by speech, gesture, or behavior. This depiction is conducted in free indirect discourse, a narrative mode alien to the poetics of Russian prose of the 1820s–50s, and constituting a marker, indeed a hallmark, of novelistic narration. How could this instance of novelistic transparency occur within a work otherwise fully conforming to the principle of external observation and the generic requirements of the novella?

The most immediate explanation for this shift in narrative technique—albeit one easily eluding the modern reader of *A Sportsman's Sketches*—is the belatedness of "The End of Chertopkhanov" as compared to the rest of the tales: it was written some twenty years after the first publication of the cycle. The first edition of *Sketches* (many of which had been published individually beginning in 1847) appeared in August 1852 and comprised twenty-two tales. In the early 1870s, Turgenev wrote and added three more tales, "The End of Chertopkhanov," "A Living Relic" ("Zhivye moshchi"), and "There Is a Clattering!" ("Stuchit!"), bringing the cycle's total to twenty-five. "The End of Chertopkhanov" first appeared separately in *The Herald of Europe* (*Vestnik Evropy*) in 1872 with the subtitle "From *A Sportsman's Sketches*" and was then included in *Sketches* as published in the 1874 and 1880 editions of Turgenev's collected works. Since then, "The End of Chertopkhanov" has been considered an integral part of the cycle, and only a glance into the reference section would reveal to the modern reader the tale's belated origin.

Turgenev wrote his major novels in the period between the first publication of *A Sportsman's Sketches* (1852) and the year "The End of Chertopkhanov" was written (1872). The tale's lone breach of the narrative organization of the cycle could thus be attributed to Turgenev's mastery of novelistic presentation of figural interiority during these intervening years. As Grossman remarks: "The first sketch of the series is separated from the last by a distance of almost thirty years, and between "Khor' and Kalinych" (1847) and "There Is a Clattering!" (1875) passed almost the entirety of Turgenev's literary activity, with his comedies, novellas, stories, and novels."[67] Moreover, as distinct from the two other latecomers to the cycle, "A Living Relic" and "There Is a Clattering!" which were based on earlier drafts from the 1840s, "The End of Chertopkhanov" was written entirely from scratch.

However, this information on the tale's history of creation and publication, while essential, does not quite suffice to explain the instance of consciousness presentation in "The End of Chertopkhanov," since not only were the other two later additions written in full accord with the cycle's narrative organization, but also, there is considerable evidence that Turgenev took great care to seamlessly integrate the tale into the cycle. When submitting his manuscript to the editor of *The Herald of Europe*, Turgenev asked that the first story about Chertopkhanov, "Chertopkhanov and Nedopiuskin," be run in the same issue of the journal, along with an editor's note that would elucidate for readers the link between the two stories. Turgenev also noted with his submission that he had mistakenly spelled the character's last name other than as in the earlier work, and requested that the proofreader A. N. Pypin correct the discrepancy:

> I have just noticed that in "The End of Chertopkhanov" I write "Chertapkhanov" throughout, but in *A Sportsman's Sketches*, it says "Chertopkhanov." This needs to be unified so that there is only one form: either *o* or *a*.[68]

Turgenev's wishes were granted, and "The End of Chertopkhanov" appeared in *The Herald of Europe* with the following introduction: "To those of my readers who have not forgotten the character Chertopkhanov from *A Sportsman's Sketches*, I would like to relate—if they don't mind listening to me—his end."[69] This sentence was followed by an editor's comment:

> Our readers would surely not mind if we . . . juxtapose that which has been separated by a significant interval of time. Here is the beginning of the story, which occupies several pages in *A Sportsman's Sketches* under the title "Chertopkhanov and Nedopiuskin."[70]

The earlier tale was then reprinted in a smaller font, followed by another editorial comment citing Turgenev's "promise [in the last paragraph of "Chertopkhanov and Nedopiuskin"] to finish the story 'some other time.'"[71] Apparently, all these measures were meant to drive home to Turgenev's audience that the hero of the new tale was the "same" Chertopkhanov they had already encountered in "Chertopkhanov and Nedopiuskin" twenty years earlier.

Certain perceptive readers, however, immediately noted the discord between "The End of Chertopkhanov" and the rest of the tales in *A Sportsman's Sketches*. One of these, Pavel Annenkov, a prominent literary critic and close friend of Turgenev, greatly admired the new work, but argued that it presented "a quite obvious and palpable disparity"[72] with the rest of the tales, and tried to convince Turgenev not to include it in the cycle. Turgenev himself sensed this "disparity": in both the 1874 and 1880 editions of *Sketches*, "The End of Chertopkhanov" was the only tale given a date of authorship (September 1872), which marked its distinct chronological position within the cycle.

Nevertheless, Turgenev was determined to incorporate the tale into his earlier work, justifying his resolve with reference to the story of Chertopkhanov's real-life prototype, an impoverished landlord named Chertov who had been Turgenev's own neighbor. In response to Annenkov, Turgenev explains that he was inspired to write a sequel to "Chertopkhanov and Nedopiuskin" by events in the life of this individual: "I just want to tell you how this thing occurred to me: my neighbor Chertov (the real name of Chertopkhanov) experienced what I related; this was told to me by his own daughter, who will, perhaps, be indignant at my indiscretion."[73] As a "true" story told by a reliable witness—in this case the character's own offspring—"The End of Chertopkhanov" should have fully conformed to the principle of external observation maintained in *A Sportsman's Sketches* and, in general, in Russian prose of the 1830s–50s. However, the instance of unmediated access to Chertopkhanov's mind attests to the fact that, even as he seeks to integrate a new Chertopkhanov story into the cycle, and obey the narrative principles thereof, Turgenev unequivocally and blatantly violates, at least once, the law of external observation.

What narrative circumstances, then, motivated Turgenev to reveal in this work his now full-fledged mastery of the novelistic technique of rendering character consciousness? What conditions induced in this particular instance a breach of the established norm of external observation otherwise sustained throughout the cycle, even in its belated additions? Due to its composition-publication history, "The End of Chertopkhanov" stands as a rare (perhaps even unique) case of what might be called the "second emergence" of the transparent rendition of consciousness in the course of Russian fiction's transition from novella to novel and, specifically, from exteriority to interiority vis-à-vis character hearts and minds. That is, the literary-historical *event* of the figural mind's transparification occurs, and the generic boundary between novella and novel is crossed, *within* the text of "The End of Chertopkhanov" itself. The tale thus provides an exceptional opportunity to inquire into this event's architectonics and enabling factors.

The life story of Pantelei Chertopkhanov unfolds in tripartite fashion, like a fairy tale, with the hero proceeding from the discovery of one love object to the next. Introduced to the reader as a solitary misanthrope—"he was too proud to visit the rich, and he disdained the poor"[74]—he first obtains a devoted friend, then the love of a beautiful woman, and then a trusted horse. But this is decidedly "like," but not equal to, a fairy tale, because Chertopkhanov loses each one in turn; his mounting grief manifests itself in progressively heavier drinking, and leads to his "end"—a demise quite in contrast to any would-be "happy ending."[75] It is during his third "calamity," when Chertopkhanov recognizes the irretrievable loss of his final true love Malek-Adel, that the sustained position of external observation breaks down, and the novelistic author is revealed in the unmediated presentation of the character's consciousness.

Notably, the problematization of the external vantage point is set in motion on the level of narrated events. Having fallen in love with Malek-Adel, Chertopkhanov perceives the horse as an indissoluble blend of physical (external) properties and (internal) personality traits:

> And what a horse it was! All fire—simply explosive as gunpowder—and stately as a boyar! Untiring, enduring, obedient, whatever you might put him

> to. . . . Sinews of steel: for him to stumble was a thing never recorded! To take a ditch or a fence was nothing to him—and what a clever beast! At his master's voice he would run with his head in the air; if you told him to stand still and walked away from him, he would not stir. . . . And afraid of nothing.[76]

It is perhaps due to this already established total congruence between Malek-Adel's body (with its gray color) and the animal's remarkable inner qualities that Chertopkhanov forgets that "gray horses turn white over time" when he sees the "other" Malek-Adel at the fair; that is, assuming a priori an inextricable connection between the inner and the outer, he relies on the latter horse's appearance in order to recognize him as Malek-Adel. As his suspicions grow, Chertopkhanov confronts the fact that two identical bodies, both purportedly hosting his one beloved individual, may contain quite different "contents." In the passage below, Chertopkhanov attempts to extract, as it were, Malek-Adel's internal qualities from his exterior:

> Chertopkhanov was not so much confused by the physical differences between *this* Malek-Adel and *that* one . . . there were few such differences. . . . What confounded Chertopkhanov most were, so to say, the moral differences. The habits of that one had been different: all his ways were not the same. For instance, *that* Malek-Adel had looked round and given a faint neigh every time Chertopkhanov went into the stable; while *this* one went on munching hay as though nothing had happened, or dozed with his head bent. Both of them stood still when their master leaped out of the saddle; but *that* one came at once at his voice when he was called, while *this* one stood stock-still. . . . *This* one, it struck Chertopkhanov, kept twitching his ears in such a stupid way, while with *that* one it was quite the contrary: he used to lay one ear back, and hold it so, as though on the alert for his master! . . . *This* was a coarser beast—coarser! And there wasn't the gentleness in it, and hard in the mouth it was—no denying it! *That* horse was a darling, but *this* . . . .[77] (Emphasis added to match Turgenev's original)

Having failed to recognize the object of his love, Chertopkhanov strives to bypass the external vantage point from which the two horses are indistinguishable, and break through to the "inner" Malek-Adel. In doing so, he occupies an analogously configured view upon himself. If Chertopkhanov blames Capt. Yaff for Masha's betrayal—his anger and despair correspondingly directed outward and fully manifested, as shown above, in speech and action—for his failure to recognize Malek-Adel, Chertopkhanov seeks an external source of blame, but cannot find one: "But rage against whom? On whom was he to be revenged? On the Jew, Yaff, Masha, the deacon, the Cossack-thief, all his neighbors, the whole world, himself? His brain was giving way."

There is no outside entity to blame; the very essence of Chertopkhanov's falling victim to this "deception" consists in his reliance on external factors when identifying the horse at the fair, his failure to see, through these, Malek-Adel's unique interiority. This principal inability to locate any external causes, any spatiotemporal circumstances potentially explaining, or at least mitigating, his fatal mistake, makes up the hero's state of mind in the instance of unmediated presentation of consciousness cited above: "That he, Chertopkhanov, had been taken in the vulgarest way—no! That he purposely, of set intent, tricked himself, blinded his own eyes—of all this he had not now the faintest doubt!" Here Chertopkhanov cannot, that is, perceive any temporal or spatial configuration as external, but rather, as emerging solely from his own unfortunate choice.

With spatiotemporal circumstances in effect configured as aspects of a given event within the hero's consciousness, such an event has no external attributes, markers, or signifiers. From the externalist perspective, which registers the spatiotemporal parameters of an event, the hero's perception of external circumstances as resulting from his own choice is, literally, unnoticeable; his perception effects no change, however nuanced or subtle, in the observable world. The event of such perception does not disturb the spatiotemporal outlines of this world, but totally and completely coincides with them. The inside view, or presentation of consciousness—consciousness being the locale of this event—thus becomes the only possible means to narrate such an event. It is at this moment that the narration of "The End of Chertopkhanov," formerly hewing to external observation, reveals the authorial capacity for novelistic presentation of inner life. As an effect of this authorial initiative, this hero who has run up against his own temporal and spatial limitations is given, within the discursive bounds of the narrated consciousness, the otherwise unnarratable opportunity to perform his subjectivity by perceiving these limitations as consequences of his own choosing.

On the level of story, the most immediate effect of mutually conditioned author/hero activity at the moment of consciousness presentation is the hero's "end." Shortly after Chertopkhanov's killing of the false Malek-Adel in the forest ravine, his only servant Perfishka, alarmed by his master's behavior, alerts the authorities:

> First, his honor drank vodka every day, and now he's taken to his bed and got very thin. . . . I did ask him, . . . wouldn't you let me run for the priest, sir? "You hold your tongue, idiot," says he; "mind your own business."
>
> "And has he been drinking a great deal of vodka?" inquired the commissioner.
>
> "Rather!"[78]

Death, which Chertopkhanov anticipates and welcomes, is the prime indicator of the subject's temporal and spatial boundedness; in a sense, Chertopkhanov *consents* to die by way of configuring these unavoidable external bounds as emerging from his own conscious choice:

> The silence of death reigned in the room. "Why, he's dead already!" [the commissioner] thought, and raising his voice, he said, "Pantelei Eremeich! Eh, Pantelei Eremeich!"
>
> Then something extraordinary occurred. Chertopkhanov's eyelids slowly opened, the eyes, fast growing dim, moved first from right to left, then from left to right, rested on the commissioner—saw him. . . . Something gleamed in their dull whites, the semblance of a flash came back to them, the blue lips were gradually unglued, and a hoarse, almost sepulchral voice was heard.
>
> "Pantelei Eremeich of the ancient hereditary nobility is dying: who can hinder him? He owes no man anything, asks nothing from anyone. . . . Leave him, people! Go!"[79]

In its temporal and spatial outlines, Chertopkhanov's consent to die fully coincides with his body's alcoholism-related deterioration; the external observer, here personified in the commissioner and Perfishka, has no means to differentiate between the two. In the same way, at the end of *Mumu*, Gerasim's voluntary choice to be silent is indistinguishable from his physical muteness, just as his lack of need for animals or humans is indistinguishable from the "absence of love" (Frost). Gerasim's transformation lies not in the attainment of a new state of mind (either utterly defeated, or liberated at last) but rather follows from his voluntary consent—enacted through the drowning of Mumu—to coincide with the state of his mute body.

In the overall context of my argument, the problematization of the position of external observation in *Mumu* and the hero's experience of external boundaries as emerging from his own conscious choice in "The End of Chertopkhanov" can be seen as discursive effects of the perspective of utterance formation and perception that, throughout this book, I define as the story-discourse convergence and view as an essential (and exclusive) property of the artistic utterance. In the fictional narrative, narrated events do not precede their narration, but rather completely concur with it in time and space; within this perspective, any textual "move" advances both events and their representation in such a way that no boundary can be drawn between the two. In the fictional narrative, that is, the very criterion for differentiating between the represented and the means of representation—or, in terms most relevant to the problematics of this chapter, between the subject's interiority and its external manifestations—is annulled. In the history of literary prose, the "rise of fictionality" (Gallagher) came into being with the emergence and advance of novelistic discourse, which is why, I would argue, it is at the close approaches to this literary-historical event that the textual effects of the story-discourse convergence are most readily observable.

The subjective activities of the author and hero of the novelistic utterance can be seen as two mutually conditional projections of the annulment of the criterion for differentiating between the represented and the means of representation, signified and signifier. The authorial insusceptibility to the distinction between the external and internal manifests itself in the unmediated access to figural minds: the narrative mode of presenting consciousness that came into being with the emergence and advance of the realist novel. The word "access" well conveys the historical dynamics of consciousness presentation but, in fact, is imprecise; it would be more accurate to say that fictional minds become transparent not in the course of the novelistic author's penetration (at long last) of the boundary between the character's inner life and its external manifestations, but rather due to—and instantaneously with—the establishment of that authorial perspective within which the very distinction between the external and internal ceases to be operative.

The counterpart to this authorial activity of perception is the hero's principal inability to differentiate between the external and internal, his or her activity of perceiving any given chunk of space-time as the result of conscious choice—a state of consciousness pertaining to distinctly novelistic figural subjectivity and describable, in the broadest possible psychological interpretation, as the consent to die. The narrative mode of free indirect discourse, which, according to Cohn, "may be most succinctly defined as the technique for rendering a character's thought in his own idiom while maintaining the third-person reference and the basic tense of narration,"[80] is marked by the absence of a criterion by which to differentiate between represented speech and some other entity performing the representing; this mode thus perfectly captures the interdependence of the two novelistic subjectivities, author and hero, on the level of narration. In this chapter, I have traced the tangible effects of the newly emergent relationship between the two novelistic subjectivities, author and hero, in fictional narratives "bookending" the literary career of Turgenev, the first Russian writer in the realist novel tradition.

Differentiation between internal and external is a characteristic immanent in the activity of utilitarian (referential) speech production: the very notion of "reference" presupposes a dichotomy between represented object or event (whether factual or pseudo- or nonfactual) and the means of its representation. As my analysis demonstrates, the experience of the suspension of this dichotomy, of the non-differentiation between external and internal—their complete, that is, convergence, which experience is unavailable under any other communicative circumstances—occurs in the activity of the novelistic author, and in the reader's experience enabled thereby, within the discursive bounds of presented consciousness. This conclusion by no means implies that these writerly and readerly activities should be "walled off" from the cognitive mechanisms and processes studied in the real-mind disciplines; but it does seem to call for such critical methodologies as would seek out the distinctly aesthetic foundations for typological and literary-historical inquiries into fictional minds.

Chapter Six

Waking Up to the Novel: The Dream Origin of Goncharov's *Oblomov*

THE NOVEL *OBLOMOV* began with a dream. In 1849 Ivan Goncharov published a stand-alone piece titled "Oblomov's Dream" and subtitled "an episode from an unfinished novel" (*epizod iz neokonchennogo romana*) in the prominent literary journal *Contemporary*. The author, however, did not take up work on the promised novel in earnest until 1857, and it was only in 1859 that *Oblomov* was published: first serially in *Notes of the Fatherland* (*Otechestvennye zapiski*) and then as a separate edition later the same year. "Oblomov's Dream" was incorporated in the completed novel toward the end of part 1, designated therein as chapter 9. Milton Ehre estimates that "there had been an eleven- to thirteen-year interval between conception and final publication," and emphasizes the importance of the "ten-year hiatus between the publication of 'Oblomov's Dream' and the publication of the completed novel."[1] Goncharov's provisional attribution of "Oblomov's Dream" to the genre of novel attests to the fact that this fragment served him as a springboard for novelistic narration—even if it took more than a decade to bring the "unfinished novel" to completion.

On the synchronic level, within the composition of the completed work, "Oblomov's Dream" stands as a particular sort of signpost in the book; what comes after it is definitively a novel, but what precedes is somehow *not*. In scholarly evaluations of *Oblomov*, part 1 has often been categorized as markedly non-novelistic. Ehre, for instance, classifies part 1 as a "farcical comedy,"[2] describing its narration using the terminology of drama: "The comedy of Part One, written in the forties, is composed of static set scenes played out between Oblomov, his servant, and his visitors."[3] Richard Peace deems part 1 as akin to a work of Molière, featuring as it does "a central character that exhibits a stock vice (laziness) from which the comedy itself flows, channeled through the well-established comedic tradition of the relationship between master and servant."[4]

The hero's typicality also links part 1 to the discourse of the Russian "natural school," a major literary current of the 1840s: the Oblomov of part 1 can be seen as exemplifying a particular "type," namely that of a "sloth" or "sleeper," which is to be subjected to a thorough "physiological" examination. Oblomov's typicality was most assertively postulated by the radical critic Nikolai Dobroliubov, who devoted his 1859 essay "What Is Oblomovism?" ("Chto takoe oblomovshchina?"), much celebrated in Soviet literary criticism, to explicating the socioeconomic and sociohistorical causalities of Goncharov's character: "His laziness and apathy is a creation of his upbringing and surrounding circumstances. The main thing here is not Oblomov, but Oblomovism."[5] In general, dramatic narrative technique is not incompatible with naturalist discourse: Aleksandr Tseitlin, a scholar of the Russian "natural school," cites the "skit from everyday life" (*bytovaia stsenka*) as a major, often dominant, generic constituent of the physiological sketch.[6] In this regard, the successive entrances and exits of Oblomov's visitors—each representing a quintessential "type" to be found in the capital city—and a series of dialogues, in which each visitor in turn attempts to get Oblomov out of bed, not only demonstrate the narrative's drama-like qualities, but serve to fully reveal the defining trait of the hero's "physiological" profile as well. Toward the end of part 1, having successfully resisted each of his guests' appeals, Oblomov finally reaches his most suitable condition, serenely (*bezmiatezhno*)[7] drifting off to sleep, or rather going back to sleep, thereby escaping the obtrusive demands of daylight.

In part 1, Oblomov's chance of ever moving beyond his unswept Petersburg apartment on Gorokhovaia Street seems as likely as the possibility of his getting married, and while the theme of marriage lurks surreptitiously throughout the text (as Peace perceptively observes),[8] Oblomov's own attitude toward this institution is one of genuine bewilderment at the fact that "there are such jackasses who get married" (*ved' est' zhe etakie osly, chto zheniatsia*).[9] It is the remainder of the work—with a wide-awake hero who moves about (even if not venturing particularly far),[10] falls in love, is passionately loved in return, and even contemplates and proposes marriage—that justifies Goncharov's preliminary attribution of the 1849 fragment to the genre of novel.

Goncharov himself may have recognized the generic and stylistic incongruence between part 1 and the rest of *Oblomov*. In a letter to his close friend Ivan Lkhovsky, the author expresses great dissatisfaction with part 1: "In December they will begin copyediting . . . the first part of *Oblomov*. Recently I sat down to reread the latter and was horrified. In the last ten years I haven't read anything worse, weaker or paler than the first half of part 1: it's awful! I spent the next several days in a row shoveling out the muck, and there is still a good deal of it left!" In another letter, this time to Leo Tolstoy,

Goncharov pleads of his correspondent: "Do not read the first part of *Oblomov*; if you have time, however, please do read the second and third, which were written much later. Part 1, on the other hand, was written in 1849 and is no good."[11] After completing the novel, Goncharov attempted to revise its earlier chapters, but ultimately admitted his failure to resolve the work's internal inconsistency.[12]

It is "Oblomov's Dream" that marks the end both of part 1 and of Il'ia Il'ich Oblomov's "comedic" and "typical" pre-novelistic existence. The dream is interrupted by the arrival of the last in the succession of guests, Andrei Stolz, who is determined "now or never" (*teper' ili nikogda*)[13] to rescue his friend, and as distinct from all others who have made the attempt, does succeed in getting Oblomov out of bed. Thus it was *through* the narrative of "Oblomov's Dream" that Goncharov's book, both diachronically, in the history of its creation and publication, and synchronically, in its composition, characterization, and plot development, became a novel. Goncharov's struggle to reconcile the incongruence between part 1 and the rest of the work can also be viewed as a struggle to bring the narration of the beginning chapters into alignment with the novelistic (postdream) narration.[14] The question, then, arises: what characteristics of the dream narrative enabled the book's generic shift, or rather leap, from naturalist to novelistic discourse, its radical transformation, within the text itself, from dramatized physiological sketch to novel?

Previous chapters of this study have described how pre-novelistic forms of Russian prose (including the physiological sketch, one of the dominant genres of the 1840s) present characters' inner experiences via an outside observer who, unable to directly access thoughts or feelings, relies on their outward manifestations in speech, gesture, and behavior. From the position of external observation, such visions as appear to a character in a dream would seem to be entirely off-limits, even more so than his or her waking thoughts and feelings, which at least can sometimes be inferred with some measure of reliability. Indeed, there is little for an external narrator to observe when confronted with a character who is fast asleep: the few clues provided by a sleeping character's face or movements seem unlikely to provide any substantive insight into the content of dreams.

In this regard, the sleeping character, inaccessible to the narrative strategies of observation and analysis, is analogous to the deaf, mute, and facially inexpressive protagonist of Turgenev's *Mumu* discussed in chapter 5. The sleeping character presents another example of the decisive problematization of external observation in mid-nineteenth-century Russian fiction discussed in the previous chapter: in choosing such "opaque" heroes— Lermontov's characters in *Princess Ligovskaia*, who as described in chapter 3 cover their faces or turn them toward the wall, might also be recalled here—writers seem to back themselves into narrative corners, necessitating a break with the position of external observation, a qualitatively different approach to figural consciousness. This chapter suggests that in *Oblomov*, this breakthrough to novelistic characterization is accomplished via the distinct discursive properties of the narration of the dream. Foregrounding not the content or events of "Oblomov's Dream"—their utmost significance for the novel's characterization and problematics notwithstanding[15]—but rather these events' narrative-oneiric format, I propose that the hero's transition from "sleeper" to "dreamer" has transformational consequences for both the story and discourse of *Oblomov*.

In order to fully manifest his typicality, a "sleeper" character must, like any other "type," triumph over all obstacles—in this case, persistent visitors, unpaid bills, and mounting dust—and so Oblomov, as if relieved to coincide at long last with his "typical" self, finally nods off; the narrator, now facing his peacefully sleeping character, is left with literally nothing more to narrate:

> His lips and tongue stopped moving after uttering the last syllable, while his mouth remained half open. Instead of a word, there came a sigh followed by the even, stertorous breathing of someone peacefully sleeping.[16]

The metonymical ease of the move from "sleep" to "dream"—a transition especially smooth in the Russian language, wherein *son* denotes "sleep" and "dream," both the physiological state and the series of images occurring to its experiencer—opens up a narrative opportunity to exceed the generic limitations of naturalist discourse, to introduce the dream of the sleeping character. And having seized this opportunity, the narrator finds himself in a unique discursive situation informed by the architectonics of dream narration.

Dreams, albeit common everyday (or every-night) occurrences, are characterized by an intrinsic "bizarreness"; but however illogical or incongruous dream images and sequences are in relation to daylight order, there is no reason to deny their validity as mental experiences. For that matter, the content of a dream may be quite ordinary and apparently insignificant. Addressing the oneiric "problem of bizarreness," Bert States illustrates the dreamer's horizon of expectations with the following example:

> Paul and I are playing tennis; Paul wins or I win, or the dream, having something else up its sleeve, takes us both to lunch. But now and then a dream becomes extraordinary: Paul and I are playing tennis and we are interrupted by the dancing bears I saw on the TV two nights ago. . . . As we say, bizarre.[17]

The dream fuses the mundane and extraordinary in a manner disallowing the singling out of *any* event—playing tennis, or bears dancing on a tennis court—as an impossible occurrence in the specific confines of the dream. In other words, *anything* can happen.

In its capacity to accommodate the implausible, the dream narrative differs in principle from the discourse of the supernatural (whether uncanny, fantastic, or marvelous, to use Todorov's typology), since the latter is fully conditioned by spatiotemporal categories, deviation from which is essential for the classification of narrated events as either plausible or implausible. The violation of the boundary between the credible and incredible, central for supernatural narration, is predicated upon this boundary's stability and efficacy for both utterance-producer and perceiver.[18] In dream narrative, by contrast, there are no criteria for differentiating between plausible and implausible events; for the mind engaged in the production and perception of a dream narrative, the temporal and spatial constraints responsible for such differentiation cease to be operative. The beginning of "Oblomov's Dream" features exalted rhetoric and a sublime, bird's-eye perspective on the "savagery and grandiosity" (*dikoe i grandioznoe*) of the sea, "mountains and precipices . . . terrible and frightful like . . . the claws and teeth of a wild beast" (*gory i propasti . . . grozny, strashny, kak . . . kogti i zuby dikogo zveria*), and so on—all of which imagery is invoked solely in order that the narrator might "zoom in" instead on an entirely different landscape, that of the "peaceful little corner" (*mirnyi ugolok*) of Oblomovka.[19] This seemingly unwarranted elevation appears justified when understood as a thematic and stylistic effect of the narrator's sudden experience of insusceptibility to spatiotemporal bounds within the discursive confines of the dream narrative.[20]

As a result, the dream narrative possesses an indisputable validity and is immune to the judgments of truth or falsehood: there are no grounds whatsoever on which to "challenge" the content of a dream. In this regard, dream narrative and the perception thereof are most reminiscent, in the history of literary prose, of novelistic discourse, within which, according to Gallagher and other historians of the novel, the necessity of establishing a referential relationship (whether of correspondence or contradiction) between narrated events and the world beyond the text was for the first time annulled, enabling the reader's experience of the irrelevance of the credibility factor. As discussed in chapter 1, non-referential perception of the utterance, which Gallagher posits as the hallmark of novelistic fictionality, is grounded in the simultaneity of events and their narration, a synchronicity established when the utterance itself becomes the object of representation. In this unique—aesthetic proper—communicative situation, represented discourse and the performance of this representation unfold synchronously, completely converging in time and space.

As for the dream narrative specifically, the irrelevance of the credibility factor in its production and perception is also conditioned by an annulment of differentiation between represented and representing discourses; however, in this case, the annulment is due not to these two discourses' simultaneous development, but rather to what might be called the dream narrative's non-alternative, or single-option, narrative perspective. In discussing actual dream experiences, States posits their essential subjectivity as a condition of perception in the dream world: "All elements of the dream cooperate in sticking to the subject (my endangerment, my defeat of the villain, my unsuccessful love affair)."[21] According to States, the "lyric principle" is fundamental to any dream, irrespective of its content: "In a dream . . . the self always speaks to and of itself, though it might do so by converting itself into other dream creatures."[22] In narratological terms, the events of the dream are necessarily focalized through the perspective of the dreamer.[23]

Applying States's observations on the actual dream experience to the analysis of the *narration* of a character's dream, I would propose that as far as the latter is concerned, particularly salient is not only that the events of the dream are necessarily seen through the eyes of the dreamer him or herself, but also that there is no other discursive perspective the producer of the dream narrative can occupy in relation to the events of the dream; he or she does not know more—or less, or differently—about these events than the dreamer him or herself. As distinct from possible interpretations of the dream (of which there may be many), or its sources or implications (which might escape the character him or herself), the scope of knowledge in relation strictly to the content of the dream is exactly the same for both the narrator and his or her character-dreamer. For this same reason, the events of the dream cannot be questioned by the dream narrative's perceiver, or reader: such an initiative of disbelief would require an alternative perspective on these events, a temporal and spatial localization that would differ from that of the dreamer him or herself, even as the architectonics of dream narration offer no such alternative.[24] Within the dream narrative, the perspectives of narrator and character-dreamer (and with them, that of the reader) fully coincide, converging in space-time as the lone narrative perspective available.

As an experience, this convergence between represented consciousness and the one performing such representation is analogous, as mentioned, to that of the producer of the fictional narrative, specifically of novelistic narration. Throughout this book I have posited the story-discourse convergence as the major characteristic of the artistic utterance: within the discursive perspective of the story-discourse convergence, any textual action or "move" carries forward both represented events and their representation in such a way that no boundary can be drawn between the two. In the history of literary prose, this aesthetic-proper communicative situation came to define nascent novelistic fictionality both in western Europe and (over a century later) in Russia. It is the establishment of this discursive stance that informs the decisive problematization of the position of external observation in the history of Russian fiction of the 1820s–50s, which position is predicated on a spatiotemporal divergence between the narrative perspectives of the representing and represented constituents of the utterance, between the narrator's and the character's viewpoints, and thus appears inadequate in relation to the consciousness engaged in the artistic experience of the story-discourse convergence.

Due to the non-alternative, or single-option, discursive perspective of dream narration, the divergence between the narrator's and character's viewpoints is eliminated in the account of the latter's dream; the producer of the dream narrative thus finds him or herself in a situation analogous to that of novelistic discourse, that is, a convergence of viewpoints.[25] In *Oblomov*, the narrator of part 1, brought up as it were in the "naturalist school," discovers an aesthetic-proper discursive stance within the dream narrative, "waking up" as the author of a novel. I suggest that this new authorial stance, acquired through the narration of the character's dream, is the major reason (aside from the obvious aspiration to later write a longer book) for Goncharov's anticipatory attribution of "Oblomov's Dream" to the genre of novel—as well as for the manifest generic discontinuity that remains in the completed work. And it was perhaps the uncertainty of how to proceed in accordance with this newly acquired discursive perspective that resulted in the ten-year delay in Goncharov's work on *Oblomov*: the postdream narration had to be mastered on a qualitatively new—novelistic—level.

The previous chapter has posited the correlation of the two novelistic subjectivities—author and hero—as that of two mutually conditioned projections of the annulment of criteria for differentiating between the subject's interiority and its external manifestations. The authorial insusceptibility to the distinction between internal and external is most notably manifested in the transparency of figural minds; the counterpart of the author's unmindfulness of the internal-external distinction is the hero's principal inability to see any temporal and spatial configurations as external, his or her perception of any temporal and spatial configuration as emerging entirely from his or her own conscious choice. This chapter will propose that character development in *Oblomov* can best be understood as the unfolding of the hero's distinctly novelistic subjectivity, a process fueled by the imperative of non-differentiation between internal and external, of perceiving whatever element of space-time as inseparable from one's own choice. Moreover, in *Oblomov*, the hero's subjectivity reaches its utmost novelistic potential, since in this work, the external (spatiotemporal) boundaries are configured on the most basic, elementary level, as the confines of one's own body. I argue that it is this exceptionally "condensed" novelistic quality of the hero's subjectivity, rather than any social, economic, (deep) psychological, or other determinants, that has the most immediate bearing on the life and death of Il'ia Il'ich Oblomov, and also accounts for the acknowledged peculiarity of Goncharov's work in the Russian novelistic canon of the nineteenth century.

Anne Lounsbery brings together a number of definitions of the genre of *Oblomov*, all of which rely on apophatic terms to convey the work's generic distinctiveness; the book has been called an "anti-adventure novel," an "anti-odyssey," an "anti-*Bildungsroman*," and (the designation Lounsbery herself coins) an "anti-travelogue." *Oblomov* is a "story about not traveling, a story about what happens when one decides to forgo virtually all movement."[26] In accord with these generic attributions, scholarly analyses of *Oblomov* often revolve around a set of oppositions: immobility vs. itinerancy, indolence vs. activity, inertia vs. progress. Ehre's contrasting of dream and awakeness in the patterns of both character and plot development in *Oblomov* can serve as a metaphorical synthesis of all such dichotomies, as well as an example of their most immediate (literal) manifestation in the story world:

> The total pattern follows a curve similar to that of Oblomov's smaller movements—for as Oblomov turns from dream and reflection to aborted action to a decline back to dream, his book proceeds from the famous chapter "Oblomov's Dream" to a vain attempt to retrieve the dream in reality through Olga's love, to a final decline into dream and death. The novel can be described by the formula stasis-action-stasis, in which a love affair with Olga marks the turning point in Oblomov's story.[27]

Oblomov scholars substantiate the novel's formative dichotomies in a variety of ways, but the boundaries dividing the two opposing "halves" are usually aligned much like those outlined by Ehre: in the character system, these boundaries separate, most blatantly, Oblomov from Stolz; in plot development, the "action" of Oblomov's one-summer-long romance with Olga (parts 2 and 3) is bracketed by his couch-bound existence on Gorokhovaia Street (part 1), on the one side, and his life in the Vyborg district as the tenant and then husband of Agaf'ia Matveevna Pshenitsyna (part 4) on the other. In contrast to these readings, I suggest that in *Oblomov*, the very association of dreaming with "stasis" (immobility, inertia) and of wakefulness with "action" (itinerancy, progress) is radically challenged. Namely, from the perspective of non-differentiation between internal and external, discovered in the course of dream narration, Oblomov's indulgent dream viewing and Stolz's incessant pursuit of practical goals appear not as opposing, but rather as congruous and *equally* deficient modes of conduct. Both of these modes are predicated on the character's consciousness being oriented away from present, here-and-now spatiotemporal circumstances, and toward some desirable there-and-then—to be found either in the premodern past of Oblomov's childhood memories, or in Stolz's visions of Russia's bright capitalist future. Both dreaming and goal setting situate consciousness elsewhere, in the past or future, divorcing it from the space-time parameters of its present existence.

As for dreams specifically: regardless of its symbolizing function, genesis, or epistemological status, the dream experience can be said to consist of the transference of a consciousness to some spatiotemporal coordinates other than the dreamer's daylight circumstances. States sees a central paradox of the dream experience in the "Two Body Problem,"[28] citing the words of the German phenomenologist Medard Boss:

> While waking observers see him fast asleep in bed in Zurich, the dreamer may feel that he is skiing, with consummate physical grace and pleasure, down an Alpine slope. The question now is which body is the real one, the body that others see lying in bed, though the dreamer is unaware of it, or the body that the dreamer himself feels so intensely but that no waking observer can perceive?[29]

Phenomenological answers to this question aside, the dreamer's acquisition of a "second body" for the "same" consciousness can be said to constitute an essential component of the dream experience; in the well-known words of Gérard de Nerval, dreams offer "a second life."[30] For instance, in Oblomov's dream in part 1, the hero's consciousness travels to the faraway lands of his family estate and the long-ago of his childhood, while his body is rooted firmly to the couch of his Petersburg apartment and wrapped in an old robe (the only hint of travel being the Persian style of this garment). "Sleep . . . carried him off in an instant to another time, to other people, and to another place to which we will follow him in the next chapter."[31] In the moment of one's awakening—which may be charged with either relief that it was "only a dream," or to the contrary regret at having to abandon this or that idyll—consciousness is snapped back, returning to its own spatiotemporal coordinates, first and foremost, those of its own body.

Similarly to the dreamer's acquisition of a "second life" in some there-and-then dream world, orientation toward any goal—however reachable or mundane—divorces consciousness from the given external coordinates of its existence, places it in some more or less distant there-and-then; the body, these coordinates' most elementary instantiation, is made secondary. Goal-oriented activities are thus conducted in a "dream state": not in the metaphorical sense of their unreality or futility, but in their dreamlike indifference to given corporeality. A common denominator between "dream" and "goal" in the English language can be found in another meaning of the word "dream"—a "desired state or action." When dreams, in this sense, are followed or pursued, they become goals. Seen in this light, both Oblomov's dormant retreat from daytime responsibilities and Stolz's alert and socially conscious goal setting are equally fraught with the possibility that consciousness—off chasing either sweet dreams or sober objectives—might *not* come home to its body, falling victim to accidental death in a "dream state."

From the perspective, then, of non-differentiation between internal and external, a viewpoint imperative for novelistic characterization, the "dream state" can no longer be equated with "stasis" or lack of action, but rather defines *any* action, however lucid and rational, which disregards here-and-now parameters and divorces a character's consciousness from its given space-time. By the same dream-derived narrative logic, "awakeness" is configured not as "action," but rather the moment when the character's consciousness is once again embodied, returned to its here-and-now.

In Ehre's tripartite "curve" of the development of Oblomov (both character and book)—that of "stasis-action-stasis," a plotting largely shared by other Goncharov scholars—the hero's romance with Olga constitutes a clear moment of "awakening," and Oblomov himself perceives it as such: "Do you really think . . . that I can go back to sleep after such an awakening . . . !"[32] But from the perspective, established within the discursive confines of dream narration, of non-differentiation between internal and external, it is the hero's "dream" that stands as the most dynamic and "progressive" period of his life. Olga's love for Oblomov demands that he constantly pursue goals she has set for him, from climbing a steep hill to not sleeping after lunch to settling his financial affairs and making marriage arrangements. Olga compares Oblomov to Galatea and casts herself in the role of his Pygmalion,[33] devoted to providing this love object a new body, as different from the "old" one as human flesh is from clay. At the farewell meeting with Oblomov, Olga describes her commitment to her lover as an attempt to induce metamorphosis, a radical transformation of his external characteristics: "My dream was . . . about bringing you to life and making you live for me, but you've been long dead. . . . With all the effort I've put in I could have brought a stone to life."[34]

Notable in this regard is that Goncharov's critics, both contemporaneous and more recent, have consistently remarked on artistic deficiencies in the portrayal of Stolz and Olga; such judgments include, among others, "cardboard characterization";[35] "wooden and unconvincing" and a "weak point in the novel";[36] and "too good to be true and the least lifelike of any of the characters in the book."[37] Stolz's and Olga's insufficient embodiment can be seen as a discursive effect of their relentless goal setting, a mode of conduct informed by the consciousness's perpetual divorcement from its here-and-now parameters.

As with his comically drawn-out awakening in part 1 from the dream of the Oblomovka of his childhood, in the aftermath of his romance with Olga—which is, once again, a "dream," albeit a lucid one—Oblomov resists "waking up":

> "Snow, snow, snow," he repeated mindlessly. . . . "Everything's covered," he whispered despairingly and lay down on the bed where he fell at once into a leaden, comfortless sleep. . . . He was in the grip of a fever.[38]

Fittingly, Oblomov's state during his life-threatening illness is described in terms of a stark gap between the hero's mental agony and his depersonalized (either motionless, or mechanically "wound-up") body, that is, as a "dream state":

> His mind was awhirl with a chaos of ugly, formless thoughts and images; they scudded through his mind like clouds in the sky in no particular sequence or direction and he was unable to latch onto any of them. . . . Oblomov did not feel his body, he was oblivious to fatigue and all his bodily needs. He would lie like a stone for days on end, and for days on end he would move about and go through the motions of living like an automaton.[39]

In Ehre's tripartite compositional layout of *Oblomov*, part 4, which begins with Oblomov's recovery from his fever, not only describes the hero's final period of "stasis" but also concludes the novel's cyclical-symmetrical trajectory: Oblomov settles permanently in the Vyborg district, Petersburg's suburban periphery; succumbs to the undemanding and indulgent care of his landlady, the widow of modest means Agaf'ia Matveevna Pshenitsyna; and appears to revert to the same lethargy, mental and physical, that had characterized his life on Gorokhovaia Street in the city center. Once again, the driving force of Oblomov's existence is an unconquerable desire to sleep—except that instead of solicitous visitors from among his Petersburg acquaintances, it is now Agaf'ia Matveevna who (following doctor's orders) thwarts Oblomov's dozing, contriving to strategically drop utensils or chairs, or send a child to play on his couch. In other words, the "stasis" of part 4 appears to be the same "stasis" as that of part 1, except now it has returned with a vengeance, as if inveterate and fatal. Stolz, who had managed to get Oblomov out of bed with his "now or never" ultimatum at the end of part 1, arrives again with an analogous rescue mission to pull his friend "out of this hole, this bog, into the wide world of a wholesome, normal existence!"[40]—but now not even he can disturb this "stasis."

Concomitant with assertions of cyclicality in the novel's composition are critical evaluations of character development in *Oblomov*. Again, Ehre's formula of "stasis-action-stasis" is indicative of many of the novel's interpretations, which impute an abortive, frustrated nature to the "action" period in character and plot development, and assert a tautological return on the part of Oblomov, and *Oblomov*, to the initial dreamlike "static" existence, which both culminates and terminates in the hero's dying in his sleep.[41] Referring to both contemporaneous and modern readers of the novel, Galya Diment observes that *Oblomov* "mock[s] the very notions of plot, suspense, and character development that were the cornerstones of many other nineteenth-century Russian and European novels."[42] Evincing a range of interpretive frameworks, the overwhelming majority of the novel's commentators nevertheless seem to concur on Oblomov's "arrested development," even if this state is explained quite variously, from socioeconomic factors—beginning with Dobroliubov's verdict on the intertwinement of "slavery" and "aristocratic habits" (*rabstvo i barstvo*)[43] in the Russian landed gentry—to diagnoses of regressive personality in the numerous psychoanalytic readings of the novel.[44]

Lounsbery notes another interpretive tradition—"canonical and enduring . . . if highly tendentious"[45]—that can be traced back to Slavophile responses to Goncharov's work. According to these readings, Oblomov's incurable lethargy and his failure to engage with the outside world emerge as "signs of a beautiful, spiritual, soul-filled, and admirably Russian 'depth,'" as opposed to the "superficiality" manifest in Stolz's restless travel and entrepreneurship, and compounded by his "suspicious foreignness."[46] As Lounsbery's concise summary makes clear, these interpretations revolve around dichotomies whose composition is the same as those described earlier—for example, in the character system, that of Oblomov vs. Stolz—even if their ideological and axiological valuations are, in relation to those already mentioned, inverted. Such Slavophilism-informed readings are also fully in accord with the "stasis-action-stasis formula" that posits Oblomov's cyclic return, after a failed attempt to change, to his initial condition—except here the "stasis" itself is perceived quite differently: as a state *worthy* of preservation, of being protected from the ostensibly pernicious pragmatism and shallow mobility (geographical and social) of the Westernizing Other; Oblomov stands (or reclines) in this view not as an emblem of apathy and stagnation, but the champion of a tranquil spirituality.

Contrary to both (negatively or positively valued) interpretations of the "stasis-action-stasis" pattern, I envision a distinct and irreversible—that is, *non*cyclical—trajectory in Oblomov's (and *Oblomov*'s) development. This trajectory comes into view if the driving force of the hero's *Bildung* is posited not in socioeconomic or psychological but rather in aesthetic terms, namely, as the imperative of non-differentiation between internal and external, which imperative defines the subjective activity of the novelistic hero. As discussed above, from the perspective of this non-differentiation, Oblomov's dreaming and Stolz's (and Olga's) goal setting, rather than constituting opposing forces within the novel's character system, emerge as congruent and equally deficient modes of conduct, as each divorces character consciousness from its here-and-now circumstances for the sake either of idealized past or sought-after future. From this same perspective, a genuine "surplus" in Oblomov's character development can be seen in his ever-strengthening opposition to all such initiatives as situate consciousness elsewhere, whether in the past or future, as separate it from the space-time parameters of its present existence—his opposition, that is, to goal setting, daydreaming, and, ultimately, even to having dreams.

Emphasizing the economic framework for configuring the novel's conflicting forces, Lounsbery argues that Oblomov's "indolence is a thoroughly futile but nonetheless satisfying (to us, not to him) form of resistance against the new (to Russia) capitalist imperatives of activity, productivity, rational mastery, and so on."[47] This is undoubtedly true; I would add that Oblomov's resistance is directed not only against itinerancy and entrepreneurship as espoused by and personified in Stolz, but also against his *own* preferred modes of conduct, daydreaming and dreaming, against forms of "indolence" itself. Foregrounding the trajectory of this latter form of resistance can clarify the process of non-redundant, transformative development that Oblomov undergoes in the course of the novel.

According to the dream architectonics of narration established in Goncharov's book, "awakening" entails not "action" or "activeness," but rather the acknowledgment—whether joyous or bitter—of the given external coordinates of one's existence. In the Oblomov-Olga romance, this moment of acknowledgment comes *after* their breakup, that is, after the hero's final recognition of his inability to change (to acquire a new body) even for the sake of marrying his beloved. Oblomov's apparently botched "rendezvous,"[48] often perceived in critical readings as the onset of his final decline, in fact constitutes an act of resistance to goal setting, corresponding to an "awakening" within the architectonics of the novel's narration: it indicates that his consciousness has returned to its here-and-now parameters, its ever-present space-time. This "awakening" is driven by that imperative of non-differentiation between internal (the hero's consciousness) and external (his body) that defines the hero's novelistic subjectivity in *Oblomov*.

Further, Oblomov's existence in the Vyborg district is characterized not only by his decisive withdrawal from the goals incessantly set by Stolz and Olga, but also by his abstinence from daydreaming. In part 1, daydreaming is not just Oblomov's favorite pastime by far; it is, in Ehre's apt formulation, "the most serious commitment of his life."[49] His fantasies at this stage had ranged from comically inflated self-imaginings as "a conquering hero," a "philosopher or artist";[50] to changes or improvements he might make in the rooms and buildings of his country estate; to elaborately detailed scenes from his future family life. These daydreams used to fill Oblomov's entire day, morning to dusk, up to the very moment when "the vast disk of the sun sank in all its glory behind the four-story house":

> It is morning again, and time for his imagination to go to work and the daydreaming to begin. . . . No one witnessed or knew of this inner life of Ilya Ilych. Everyone thought that Oblomov just lay around eating whatever he wanted whenever he felt like it and that was all there was to him, and that he barely had two thoughts to rub together.[51]

Along with dreaming and goal setting, daydreaming is another mode of conduct that is grounded in the discontinuity between internal and external, between consciousness and its given space-time, first and foremost, that of its own body. The following description of Il'ia Il'ich, musing on his couch, captures this fundamental breach:

> He stretched his legs slowly and langorously, causing his trouser legs to ride up his calves, but he was oblivious to this minor sartorial embarrassment; his obliging fancy was wafting him clear and free, far into the future.[52]

In marked contrast to this daydreaming indulgence, Oblomov's life in part 4 is organized not by his consciousness's retreat to some all-satisfying imaginary realm (with his slovenly body left behind), but rather by his arrival at a state of consciousness within which all goals have already been achieved, such that there is no longer any need to either set or pursue them, whether in real life or fantasy:

> As he examined and contemplated his existence, as he settled ever deeper into it, he had finally concluded that he had nowhere further to go, nothing further to seek, that he had achieved his ideal.[53]

The hero's consciousness no longer yearns to escape to an idealized past or illusory future, but is content to remain in the present. Seen in this light, Oblomov's life in the Vyborg district does not constitute, as commonly assumed, a tautological relapse to the dreamlike "stasis" of part 1, but rather, quite to the contrary, emerges as the period of his consciousness's return to, or coinciding with, the here-and-now coordinates of its existence; emerges, in other words, as a state of "awakeness."

The hero's content to neither set goals *nor* conjure up reveries is signaled by the appearance of Agaf'ia Matveevna Pshenitsyna. Implicit in the dream architectonics of the novel's narration, I believe, is that we should set aside psychological (including psychoanalytic) interpretations foregrounding Oblomov's infantilism or reliance on the motherly care of Agaf'ia Matveevna,[54] and note instead a rather different dynamic between the two characters. I would stress that Agaf'ia Matveevna perceives Oblomov as, so far from helpless, absolutely self-sufficient, that is, as one who has attained all possible—physical as well as spiritual—goals:

> He looked at people boldly and freely, in the confident expectation of their deference. His features were not coarse, his face was not reddened, but white and delicate. . . . When he sat down, crossed his legs or propped his head on his hand, it was all done so naturally and gracefully and with such dignity. . . . There was much that she did not even understand but she felt instinctively that there was something intelligent, beautiful and unusual about it—and what she did understand was expressed in a way that was somehow different.[55]

Having attained all possible goals, Oblomov himself becomes the reason, or in the broadest sense *cause*, for Agaf'ia's existence:

> It was as if she had adopted a new religion and had gone about practicing it without examining its tenets or dogmas, but blindly following its dictates. . . . She learned to recognize each and every one of his shirts and knew exactly how many of his stockings had worn out heels. She knew which foot he lowered to the floor first and exactly when he was about to get a sty. . . . She knew exactly what he liked to eat and how much, whether he was in a good mood or bad, whether he had slept a lot or a little. . . . Her face shone perpetually with an unvarying happiness, a happiness that was total, fulfilled and complete.[56]

Goncharov's readers and commentators have long recognized the author's penchant for the material constituents of everyday life. Iulii Aikhenval'd describes Goncharov as "a poet of the room, a bard of the household . . . a Flemish artist."[57] Lounsbery speaks of the "concrete physical world" of the novel, most prominently—and in "minute physical detail"—represented in Agaf'ia Matveevna's Vyborg district house, where narrative "generalities give way to endless lists of *things* (household remedies, herbs, lotions, plasters, spirits, camphor, powders, incense, cleaning fluids), especially food items (cheeses, sugar loaves, Gatchina trout)."[58] In the perspective outlined here, the novel's irresistible pathos of domesticity, rather unusual in the Russian literary tradition, can be seen as another effect of the imperative of nondifferentiation between internal and external, between consciousness and the spatiotemporal coordinates of its existence, of which one's own body is the most elemental unit. Objects and things that nourish and sustain the body—most prominently, food and its sundry paraphernalia: dishes, pots, jars, and so on—become narratively validated.

Oblomov's death is predicted in part 1 by a physician who pays him a house call: "If you spend another two or three years in this climate, lounging around and eating heavy, fatty food, you'll die of a stroke."[59] And indeed, the doctor's prognosis regarding this lifestyle is apparently accurate: Oblomov comes to an early grave (in his forties), dying in his sleep: "One morning Agafya Matveevna brought him his coffee as usual, and found him resting as gently in death as he rested in sleep."[60] Critical interpreters of *Oblomov*, as noted largely concurring with the "stasis-action-stasis" formula, are in accord with the medical history thus charted, viewing the hero's death as the predictable result and fitting culmination of his "static," immobile existence. In a psychoanalytic reading of Goncharov's work, John Givens asserts that in part 4, Oblomov begins his "slow descent into a vegetative, womblike existence in the Vyborg house under Agafya's motherly care. . . . Death catches him unawares, in his sleep."[61] According to Kleespies, "[Oblomov's] death is caused by a literal excess of domesticity that he consumes without putting in much effort in return—he eats and sleeps himself to death."[62]

Within the framework developed here, Oblomov's death in sleep appears in a different light. As shown above, from the perspective of nondifferentiation between internal and external, Oblomov's life in the Vyborg district is not a "picture of fatal stagnation"[63] but rather, conversely, a period of "awakeness," characterized by the hero's emancipation from both goal setting *and* daydreaming, two modes of conduct that are equally "dreamlike" insofar as they perpetuate consciousness's separation from its here-and-now, promote its questing after this or that *other* space-time. Oblomov's death in sleep, moreover, can be seen in an analogous light, that is, as the ultimate act of the hero's resistance to such initiatives as would relegate consciousness to some alternative situation, some past or future there-and-then. Oblomov's death constitutes an act that corresponds to his daylight resolve not to set goals and not to daydream: death in sleep thus emerges as the only possible realization of the hero's determination *not to have dreams*, not to let consciousness wander in search of dream-induced "second bodies."

Conceptualized in this way, the novel no longer fits the widespread "stasis-action-stasis" pattern by which the hero experiences a cyclical and tautological return, or rather relapse to his original condition. Instead, the trajectory of plot and character development in *Oblomov* is that of the hero's unfailing and intensifying acts of resistance to all modes of consciousness-displacing conduct. Oblomov's war on goal setting is carried out through his breakup with Olga; on daydreaming, through his life in the Vyborg house, marked by the acknowledgment that he has "nothing more to seek"; and, ultimately, in a crowning act of resistance, his determination not to have dreams is actualized through his death in sleep.

The resolution not to have dreams is another event that, as with Gerasim's falling silent (*Mumu*) and Chertopkhanov's consent to die ("The End of Chertopkhanov") discussed in the previous chapter, has no attributes, markers, or signifiers, and is therefore absolutely unavailable to the outside observer. From the position of external observation, Oblomov's decision not to have dreams utterly coincides with his body's collapse from years of overeating and sedentariness—just as in *Mumu*, Gerasim's self-imposed silence coincides with his physiological muteness, and in "The End of Chertopkhanov," the hero's consent to die is indistinguishable from his progressive alcoholic deterioration (and is perceived as such by the servant Perfishka and the commissioner). In the final chapters of *Oblomov*, the role of external observer is given to Stolz:

> "Ilya, Ilya, get out of here, come with me now! What's become of you? How low you've sunk! That woman, what is she to you?"
>
> "My wife," Oblomov said quietly.
>
> Stolz was dumbfounded.[64]

Notably, it is now the ever-itinerant Stolz who finds himself in a "petrified" state (the literal meaning of his being dumbfounded, *okamenel*), exhibiting thus the utmost immobility or "stasis"; such a characteristic marks an impasse—that insurmountable limit of the position of external observation, from which an event in the life of consciousness is completely inaccessible. Opposed to Stolz's "petrification" is Oblomov's "content" or "peace" (*pokoi*), indicating not the hero's resignation or ascension to some higher spiritual plane, but rather an inner experience that, having no external markers or signifiers, does not impinge upon visible, observable space-time, but leaves it "in peace" (*v pokoe*). Death in sleep—understood as a voluntary choice not to be transferred to some "second," dream-fed there-and-then—occurs entirely within the hero's consciousness: spatial and temporal circumstances themselves appear as aspects of this event, rather than its underlying conditions.

The novel's compositionally unmarked epilogue (chapters 10 and 11 of part 4) apprises the reader of Oblomov's death and briefly attends to other characters' whereabouts five years thereafter. This section features several more instances interpretable as discursive consequences of the imperative of non-differentiation between internal and external, between consciousness and its here-and-now circumstances, that informs the unfolding of the hero's distinctly novelistic subjectivity in *Oblomov*. Concomitant with this imperative, all these instances underscore the deficiency of the position of external observation, effecting as they do no change in spatiotemporal circumstances, and having thus no visible signs or symptoms. In the first example, Agaf'ia Matveevna's reflection upon the seven years of her life with Oblomov is described emphatically as an unobserved, unseen from without, experience:

> She understood that life had favored and smiled at her for a while, that God had put a light into her life and then snuffed it out. . . . Yes, forever—but at the same time it was forever that her life had been given meaning and she knew now why she had lived and that she had not lived in vain. . . . There was no one else she could tell and there never had been. And no one around her would have understood in any case. What language could she have used?[65]

The experience of a light being put in and out of one's life has no bearing on this life's external, temporal and spatial outlines; indeed, the reader learns that after Oblomov's death, "Agafya Matveevna remained the driving force in the house. She still presided over the kitchen and the table, supplied everyone with tea and coffee, did everyone's sewing and supervised the laundry, the children, Akulina, and the gatekeeper."[66] This illumination/delumination is, rather, an event taking place entirely within the character's consciousness, and is thus both completely inaccessible from without and unrenderable into direct, externalized speech.

The second instance in the epilogue underscoring the inadequacy of the position of external observation explicitly links this issue to the problems of literary representation. The very last chapter of the novel introduces an acquaintance of Stolz's, a "writer . . . stout, with an inexpressive face and thoughtful, seemingly sleepy eyes."[67] The two are slowly walking along the wooden sidewalks of the Vyborg district when they come across a church just as a service has ended, and a crowd of worshippers, headed by "a large and various collection of beggars" (*kollektsiia . . . nishchikh . . . bol'shaia i raznoobraznaia*),[68] is pouring into the street. The conversation that follows makes explicit the two companions' enmeshment in the ideological and artistic aspirations of the Russian "natural school":

> "I'm curious about where all these beggars come from," said the literary gentleman as he regarded them.
>
> "What do you mean 'where from'? They crawl out of every nook and cranny [or "corner," *uglov*] . . ."
>
> "No, that's not what I'm asking," the literary gentleman interjected. "What I want to know is how people become beggars, how they get into that situation. Does it happen gradually or suddenly? Is it genuine or are they putting on an act?"

"But why? Do you want to write a sequel to *Mystères de Paris* called *Mystères de Pétersbourg?*

"Maybe . . ." said the literary gentleman, yawning lazily.[69]

Concerns with the sociohistorical genealogy of destitution; the perception of a group of beggars as a "collection" of human types to be examined and catalogued, and of their dwellings as "corners" (*ugly*); the reference to Eugene Sue's novel *Mystères de Paris*, widely popular in the 1840s, and inspiring not a few Russian naturalists to undertake an analogous project on their native soil—all these facets of the two characters' exchange reveal the inquisitive writer as a representative of mid-century Russian naturalism, and Stolz as a well-informed, engaged participant in contemporary literary culture. In response to his companion's inquiries, Stolz suggests summoning one of the people coming out of the church, who in his view should, being beggars, be willing to share their story for a sum of money; his choice falls on an old man whom he confidently defines as "the most standard type, it seems, of beggar" (*tip nishchego, kazhetsia, samyi normal'nyi*).[70] However, the beggar turns out to be Zakhar, Oblomov's former serf and manservant, who, in the course of the ensuing conversation, rejects Stolz's offer of housing and help in leaving the city—an offer a "standard" beggar would no doubt have capitalized on—exhibiting an intensely personal attachment to his late master that exceeds the "typical" and "comedic" noble-serf relationship: "But I wouldn't like to leave, sir, here's where he's buried. . . . What a master the Lord took from us! . . . A master in a million!"[71]

The boundary dividing Zakhar-the-beggar—a nexus in human shape of socioeconomic causalities, and potential object of a "physiological" description—and Zakhar as subject, suffused with disinterested commitment to the deceased, is precisely the sort of boundary that separates Oblomov's life story as a "typical" (socioeconomically or psychologically determined) failure from the same life, identical in its fabulaic outlines, informed most pertinently by resistance to such modes of conduct as situate consciousness in some desirable there-and-then of the past or future, which resistive imperative defines the subjective activity of the novelistic hero. This boundary also separates, *within* the writer whose appearance is reminiscent of both Il'ia Il'ich Oblomov and Ivan Goncharov,[72] the naturalist observer-analyst of part 1 from the author of the novel *Oblomov*:

"Who was that Ilya Ilych he [Zakhar] mentioned?" asked the writer. . . .

"I'll tell you but give me a moment to collect my thoughts and sort out my memories. And you write it down; who knows, it might be useful to someone sometime."

And the story he told was the one you have just read.[73]

Confronting the embodied author of the book he or she has just read, the reader performs his or her own "awakening" from the fictional realm of *Oblomov* to the fleshed-out world of writers and readers, specifically, to the corporeal source of the narrative, an ordinary-looking littérateur leisurely strolling the streets of Petersburg. These final embodying conversions of author and reader are accomplished in full accord with the imperative of non-differentiation between internal and external, between consciousness and the space-time parameters of its existence, that enables and carries forward plot and character development in *Oblomov*. And it is therefore not surprising that the author of *Oblomov* has his hero's "sleepy" (*kak budto sonnye*) eyes—the eyes, that is, of someone who has just awoken from, or who is about to engage in, novelistic narration, perhaps the most involved and absorbing of all literary dreams.

Afterword and Afterward

Tolstoy's *After the Ball*

THE POINT OF DEPARTURE of my inquiry into the development of artistic prose has been the identification of an unprecedented situation in the production and perception of the utterance, in which the utterance itself—whether an oral story or a "found" manuscript—became the object of representation within the compositional form of the frame narrative. I define this situation as that of the story-discourse convergence, since it engendered a narrative perspective from which both events and their representation appeared as concomitant in time and space: events did not precede their narration, but rather occurred and developed with and within it. This hitherto-unseen narrative perspective facilitated a release from the requirement—obligatory in *any other* communicative situation—to interrogate an utterance's relationship to reality, and thus differentiated nascent novelistic fictionality from any "serious" or "natural" narrative, as well as from previous forms of literary prose. I have posited the story-discourse convergence as a foundational characteristic of fictional narration, viewing it as a major formative resource and enabling factor for the development of fiction in general, and in particular as a phenomenon useful for tracing the path of prose narrative toward the genre of the realist novel. The "rise of the novel" thus emerges as one of the culminations in the unfolding of the potential of the narrative situation—properly speaking, aesthetic—of the story-discourse convergence.

My task in this book has been to explore the situation of the utterance's production and perception thus configured on the analytically rich material of Russian fiction, which underwent a remarkably swift and "condensed" development in the course of the nineteenth century. This analysis has examined, along both chronological and typological lines, some of the major literary-historical landmarks of this development in the 1820s through 1850s, focusing especially on the major shift from shorter prose forms (the novella, the cycle of tales, the sketch) to the emergence of the realist novel's discourse. In answering the question of how something "new" came about—a new literary movement or "school," genre, narrative strategy, character-form, and so on—my methodology has been to postulate the unconditional priority of an event occurring *within* the bounds of artistic discourse, or an intraverbal event, over paradigms of influence and sociohistorical or (in a narrow sense) formal developments. The sequence of such events and their discursive implications constitute the history of nineteenth-century Russian literary prose as it is understood in my study.

In its examination of the architectonics of the realist novel's narration, this book has posited the correlation of the two novelistic subjectivities, authorial and figural, as that of two mutually conditioned projections of the annulment of criteria for differentiating between the subject's interiority and its external manifestations—an annulment standing as one of the most prominent effects of the story-discourse convergence in the fictional narrative. The authorial unmindfulness of the distinction between internal and external (a state definable as that of excessive knowledge) manifests itself in the transparency of figural minds—the hallmark of the realist novel's narration. The counterpart of the author's insusceptibility to the internal-external divide is the hero's activity of perceiving any single external (spatiotemporal) moment as the result of his or her conscious choice (a state definable as that of excessive ignorance). The interdependence of these two novelistic subjectivities is established and sustained within the discursive bounds of the narrated consciousness, and is most perfectly captured by free indirect discourse, a mode of consciousness presentation marked by a lack of any decisive criterion by which to differentiate between represented and representing speech.

In concluding my study, I would like to provide a few additional examples of the narrative situation, central to the discourse of the realist novel, of represented speech and thought, and to reflect upon its further implications for full-fledged novelistic characterization; and for certain post-novelistic developments in the history of nineteenth-century Russian prose, particularly vis-à-vis the reappearance in Tolstoy's late, post-novelistic fiction, in the aftermath of the "age of the novel," of the frame narrative, the compositional form that had dominated the 1820s–30s—the approaches to this "age."

My examples of consciousness presentation in novelistic discourse come from Tolstoy's *War and Peace* (*Voina i mir*), and are readily recognizable as classic cases of estrangement (*ostranenie*, also rendered in English as defamiliarization, de-automation, etc.), the concept introduced by Viktor Shklovsky in his 1917 essay "Art as Device" ("Iskusstvo kak priem"), a programmatic piece of Russian formalist theory.[1] The first example is Natasha Rostova's perception of a performance at the Moscow Opera Theater:

> The floor of the stage consisted of smooth boards; at the sides was some painted cardboard representing trees. . . . In the center of the stage sat some

> girls in red bodices and white skirts. . . . They all sang something. When they had finished their song the girl in white went up to the prompter's box and a man with tight silk trousers over his stout legs, and holding a plume and a dagger, went up to her and began singing, waving his arms about. . . . Natasha could not follow the opera nor even listen to the music; she saw only the painted cardboard and the queerly dressed men and women.[2]

The second example is Prince Andrei Bolkonsky's observation of hand-to-hand combat—during the battle at Austerlitz, in which he himself participates—between a French and Russian soldier:

> Prince Andrei . . . was looking only at what was going on in front of him—at the battery. He now saw clearly the figure of a red-haired gunner with his shako knocked awry, pulling one end of a mop while a French soldier tugged at the other. . . . "What are they about?" thought Prince Andrei as he gazed at them. "Why doesn't the red-haired gunner run away as he is unarmed? Why doesn't the Frenchman stab him? He will not get away before the Frenchman remembers his bayonet and stabs him."[3]

For Shklovsky, Natasha's estranged view of the operatic performance has little to do with the relative quality of the production or the worthwhileness of any such performance, Tolstoy's well-known antipathy toward opera notwithstanding: according to Shklovsky, estrangement challenges the desensitized perceptual habits that suffuse *all* experience, personal and communal, of whatever significance. In Shklovsky's famous words: "Automatization eats away at things, at clothes, at furniture, at our wives, and at our fear of war."[4] Neither does this moment of estranged perception, in Shklovsky's view, have any bearing on character or plot development in the novel; in a later study of *War and Peace*, he rejects the idea, advanced by other commentators, that Natasha's incomprehension of the opera (or the opera's invitation as it were to overlook a patent falsehood) is somehow linked to her falling victim to Anatole Kuragin's seduction plot, which is set in motion during the performance:

> In Tolstoy's original characterization of Natasha it is said that she wants to get married in general. . . . There is nothing strange about this "in general." Tolstoy himself writes: "Natasha needs a husband, or maybe even two." She wants to live with men; she has a love, and is selecting a lover. Therefore additional motivations for Natasha's betrayal weren't needed in any theater: the motivation for the betrayal was physiological. . . . Thus it would be a stretch to use the scene in the theater to characterize the change in Natasha's psychology.[5]

Other critics, on the contrary, establish a direct relationship between the initiative of estrangement and the properties of its targets. For instance, Carlo Ginzburg, in his discussion on the prehistory of estrangement (which he traces back to Roman antiquity and the tradition of the French Enlightenment), takes issue with the formalists' view: "A purely formalistic approach inevitably misses what Tolstoy learned from Voltaire: the use of estrangement as a delegitimizing device, operating at every level—political, social, religious. . . . Within this tradition, estrangement is an instrument to overcome appearances in order to achieve a deeper understanding of reality."[6] Estrangement is thus understood as a method for exposing the meaninglessness of societal conventions, an eye-opener enabling characters to penetrate the "conventional" in order to see the "essence." In the discussion below I will suggest that the moments of estranged perception do bear on plot and character development in *War and Peace*; however, this impact has to do not with the "illegitimacy" of the exposed conventions—artistic, military, and so on—but rather with the figural excess actualized in the realist novel, an excess in relation to which *all* forms, whether social or natural, appear as equally deficient.[7]

Narrative situations of estranged perception constitute par excellence examples of consciousness presentation, since at these moments direct figural speech is impossible: the characters cannot name what it is that they see. Their bewilderment can be described as a suspension of (re)cognition, a state contingent upon their forgetting of vocabulary ("opera," "battle") previously automatically and unthinkingly available to them. Presentation of figural consciousness thus becomes the *only* means to "record" the characters' mental state. Narrative situations of estranged perception most immediately illustrate the distinctly novelistic correlation of the authorial non-differentiation between external and internal—manifested in the transparent rendition of figural minds—and characters' excessive mindfulness of such differentiation, their perceiving external boundaries as consequences of their own choosing. In moments of estranged perception, it is first of all a linguistic boundary—an element of the semantic, syntactic, and other normative linguistic resources constituting a "system of language"—that characters are unable to comprehend, and so strive to establish themselves.

Notably, in one example, this moment of incomprehension is led up to by a diametrically opposed narrative situation, that is, one of axiological congruence: just before Prince Andrei views the fight between a Russian and French soldier as the mere back-and-forth snatching at a mop, he has turned around the fleeing troops of his battalion by seizing the faltering standard and rushing ahead despite the hail of enemy fire. Andrei's query—"why doesn't the red-haired gunner run away as he is unarmed?"—signals incomprehension of military honor, the constituent of military experience that differentiates human war from animal fight (or flight) for survival; but what directly precedes this moment of incomprehension is the prince's *own* consummate heroic deed.

Or, to describe the opposition of these two narrative situations in the terms outlined above: while in the moment of estranged perception of the two soldiers' struggle, Prince Andrei is unable to cognize an external boundary (in this case pertaining to a military behavioral code), in the preceding moment, to the contrary, he unconditionally embraces this very boundary in his readiness to sacrifice his life for the common, hence external, cause. Here I would take a further interpretive step and suggest that it is precisely Prince Andrei's ultimate acceptance of an external boundary (in the act of self-sacrifice on the battlefield) that casts the hero into the inverse experience of excessive ignorance, that same boundary's utter incomprehensibility. The moment of estranged perception thereby marks not the meaninglessness of warfare as an institution or convention, but rather the character's excess in relation to social form, an excess revealed only *after* the demands of this form have been completely fulfilled.

Immediately following Prince Andrei's estranged perception of the almost slapstick struggle between the French and Russian soldiers comes one of the most celebrated passages of *War and Peace*: Andrei's seeing of the "lofty sky" (*vysokoe nebo*) over Austerlitz. Wounded, he falls flat on his back so that there is literally nothing before his eyes but the heavens:

> He opened his eyes, hoping to see how the struggle of the Frenchmen with the gunners ended, whether the red-haired gunner had been killed or not and whether the cannon had been captured or saved. But he saw nothing. Above him there was now nothing but the sky—the lofty sky, not clear yet still immeasurably lofty, with gray clouds gliding slowly across it.[8]

Observing the sky over Austerlitz, Prince Andrei experiences, as he later recalls, one of his "finest moments" (*luchsie momenty zhizny*);[9] at the Moscow Opera Theater, by contrast, Natasha comes very near disaster, falling victim to Kuragin's seduction scheme:

> But looking into [Kuragin's] eyes she realized with fright that there was not that barrier of modesty she had always felt between herself and other men. She did not know how it was that within five minutes she had come to feel herself terribly near to this man. . . . She smiled just as he was doing, gazing straight into his eyes. And again she felt with horror that no barrier lay between him and her.[10]

Despite the obvious contrasts, however, I would suggest that Prince Andrei's encounter with the boundless sky and Natasha's "shamelessness" vis-à-vis Kuragin can be seen as analogous narrative situations, each informed by the characters' experiences of estrangement. The defamiliarization of one "convention," be it of opera or battle, "makes strange" all other forms of social life, in Andrei's case, the honor expected in battle, in Natasha's, the shame governing (or barring) sexual relationships. Fully unfurled, the experience of estrangement results in the suspension of *all* cognitive and ethical boundaries; it is this suspension that is marked by, or rather coincides with, the characters' gravitation toward natural (asocial) forms of life.

Prince Andrei:

> All is vanity, all falsehood, except that infinite sky. There is nothing, nothing, but that. But even it does not exist, there is nothing but quiet and peace. Thank God![11]

Natasha:

> Natasha little by little began to pass into a state of intoxication she had not experienced for a long while. She did not realize who and where she was, nor what was going on before her. As she looked and thought, the strangest fancies unexpectedly and disconnectedly passed through her mind: the idea occurred to her of jumping onto the edge of the box and singing the air the actress was singing, then she wished to touch with her fan an old gentleman sitting not far from her, then to lean over to Hélèn and tickle her.[12]

Andrei himself (and a number of Tolstoy scholars after him)[13] interprets his experience in terms of the opposition between the human realm, with its petty squabbles, and the sublime world of nature:

> "How quiet, peaceful, and solemn; not at all as I ran," thought Prince Andrei—"not as we ran, shouting and fighting, not at all as the gunner and the Frenchman with frightened and angry faces struggled for the mop: how differently do those clouds glide across that lofty infinite sky!"[14]

Prince Andrei blames himself for the complete immersion in dreams of worldly glory that previously precluded him from contemplating the sky: "How was it I did not see that lofty sky before? And how happy I am to have found it at last!"[15] However, there is yet another immediate cause for Andrei's prior imperception of the sky's "loftiness," and this cause is a strictly natural one: fog, which has since dissipated. The critical mistake of commanders leading to the crushing Russian defeat at Austerlitz consisted precisely in not taking the natural law of fog dissipation—from the heights on down—into account; by contrast, Napoleon initially deploys his troops on high ground, where the fog clears first:

> It was nine o'clock in the morning. The fog lay unbroken like a sea down below, but higher up at the village of Schlappanitz where Napoleon stood with his marshals around him, it was quite light. Above him was a clear blue sky.[16]

The Russian troops, however, were ordered to descend from the hills and march into the hollow where the fog is both the deepest and slowest to burn off. When the fog finally does evaporate around them, the failure of this strategic maneuver becomes (literally and metaphorically) clear:

> The fog had begun to clear and enemy troops were already dimly visible about a mile and a half off on the opposite heights. . . . The two generals and the adjutant took hold of the field glass, trying to snatch it from one another. The expression on all their faces suddenly changed to one of horror. The French were supposed to be a mile and a half away, but had suddenly and unexpectedly appeared just in front of us.[17]

Thus, the "loftiness" of the sky observed by the wounded Andrei on the field at Austerlitz results from a sequence of natural, namely, meteorological events occurring simultaneously with military ones, such that, by the time Andrei falls to lie on his back, the fog has finally dissolved, and the sky is clear. Later in the day, when Andrei, having lost and then regained consciousness, opens his eyes again, he sees "the same lofty sky with clouds that had risen and were floating still higher, and between them gleamed blue infinity."[18] The sky becomes even "loftier" and clearer toward evening since, according to the natural (meteorological) course of events, the fog continues to dissipate.

Kuragin's efforts to seduce Natasha are dictated by similarly natural phenomena, specifically, the physiological impulses governing his behavior with women; his entire way of life is described as animal- rather than human-like:

> He was instinctively and thoroughly convinced that it was impossible for him to live otherwise than as he did and that he had never in his life done anything base. . . . He was convinced that, as a duck is so made that it must live in water, so God had made him such that he must spend thirty thousand rubles a year and always occupy a prominent position in society.[19]

The sheer physiological incentive of Kuragin's interest in Natasha is obvious to everyone, except Natasha herself. Her obliviousness is similar to that of Prince Andrei, who does not take into account the daily meteorological pattern as a possible source of the sky's seemingly sudden "loftiness." In Natasha's eyes, physiology-driven Kuragin acquires some sort of supreme authority, much like the sovereign majesty Andrei ascribes to the cloudless sky: "One can't doubt him! One can't, one can't! Don't you understand!"[20]—Natasha says to Sonya.

In the trajectories of character and plot development described above, the hero projects the excess he or she experiences in relation to a social form—revealed through his or her ultimate acceptance of it—onto natural forms, endowing strictly natural (meteorological, physiological) phenomena with cognitive and moral urgency that in and of themselves these phenomena do not possess. Having emerged from the experience of estranged perception—of perceiving an external boundary as resulting from his or her own choice—that registers this excess, both Prince Andrei and Natasha immediately establish new cognitive and moral hierarchies, new external parameters for offering up a sacrifice: Andrei: "All is vanity, all falsehood, except that infinite sky"[21] (*Vse obman, vse zlo, krome etogo beskonechnogo neba*);[22] Natasha: "Whatever [Kuragin] commands, I shall do"[23] (*Chto on mne velit, to ia i sdelaiu*).[24] Both social and natural forms thus emerge as deficient in relation to their capacity to sustain the novelistic hero's excess; yet it is this excess—the experience of any external (social or natural) boundary as a result of conscious choice—rather than the inherent properties of social and natural phenomena themselves (e.g., the opera or the sky) that informs the above examples of character and plot development in *War and Peace*.

In more general terms, these trajectories of character and plot development can be described as a dual process of de-symbolization/symbolization: if in the moment of estranged perception, an object is momentarily stripped of its symbolic significance (e.g., painted pieces of cardboard no longer signify "trees"), in the next moment, another object is signified *excessively*, granted a symbolic meaning it has hitherto—for the perceiver, in any case—not possessed: thus for Andrei, de-symbolization of the battle results in *excessive* symbolization of the cloudless sky, which comes to signify "loftiness."[25]

I would suggest that these two correlative "sides" of the estranging process—de-symbolization and excessive symbolization—are informed by the narrative perspective of the story-discourse convergence, within which any textual action or "move" carries forward both events and their representation such that no boundary can be drawn between the two. One consequence of the situation of utterance production and perception thus configured is that applying any "device" or "technique" on the level of narration has instantaneous (utterly coincident in space-time) "equalizing" corollaries on the level of story: the estranging, de-symbolizing description of an object, that is, has a correlative effect in a character's excessive symbolization of another object. It is perhaps the writer's susceptibility to the two-sidedness of estrangement, to the immediate and decisive consequences that applying this "device" produces on the level of narrated events, that differentiates the effortless manufacture of estranged descriptions—of which indeed any object can become a target[26]—from estrangement as an aesthetic event.

As the examples above demonstrate, in the figural perspective, the mutual conditioning of the two sides of the (de-)symbolization process, their utter simultaneity (enabled, in turn, by the story-discourse convergence) unfolds into a series of *consecutive* states, or stages, each with its own intellectual, psychological, or emotional content. The "device" of estrangement thus propels the novelistic character's progression through a series of potentially endless constructions of meanings and judgments, which lay claim by turns to sovereign cognitive and moral authority; whereas the true driving force of this progression—the correlative forms of authorial and figural excess in relation to any social or natural configurations—remains inaccessible from within the narrated world, and unexplained therein. I would suggest that one of Tolstoy's last works, the short novella *After the Ball* (written in 1903 and published only posthumously, in 1911) can be seen as an artistic response to the novelistic patterns of character and plot development enabled by the workings of this (de-)symbolization process.[27]

After the Ball centers on a transformative moment in the life of its narrator-protagonist Ivan Vasil'evich, who at a casual gathering of friends recounts a story from his youth about how his "whole life was changed because of one night, or rather one morning."[28] Indeed, though the events narrated by the hero occurred long previously, when he was a university student, they have had lasting consequences for him: as a result of what had happened that fateful morning, Ivan Vasil'evich has never entered service, either military or civil, and never married. As distinct from the succession, potentially infinite, of alternative states that characters undergo in *War and Peace*, the hero's change in *After the Ball* is decisive and final, resulting in a figural state of consciousness that is unalterable; this transformation, that is, harbors the principle of arrest or restriction of any and all further development. It is the finality of the hero's transformative moment in *After the Ball* that my reading of the novella foregrounds and attempts to explicate.

As the title suggests, the novella has a clearly demarcated dual structure: first, there is the "ball," a provincial high society gathering, where the hero dances all night long with the beautiful Varenka, a young woman he is in love with, under the approving and reassuring gaze of all present, particularly Varenka's father, a decorated colonel and "a very handsome, stately, tall, and well-preserved old man";[29] and then there is the "after," when, unable to fall asleep after the dance has ended, Ivan Vasil'evich goes out for a walk toward Varenka's house on the other side of town. Arriving there by morning, the hero becomes an accidental witness as Varenka's father presides over the brutal punishment of an army deserter, who is forced to run the gauntlet. It is as a result of this "one morning" that not only the hero's love for Varenka "came to naught,"[30] but also his "whole life was changed."

This ball was only the latest of many for the hero, whose greatest pleasure during his student years, as he himself explains, was the attendance of such soirees; but this particular ball is where his love for Varenka reached its apex: strong to begin with ("I was in love many times but this was the deepest of my loves"),[31] the feeling continues to grow as the evening goes on, coming to encompass not only the young woman but also her father. Ivan Vasil'evich begins to experience a tender adoration toward the colonel focused, in particular, on his sturdy handcrafted boots:

> Obviously, the boots were made by a regimental cobbler. "In order to dress his favorite daughter and bring her out into society, he doesn't buy fashionable boots, but wears his everyday ones," I thought, and I was moved especially by the square toes of those boots.[32]

The hero's love continues to expand, attracting into its orbit literally everyone and everything in his field of vision:

> [I embraced the whole world then with my love.] I loved the hostess in the diadem with her Yelizaveta Petrovna bust, I loved her husband and her guests and her servants, and I even loved the engineer Anisimov who was feeling a bit peeved with me. . . . Despite the fact that I seemed to be infinitely happy, my happiness kept on growing and growing.[33]

The "worldwide" capacity of the hero's feeling is confirmed when after the ball he returns home and finds there yet more objects to draw into his all-encompassing love:

> I stared at [my brother's] head buried in his pillow and half-covered with his flannel blanket and I started to feel lovingly sorry for him, sorry that he did not know nor share that happiness that I was experiencing. Our household serf Petrusha came in with a candle and wanted to help me undress, but I didn't let him. The sight of his sleepy face and tousled hair touched and moved me.[34]

In the terms introduced above, the hero's stance—defined by Ivan Vasil'evich himself as love for "the whole world"—can be described as that of excessive symbolization gone *total*: each and every object, from the colonel's rectangular boot toe-caps to the house-serf's tousled hair, acquire a significance they have heretofore not possessed. This state is analogous to Prince Andrei's granting of "loftiness" to the clear, fogless sky, and to Natasha's perception of the "instinctual" Kuragin as a man of utmost honor—except that for Ivan Vasil'evich, *all* objects ("the whole world") are pulled into the process of excessive symbolization.

It is this overwhelming state that draws Ivan Vasil'evich out of the house in the early morning after the ball: "I was too happy, I could not sleep."[35] The process of total symbolization continues up to the very moment when the hero, having walked across town, reaches its edge, and comes to a field near Varenka's house. Thus it is from within the perspective of his world-encompassing love that Ivan Vasil'evich observes the violent beating of a deserter:

> And the horses rhythmically swaying their soaked heads under the glistening shaft-bows, and the cabbies covered with bast matting, thudding along in their huge boots beside their cabs, and the houses on the street, which in the fog appeared very tall—all this seemed to me especially dear and meaningful.
>
> When I came to the field where their house was, I saw something huge and black at the end of it, in the direction of the parade ground. And from there I heard the sounds of a fife and drum.[36]

Like Natasha at the opera and Prince Andrei on the battlefield at Austerlitz, the hero cannot fully comprehend what it is that he hears ("this was some other kind of music, harsh and unpleasant") and sees: "As the procession passed the place where I was standing, between the rows of the soldiers I caught sight of the back of the man being punished. It was something so motley, wet, red, and unnatural that I could not believe it was the body of a human being."[37] Despite his perfect view on this potentially lethal beating (the procession goes right by him) and the readily available and thorough definition of the event's social-institutional meaning ("They are beating a Tatar for desertion," answers another passerby when Ivan Vasil'evich asks what is happening), the pieces of information do not cohere even after the hero leaves the scene:

> "Obviously, he knows something that I don't," I thought with the colonel in mind. "If I knew what he knows, I would understand even what I saw and it wouldn't torment me." But no matter how much I thought about it, I could not understand what it was the colonel knew, and I managed to fall asleep only toward evening and then only after going over to a friend's and getting completely drunk with him.[38]

In *War and Peace*, as discussed, the event of the de-symbolization of an object or phenomenon instantly generates the discursive effect of excessive symbolization of another object or phenomenon; this two-sided process drives forward character and plot development in the novel. In *After the Ball*, however, this narrative development, called forth by the dynamics of estrangement, is interrupted, or rather blocked, because no objects or phenomena are available, "vacant," so to speak, as potential material for symbolization: everything has already been excessively symbolized to capacity, endowed with significance by the hero's world-encompassing love. This definitive absence of any social or natural forms available for excessive symbolization, for being invested with the sort of intellectual and moral authority Prince Andrei grants to the sky, and Natasha does to Kuragin, leads to the suspension of the hero's capacity for cognitive and ethical valuation and his resulting withdrawal from all societal forms of life:

> So do you think that it was then that I decided that what I saw was a wicked thing? Not in the least. "If it was done with such assurance and deemed necessary by everyone, then they must have known something I didn't," I thought, and I tried to find out what it was. But no matter how hard I tried, I could not find out what it was, not even later. And since I couldn't find out, I couldn't enter military service, as I had formerly wanted to, and so I didn't serve in the military nor in the civil service and have been quite useless, as you can see.[39]

In *After the Ball*, the hero's exemption from a particular subset of the estranging process—from the dynamic that, in *War and Peace*, fuels characters' progression through a series of mental states with changeable, often antithetical, intellectual, psychological, and emotional content—is marked by the emergence of what might be called *direct* symbolization; by the establishment, that is, from within the figural perspective, of a connection between signifier and signified that is absolutely invariable, stable in relation to contextual and spatiotemporal heterogeneity. Ivan Vasil'evich explains how his love for Varenka "began to fade"[40] thus:

> When [Varenka] would grow pensive with that smile on her face, as she often did, I would immediately remember the colonel on the parade ground and it would become somehow uncomfortable and unpleasant for me, and so I started seeing her less.[41]

For the hero, now "Varenka," whatever she is smiling or thinking about, means *only* "the colonel on the parade ground." The relationship between signified and signifier in the "Varenka-colonel" association is independent from any temporal and spatial variables. It is from the perspective of the absolute certitude of this newly formed "word" that all other spatiotemporal forms, whether social or natural, appear deficient to Ivan Vasil'evich.

As the possessor of this word that yields not to spatiotemporal diversity—this fully reliable word—the narrator-protagonist acquires a discursive status congenial to that of the fictional utterance's producer, or author, whose narrative position is self-sufficient regardless of the referential relationship between the text and the (spatiotemporally heterogeneous) world outside it. This analogy between the authorial and figural perspectives in *After the Ball* underscores the hero's status as his own narrator and thus brings forth, or brings *back*, the compositional form of the frame narrative, dominant in Russian fiction of the 1820s–30s (as well as in early forms of the western European novel) and then overshadowed by the rise and advance of the realist novel's discourse. This return to a pre-novelistic compositional form is, however, far from redundant: as my reading of Tolstoy's novella shows, its narrator-protagonist's discursive perspective sustains and consummates the novelistic hero's excess in relation to all spatiotemporal configurations, and thus has the "age of the novel" as its *terminus post quem*. Like major events on the level of the novelistic story, namely, events in the life of figural consciousness that are imperceptible from the position of external observation, this trajectory of the development of the novella genre, from the frame narrative of the 1820s–30s to the frame narrative on the "other side" of the Russian "age of the novel," cannot be substantiated on the compositional level—external in relation to the architectonics of the authorial and figural discursive perspectives—where the frame narratives "before" and "after" the novel are impossible to differentiate.

In *After the Ball*, the narrator-protagonist's depletion of social and natural forms potentially endowable with cognitive or moral authority acquires a positive valuation when he is envisioned as a subject in need of some *other*, as yet absent, form, one that would differ from *all* available social and natural configurations, whether given here-and-now or projected into the past/future. There is a moment in Tolstoy's novella that reveals a textual trace of figural subjectivity thus conceived: one of Ivan Vasil'evich's listeners, responding to his concluding statement that, having made no socially accepted career, he "ha[s] been quite useless," protests by saying that "many people would be useless if it hadn't been for [him]."[42] The reader never learns exactly how Ivan Vasil'evich helps other people to become "useful"; presumably it is the Tolstoyan-anarchist subtext—at the outset of the novella, the gathered friends have touched upon the "necessity of changing the conditions in which people live"[43]—that is the key to the unavailable moral authority, which is displaced, that is, onto some non- or post-statist plane of reality. In any case, the hero's non-participation in either civil or military service emerges as enabling some *other* form of serving, one that has tangible, decisive effects, yet exceeds all available classifications.

Ivan Vasil'evich finds his listener's remark greatly displeasing: "'Well that's just sheer nonsense,' Ivan Vasilievich said with genuine vexation."[44] The hero's annoyance attests to the fact that this other form, undetectable in societal terms, is also unavailable to the hero himself; it is uncognizable, or, to make use of Bakhtin's fundamental concept, it is situated *outside* in relation to the hero's cognitive and ethical susceptibilities, within which he genuinely perceives himself as a good-for-nothing. Notable in this regard is that, in elaborating the notion of outsideness, Bakhtin invokes a metaphor of birth that conveys the non-causal, non-derivative relationship between the cognitive and ethical imperatives of reality and the aesthetic experience—the incongruity of, or discontinuity between, the two major participants in aesthetic activity, author and hero:

> Such [a "fundamental, aesthetically productive"] relationship of the author to the hero . . . places the hero beyond [*iz"emlet*, lit., takes him out of, extracts him from] mutual surety, collective liability, and solitary responsibility and gives birth to him as a new human being on a new plane of existence—a plane of existence where the hero himself is incapable of being born for himself and through his own power; or, in other words, it invests or embodies the hero in that new flesh which is not essential and does not exist for the hero himself.[45]

In terms of methodology, Bakhtin's metaphor for the study of verbal art seems to imply that any critical effort to identify some set of markers or attributes that would distinguish utilitarian from artistic utterances is as futile as attempting to pinpoint the ultimate cause of the birth of a human being. Likewise unproductive are assertions of the inexplicability of the origins of life and art. In both methodological attitudes, the indeterminacy involved in the creative process is removed from analytical consideration: either explained away or left completely inviolable. In contrast to these attitudes, my study has posited this very indeterminacy as a meaningful, operative component in the production and perception of the artistic utterance. In the communicative situation of the simultaneous unfolding of story and discourse, the speaking subject finds him or herself privy to at least two discourses—one being represented, the other performing the representing—that utterly converge in space-time; his or her every textual action or "move" on one level, then, has immediate—utterly coincident in time and space—and unforeseeable discursive consequences on the other. Moreover, the very differentiation into levels emerges as derivate, secondary in relation to the process of constant and continuous mutual crossings from one level to another, a process standing as the propulsive power of the artistic utterance's *self*-development. The stages and shifts of this process—here examined on the material of some of the key moments in the history of nineteenth-century Russian prose—emerge as events *within* the bounds of the artistic utterance, or intraverbal events; such events have no external generative causes, and so can properly be defined as both creative and fully reliable.

Notes

INTRODUCTION

1. Letter to P. Viazemsky, November 4, 1823; Pushkin, *Sobranie sochinenii v desiati tomakh*, 9: 77. (Uncited translations in this book are my own; all others belong to the translators indicated in the respective editions.) Other examples of Pushkin's "prose in verse" include 1833's "The Bronze Horseman" ("Mednyi vsadnik"), subtitled "A Petersburg Tale" ("*Peterburgskaia povest'*"), and 1828's "Count Nulin" ("Graf Nulin"), published together with Evgenii Baratynsky's "The Ball" ("Bal") in a single volume under the heading "Two Tales in Verse" ("Dve povesti v stikhakh").

2. Cited in Eikhenbaum, "Put' Pushkina k proze," 224. Notably, Pushkin's unfinished prose fragments played a key role in Leo Tolstoy's conception of *Anna Karenina*; see Eikhenbaum, *Lev Tolstoi: Semidesiatye gody*, 147–60.

3. Eikhenbaum, *Lermontov: Opyt istoriko-literaturnoi otsenki*, 134. In 1924 Eikhenbaum and Iurii Tynianov edited and published a collection of essays, *Russkaia proza*, devoted to Russian prose from the end of the eighteenth century to the 1830s that contained works on particular authors (Karamzin, Marlinsky, Senkovsky, Vel'tman, Viazemsky), as well as on popular literary genres of the time. Alessandra Tosi's recent study *Waiting for Pushkin: Russian Fiction in the Reign of Alexander I (1801–1825)* examines prose fiction of the first quarter of the nineteenth century, including some of the period's most obscure (in some cases unpublished) writings.

4. Other examples of longer prose narratives bearing uncertain generic designations are Goncharov's *A Common Story* (*Obyknovennaia istoriia*, 1847) and Nikolai Chernyshevsky's *What Is to Be Done?* (*Chto delat?* 1863).

5. Eikhenbaum observes: "Chief attention is directed precisely to the novel, to the large form. The question of the essence of the genre is actively discussed in journal articles and reviews. . . . The issue of the novel becomes a favorite topic of theoretical discussions. Finally, even scholarly dissertations devoted to this topic appear: thus in 1844, M. A. Tulov (a teacher at Count Bezborodko's Nezhin Lyceum), defended a dissertation 'On the Novel as One of the Forms

of the Verbal Arts' in Kiev. But in practice, the large form had a long way to go before it would succeed." Eikhenbaum, *Lermontov: Opyt istoriko-literaturnoi otsenki*, 138.

6. Freeborn, *The Rise of the Russian Novel: Studies in the Russian Novel from "Eugene Onegin" to "War and Peace,"* 1.

7. Watt, *The Rise of the Novel: Studies in Defoe, Richardson, and Fielding*, 31.

8. De Armas Wilson, "Of Pilgrims and Polyglots: Heliodorus, Cervantes, and Defoe," 47.

9. Examples of this broader scope are too numerous to list with any exhaustiveness here. Recent scholarly publications that expand the geographic boundaries of the novel's origins include Cohen and Dever, *The Literary Channel: The Inter-National Invention of the Novel*; Mander, *Remapping the Rise of the European Novel*; and essays on novelistic traditions the world over in Franco Moretti's anthology *The Novel: History, Geography, and Culture*.

10. Todd, "The Ruse of the Russian Novel," 404. In comparison to the Russian eighteenth-century literary scene, both readership and commercial opportunities increased significantly in the first half of the nineteenth century; nonetheless, the scale of these new opportunities remained out of step with those extant in western Europe. In her *Romantic Encounters: Writers, Readers, and the Library for Reading*, Melissa Frazier—despite focusing more on the "imaginary" rather than "real" literary marketplace of 1830s Russia—provides (18–40) a detailed and informative account of the latter.

11. Woloch, *The One vs. the Many: Minor Characters and the Space of the Protagonist in the Novel*, 30.

12. One of the most recent attempts, aside from that of Woloch, to bring together sociocultural and literary forms in relation to the novel's rise is Kent Puckett's *Bad Form: Social Mistakes and the Nineteenth-Century Novel*.

13. McKeon, "Generic Transformation and Social Change: Rethinking the Rise of the Novel," 382. Specifically, McKeon demonstrates the instability of Watt's conceptual categories (including those of the "middle class" and the "novel") during the sociocultural transformations he describes.

14. These approaches, which dominate in non-Eurocentric accounts of the novel, refute Watt's pinpointing of eighteenth-century England as uniquely fertile soil for the rise of the novel, but remain faithful to his central methodological premise of the sociological study of narrative forms. Jenny Mander aptly summarizes: even though "Watt's thesis regarding the origins of the novel has now become highly debatable," his "exploration of the dynamics of the reading public and the interplay between the form of the novel and cultural and philosophical influences opened up studies to the perspectives of social history" (Mander, *Remapping the Rise of the European Novel*, 4).

15. Schwarz, *Misplaced Ideas: Essays on Brazilian Culture*, 29.

16. Ibid.

17. Of the numerous studies devoted to the role of Western models in the development of Russian fiction in the first half of the nineteenth century, I would single out Viktor Vinogradov's works on Sir Walter Scott (*Gogol' i natural'naia shkola*) and Jules Janin (*Zhiul' Zhanin i Gogol'*); Viktor Shklovsky's on Sterne (*'Tristram Shendi' Sterna i teoriia romana*); Donald Fanger's influential study of the Dickens-Balzac-Gogol-Dostoevsky connection (*Dostoevsky and Romantic Realism: A Study of Dostoevsky in Relation to Balzac, Dickens, and Gogol*); and Ronald LeBlanc's hypothesis of Gogol's artistic appropriation of Fielding's *Tom Jones* in *Dead Souls* ("A la recherche du genre perdu: Fielding, Gogol, and Bakhtin's Genre Memory"). More recent book-length publications include Dolinin, *Pushkin i Angliia* and the above-mentioned Frazier, *Romantic Encounters*.

18. For an overview of the reformulations of Schwarz's argument (and one that offers its own revision), see Palti, "The Problem of 'Misplaced Ideas' Revisited: Beyond the History of Ideas in Latin America."

19. Aleksandr Veselovskii, *Zhurnal ministerstva narodnogo prosveshcheniia* 12 (1863): 557–58. On Veselovsky's legacy, his formative impact on major Russian literary theorists (including the formalist school, Ol'ga Freidenberg, Vladimir Propp, and Mikhail Bakhtin), and the reception of his ideas both in Russia and the West, see Maslov, "Comparative Literature and Revolution, or the Many Arts of (Mis)reading Alexander Veselovsky." Maslov performs a reclamation of Veselovsky's theory and methodology in response to the perceived need to interrogate "how the objects of literary analysis—and the objects of comparative literary analysis—were constituted, maintained, revised, rejected, or neglected." Precisely what constitutes the object of analytical inquiry into the novel's "rise" is a question central to contemporary reevaluations of Schwarz's approach to Brazilian literary history, as well as to my own examination of the development of Russian fiction. In addressing the dynamics of the core-periphery relationship in literary history, Ilya Kliger evokes another Russian theoretician, opposing the paradigms of world literary development offered by Franco Moretti and Pascale Casanova to those represented by Russian cultural semiotician Yuri Lotman. For the former two, a single center or core unilaterally dominates the periphery, whereas the latter envisions every cultural moment as "an intersection point between numerous global asymmetries in which core and peripheral processes interact to invariably unique effects" (Kliger, "World Literature Beyond Hegemony in Yuri M. Lotman's Cultural Semiotics," 270).

20. Todd, "The Ruse of the Russian Novel," 405.

21. Eikhenbaum, "*Geroi nashego vremeni*," 283.

22. In this way, my analysis complements studies of the emergence and development of novelistic discourse that foreground social context and reception. On the sociohistorical, institutional, and ideological context of the novel's rise in Russia, see William Mills Todd's landmark study *Fiction and Society in the*

Age of Pushkin: Ideology, Institutions, and Narrative, which deals with such factors as literary patronage and commercial interests, discourse and intercourse in polite society, the role of salons and circles of friends, and more. As mentioned earlier, Frazier in her *Romantic Encounters* provides (18–40) a detailed account of the literary market in Russia in the 1830s. As for reception studies, several scholarly works single out specific influences that were operative in the genesis of the Russian novelistic tradition. David Budgen discusses Fedor Emin's pioneering effort to break away from the traditions of the chivalrous tale and romance in "Fedor Emin and the Beginnings of the Russian Novel." In *The Rise of the Russian Novel: Carnival, Stylization, and Mockery of the West*, David Gasperetti analyzes the formative role of eighteenth-century prose, specifically that of Emin, Chulkov, and Komarov, in the Russian novelistic tradition. Frederick Griffiths and Stanley Rabinowitz argue (*Novel Epics: Gogol, Dostoevsky, and National Narrative*) that, beginning with Gogol's *Dead Souls*, the development of the Russian novel was catalyzed by the epic tradition. Andrew Kahn emphasizes the influence of the Greek romance and a large corpus of translated Western novels in his recent study "The Rise of the Russian Novel and the Problem of Romance." For an overview of the genre of *povest'* in Russian literature from the Kievan period to the early nineteenth century, see Di Salvo, "Povest'"; the author poses the question of "continuity between the novel and *povest'*" at the end of her essay, but does not pursue it further.

23. On the other hand, the problematics of narrative construction notwithstanding, "the idea that history is committed to verifiable documentation and that this commitment is suspended in fiction has survived even the most radical dismantling of the history/fiction distinction." Cohn, *The Distinction of Fiction*, 112–13.

24. Gallagher, "The Rise of Fictionality," 339–40.

25. Ibid., 337.

26. It is for this reason that I have made the choice to focus my study on fiction and "fictionality," even though there is no doubt, as has been shown, that other discourses, such as history writing, bureaucratic prose, and newspaper reportage, have played a role in the "rise" of the novel. For the Russian novel, albeit at a later stage, this has been demonstrated by Konstantine Klioutchkine in "The Rise of *Crime and Punishment* from the Air of the Media."

27. Miller, *The Novel and the Police*, 24.

28. Cohn, *The Distinction of Fiction*, 165. This debate was conducted on the pages of *New Literary History*. See Cohn, "Optics and Power in the Novel"; Bender, "Making the World Safe for Narratology: A Reply to Dorrit Cohn"; and Cohn, "Reply to John Bender and Mark Seltzer."

29. Here might be mentioned other notable attempts to bring together the genre of the novel and notions of power and authority. Audrey Jaffe (*Vanishing Points: Dickens, Narrative, and the Subject of Omniscience*) defines the omni-

science of the novelistic author as a fantasy of unlimited knowledge and mobility actualized through a set of narrative strategies employed in the novel to produce this effect. One of these strategies is the construction of characters (who are bereft of mobility and freedom) in relation to and at the expense of which the author defines him or herself as omniscient. Another influential paradigm often applied to the novel is the Freudian metaphor, with the novelistic text embodying the son-as-writer's attempts to usurp paternal authority. For a conceptualization of the paternal metaphor, see Barthes, *The Pleasure of the Text*; for examples of its application to specific novels, see, for instance, Brooks, "The Novel and the Guillotine, or Fathers and Sons in *Le Rouge et le noir*"; and Sadoff, "Storytelling and the Figure of the Father in *Little Dorrit*." My concept of the reliability imperative is concerned with the writer's quest for *aesthetic* authority—an aptitude for engendering and sustaining non-referential discourse—rather than for a reenactment of political/penitentiary power, unlimited knowledge, or "Oedipal pleasure" (Barthes).

30. Here and elsewhere in the book, *povest'* will be rendered by "tale" with reference to cycles of tales; and by "novella" with reference to the pre-novelistic form as developed in Russian prose of the first half of the nineteenth century. Of course, *povesti* (whether "tales" or "novellas") continued to be written and read throughout this century, even as the novel appeared and advanced. Although a detailed discussion of the post-novelistic novella exceeds the scope of this study, the afterword describes the prominent return of the framed novella in the "aftermath" of Russia's "age of the novel," specifically, in Tolstoy's late fiction.

31. I employ the term "presentation of consciousness" exactly as does Cohn—as a portrayal of the "unspoken thoughts, feelings, perceptions of a person other than the speaker" (*Transparent Minds: Narrative Modes for Presenting Consciousness in Fiction*, 7). When "consciousness" (or "inner life") is construed as the object of presentation regardless of the narrative position from which such presentation is undertaken, the discussion can lose its focus. Thus, in a recent study on the presentation of consciousness in the ancient Greek novel, Margaret Anne Doody dismisses the realist novel's exclusive prerogative vis-à-vis the portrayal of inner life, arguing instead that "writers of novels—of all kinds and in all periods—give a major place to the workings of the mind itself" ("The Representation of Consciousness in the Ancient Novel," 36). However, the examples from ancient Greek prose that Doody adduces to support her claim highlight precisely a discontinuity in the representation of inner life. That is, in each instance, the inner life of the character, however intense, complex, and dynamic, is expressed entirely in his or her own words–even when there is no one around to hear them. Doody's conclusion that the earliest novel "gives voice to the voiceless" (ibid., 42) underscores how qualitatively different is the narrative mode of representation of consciousness in the ancient Greek novel from that of the realist novel. The hallmark of the latter is the presentation of the invisible, inaudible, and

often *nonverbal* workings of the characters' hearts and minds, which are inaccessible to both external observation and first-person narration.

32. Bakhtin, *The Dialogic Imagination: Four Essays*, 123.

33. Bakhtin's observations resonate with Miller's argument that the practice of novelistic representation appropriates with unsurpassed efficiency the policing procedures of examination and interrogation—procedures transposed "out of the streets . . . [and] into the closet—into the private and domestic sphere on which the very identity of the liberal subject depends," which sphere is technically off-limits to the police (*The Novel and the Police*, viii–ix). Neither critic, however, addresses the essential difference between access to the private/domestic sphere and access to inner life: the latter is off-limits not only to the police as typically understood institutionally, but, indeed, to *any* initiative of observation and interrogation. It is precisely this boundary that in the history of Russian fiction (and, albeit less rigidly, that of western Europe as well) separates shorter prose works from the novel, and that therefore constitutes the primary focus of my examination of the Russian novel's "rise."

34. Cohn, *Transparent Minds: Narrative Modes for Presenting Consciousness in Fiction*, 5–6.

35. For some of the reconceptualizations and critiques of the notion of omniscience that center on the presentation of consciousness in fictional narrative, see Jonathan Culler's "Omniscience"; Monika Fludernik's book *Toward A Natural Narratology*, particularly chapters 4 and 5, and her subsequent essay "Naturalizing the Unnatural: A View from Blending Theory"; as well as a number of studies undertaken within the framework of "unnatural narratology." (For a concise introduction to this latter approach, see Alber, Iversen, Nielsen, and Richardson, "Unnatural Narratives, Unnatural Narratology: Beyond Mimetic Models.")

36. Costlow, *Worlds within Worlds: The Novels of Ivan Turgenev*, 13.

37. I have chosen not to employ Gérard Genette's widely accepted terminology for narrative perspectives in fictional discourse because, while undoubtedly useful in synchronic analysis of a literary text, this terminology loses its explanatory value within the diachronic perspective assumed in my study. A narrator can be "heterodiegetic" (external to narrated events) in novella and novel alike, but with a fundamental distinction: in the novella, exteriority prevents the narrator from accessing a character's inner life, while in the novel, this access is granted. Further division of narrators into "overt" and "covert" (Rimmon-Kenan, *Narrative Fiction: Contemporary Poetics*) does not address this difference either: a heterodiegetic narrator might be "covert" whether in novella or novel. Consequently, while throughout the book I rely on a number of insights gleaned from the field of narratology, my discussion of the narrative perspectives actualized in nineteenth-century Russian prose avoids such terminology as might blur the boundaries I strive to bring into view.

38. These works include "Author and Hero in Aesthetic Activity" ("Avtor i geroi v esteticheskoi deiatel'nosti"), "Toward a Philosophy of the Deed" ("K filosofii postupka"), and "The Problems of Content, Form, and Material in Verbal Art" ("Problemy materiala, soderzhaniia i formy v slovesnom khudozhestvennom tvorchestve").

39. Bakhtin, *Art and Answerability: Early Philosophical Essays*, 14.

40. Ibid., 15.

41. For an insightful overview of the debates on "outsideness," see chapter 5, "Outsideness as the Ethical Dimension of Art (Bakhtin and the Aesthetic Moment)," in Emerson, *The First Hundred Years of Mikhail Bakhtin*.

42. Vinogradov, "Etiudy o stile Gogolia," 257–58.

43. Analyzing a different trend of this period (specifically, changes in conceptualization of the literary marketplace), Frazier hints at the eternal quest for imported predecessors with the pointed question: "Perhaps [it derives from] someone further West?" (Frazier, *Romantic Encounters*, 18).

44. In its overarching theoretical framework, Frazier's *Romantic Encounters* is a worthy and encouraging example of an approach to Russian literature's relationship with the European tradition that eschews the "model-creative appropriation" paradigm. With Russian romanticism as her source material, Frazier convincingly argues that the Russian romantics' artistic concerns (including those of marginality and authenticity) go to the very essence of romanticism as a literary phenomenon. For Frazier, Russian literature's social, economic, geographical, and institutional marginality provide a particularly advantageous focal point from which to explore not only Russian but European romanticism as a whole. Explaining her methodology, Frazier states: "I would . . . put all these Romantic literatures striving to find (or create) their own essence on an equal footing, and use the particularly Russian anxiety of influence only to argue that absolute presence not only eludes them all but also on a fundamental level was intended to do exactly that" (*Romantic Encounters*, 4). Likewise, Anne Lounsbery explicitly forgoes the influence paradigm in her recent side-by-side reading of Nikolai Gogol and Nathaniel Hawthorne, convincingly demonstrating a number of significant parallels (particularly in models of author- and readership) between these two contemporaneous writers who "never read each other's work" (*Thin Culture, High Art: Gogol, Hawthorne, and Authorship in Nineteenth-Century Russia and America*, 1).

45. Booth, *The Rhetoric of Fiction*, 300. For further advances in the concept of reliability as proposed by Booth, see Martínez-Bonati, *Fictive Discourse and the Structures of Literature: A Phenomenological Approach*, in which an attempt is made to discover unreliable narration in third-person fictional texts. In general, remarks Dorrit Cohn (*The Distinction of Fiction*, 130), "the discovery of unreliable narrators in heterodiegetic novels has of late been on the rise, fulfilling Booth's prediction that the 'pervasive irony hunt' would ultimately reach

'even the most obviously omniscient and reliable narrators.'" These recent developments of Booth's concept are still concerned with the (un)reliability of the narrator, while the implied author remains the ultimate source of the pervasive irony that is the object of the reader/interpreter's hunt.

CHAPTER ONE

1. On the distinction between these renderings as used in this book, see the introduction, note 30.

2. Iezuitova notes this characteristic of Russian novellas of the 1820s–30s ("Puti razvitiia romanticheskoi povesti," 89–90), but does not elaborate upon it. In "Fedor Emin and the Beginnings of the Russian Novel," Budgen considers Emin's "consistent, almost obsessive" assertions of the historical accuracy of his works to be the most original aspect of his fiction (86). Though Emin's oeuvre is beyond the scope of this discussion, it is notable that Budgen's article links Emin's historicity claims with the origins of the novelistic genre in Russian prose.

3. Goody, "From Oral to Written: An Anthropological Breakthrough in Storytelling," 21. Citing numerous analogous examples from eighteenth-century French fiction, Lennard Davis concludes: "After 1710 there was a general tendency for French novelists to claim that their works were true" (*Factual Fictions: The Origins of the English Novel*, 36).

4. The exceptions affirm the rule. On the reception of Defoe's novels—"issued as histories, branded as lies, and eventually read as novels"—see Mayer, *History and the Early English Novel: Matters of Fact from Bacon to Defoe*, 4.

5. Gallagher, "The Rise of Fictionality," 345. Other important studies have examined the shifting relationship between "real" and "fictional" as central for understanding the genealogy of novelistic discourse. These include Mayer's work referenced just above; Davis's case (*Factual Fictions: The Origins of the English Novel*) for the existence of a period (late sixteenth and early seventeenth centuries) of genuine categorical confusion between "fact" and "fiction," from which the genre of novel emerged; and Michael McKeon's argument (*The Origins of the English Novel, 1600–1740*) that the novel arose within the context of the early modern historicist revolution, specifically in the epistemological shift by which the expanded boundaries of the notion of "truth" came to include "verisimilitude." In the discussion that follows, I will argue that the fact/fiction dichotomy is inadequate to fully account for the novel's origins, since the essence of novelistic fictionality consists precisely in the annulment of the relevance of this dichotomy.

6. Gallagher, "The Rise of Fictionality," 340.

7. Ibid.

8. Goody sees the early European novels' claims to historical truth as the new genre's "strategy of legitimation," one called for due to a fundamental and

essentially universal (observable in oral cultures, and from Plato to our own day) ambivalence toward representation in general, and especially toward fictional, that is, nontruthful and nonserious, representation. "Doubts about fiction, about the novel, have dogged the history of this genre, because such worries are embedded in the human situation." Goody, "From Oral to Written: An Anthropological Breakthrough in Storytelling," 32.

9. Bakhtin, *The Dialogic Imagination: Four Essays*, 328.

10. Bakhtin, "Slovo v romane," 150.

11. Letter of August 13, 1831, originally appearing in *Russkii vestnik* 32 (1861): 305; cited in Bestuzhev-Marlinskii, *Sochineniia v dvukh tomakh*, 623.

12. Ibid., 624.

13. Ibid., 623.

14. Ibid., 624–25.

15. Moeller-Sally, "0000; or, The Sign of the Subject in Gogol's Petersburg," 325.

16. Raven, "Britain, 1750–1830," 441.

17. Odoevskii, *Sochineniia v dvukh tomakh*, 2: 81.

18. Zhukova, *Vechera na Karpovke*, 117.

19. Vel'tman, *Povesti i rasskazy*, 144.

20. Pavlov, *Tri povesti*, 13.

21. Ibid., 34.

22. Somov, *Byli i nebylitsy*, 309.

23. For a thorough examination of the tradition of the familiar letter in early nineteenth-century Russia, see Todd, *The Familiar Letter as a Literary Genre in the Age of Pushkin*. Notably, Todd remarks in his conclusion that "the brief cult of familiar letters did not, however, spill over into a multitude of epistolary novels, as had been the case in Western literatures" (187). At the same time, as the examples above demonstrate, despite the absence of epistolary novels in Russian fiction of the 1820s–30s, the compositional form of the embedded letter (or two, or six, or seven letters) was common in Russian prose of the time. In this regard, it is interesting to note that the epistolary novel is the prose form by which Fyodor Dostoevsky chose to begin his career as novelist.

24. Somov, *Byli i nebylitsy*, 108–9.

25. For an extensive discussion of the traveling author in sentimental and romantic travelogues of the late eighteenth and early nineteenth centuries, see Tosi, *Waiting for Pushkin: Russian Fiction in the Reign of Alexander 1 (1801–1825)*, 263–96. In *Romantic Encounters: Writers, Readers, and the Library for Reading*, Melissa Frazier provides an innovative examination of early nineteenth-century Russian fiction's "chameleonlike figure of the writer as editor, plagiarist, and/or critic" (69) in the context of romantic notions of authorship.

26. Lodge, "Mimesis and Diegesis in Modern Fiction," 95.

27. Davis, *Factual Fictions: The Origins of the English Novel*, 35. Summariz-

ing the characteristics distinguishing novel from romance, Davis maintains that "novels of the eighteenth century tend to be written in the first person and in the letter form; romances are never written in these forms" (40). In support of this statement, Davis cites (229, n. 40) Silas Paul Jones's *A List of French Prose Fiction from 1700 to 1740* (1939), which tallies "200 novels written in the first person out of a total of 946."

28. For instance, William Burling states in his review of *Factual Fictions*: "No one will deny that fiction writers often relied on this frame, but to claim that any writer who did not was therefore writing romance is only a circular argument. Consider the case of Congreve, who in the Preface to *Incognita* (1692) makes no claim to truth, calls his fiction a novel (stressing its non-romance features), and cites the influence of drama on his fiction. The reverse of Davis's argument also proves unconvincing. Mary Manley claimed she *was* writing fiction in her *New Atlantis* (1705) yet every informed reader knew she was writing about actual people" (283).

29. McKeon, review of *Factual Fictions: The Origins of the English Novel*, by Lennard J. Davis, 86.

30. McKeon, "Generic Transformation and Social Change: Rethinking the Rise of the Novel," 383.

31. My emphasis on this correlation is not meant to ignore the "monumental" (Burling, review of *Factual Fictions*, 283) diversity of prose fiction and the categorical uncertainty of artistic discourse in the seventeenth and eighteenth centuries; or to exclude, as does Davis, the centuries-long romance tradition (or, for that matter, any speech practices of the time) from participation in the process by which the realist novel, to use McKeon's apt formulation, "has come to the end of its origins" ("Generic Transformation and Social Change: Rethinking the Rise of the Novel," 397). On the contrary, I believe that an examination of the effects of narrative embedding from the perspective of the utterance's perception, specifically that of the annulment of its attribution to reality, can provide a clearer understanding of the ways in which prose genres, literary and nonliterary, interacted, coalesced, or "subdivided" (Davis) in the early modern period.

32. Bakhtin, *The Dialogic Imagination: Four Essays*, 332.

33. Ibid.

34. These are the "forms that are defined by their use of a personified and concretely posited author (written speech) or teller (oral speech)" (ibid., 312). Bakhtin's examples include narrators from the prose of Pushkin, Gogol, and Lermontov, among others.

35. Ibid., 321.

36. Ibid., 333.

37. Smith, "Narrative Versions, Narrative Theories," 228.

38. Culler, "Fabula and Sjuzhet in the Analysis of Narrative: Some American Dimensions," 35.

39. Ibid., 29. "Point of view" studies make no accounting for the story's state of having been conditioned by discourse: "For the study of point of view to make any sense, there must be various contrasting ways of viewing and telling a given story, and this makes 'story' an invariant core, a sequence of actions which can be presented in any of various ways. Action becomes something that exists independently of narrative presentation; in principle it exists prior to any narrative presentation and could be presented in other ways" (ibid., 28).

40. Smith, "Narrative Versions, Narrative Theories," 229.

41. Ibid.

42. Here I find support in Dorrit Cohn's fundamental disagreement with the conception of the story-discourse relationship as analogous in fictional and nonfictional domains. Cohn asserts that in nonfictional narratives, this relationship is decisively affected by the attribution to reality: "The level of reference introduces a diachronic dimension into the three-level model of historical narrative that is absent from the bi-level model of fictional narrative. . . . Outside the realm of fiction, the synchronous interplay of story and discourse is undergirded—no matter how shakily—by the logical and chronological priority of documented or observed events." Cohn, *The Distinction of Fiction*, 115.

43. Culler, "Fabula and Sjuzhet in the Analysis of Narrative: Some American Dimensions," 34.

44. Gérard Genette defines metalepsis as "any intrusion by the extradiegetic narrator or narratee into the diegetic universe, or the inverse" (*Narrative Discourse: An Essay in Method*, 234–35).

45. Malina, *Breaking the Frame: Metalepsis and the Construction of the Subject*, 7. In his influential study of the eighteenth-century comic novel, Robert Alter describes Fielding as a writer who "is continuously and finely conscious of the status of his novels as artifacts" (*Fielding and the Nature of the Novel*, 101). Alter later calls Fielding a "principal model for the self-conscious novel, a writer who realized its possibilities with a superbly confident artistic poise that has not been surpassed" (*Partial Magic: The Novel as a Self-Conscious Genre*, xiv).

46. Another good example of the Russian-doll framing technique is Bestuzhev's *Cuirassier: From the Notes of a Partisan Officer* (*Latnik: Iz zapisok partizanskogo ofitsera*, 1832).

47. Vel'tman, *Povesti i rasskazy*, 182.

48. An analogous, albeit more complex, moment occurs in Zhukova's *Evenings on the Karpovka*, when one of the narrators, the doctor, accuses another of inaccurate reportage, of "sinning against the truth" (*pogreshil protiv istiny*). The doctor then supplies a "true" version, anchoring his narrative authority in his having personally witnessed the events in question.

49. Pogorel'skii, *Dvoinik: Izbrannye proizvedeniia*, 162.

50. Ibid., 322.

51. Somov, *Byli i nebylitsy*, 111.

52. Ibid., 135.

53. Odoevskii, *Sochineniia v dvukh tomakh*, 2: 312.

54. Ibid.

55. Ibid., 313.

56. Ibid., 317.

57. Ibid., 310.

58. Rostopchina's *Rank and Money* similarly moves from an internal to an external perspective: the hero's letters and diaries are followed by an account provided by a friend who happened to witness the story's events.

59. Odoevskii, *Sochineniia v dvukh tomakh*, 2: 126.

CHAPTER TWO

1. The cyclical organization of prose persists into the 1850s, as witness the collections of physiological sketches and Turgenev's *A Sportsman's Sketches*.

2. *Russian Nights* evolved from a cyclical project tentatively entitled *House of Madmen* (*Dom sumasshedshikh*) that Odoevsky contemplated in the first half of the 1830s.

3. As envisioned by Odoevsky, this cycle was to include stories devoted to various types of possession; *Orlakh Peasant Girl* remained not only the first, but only work written for it.

4. "A variety of forms of cyclization, such as episodes, stories, sketches, and tales, constitute the defining characteristic of Russian prose in the 1830s. In some cases, these are collections such as *Evenings on a Farm near Dikan'ka*, or *Tales of the Late Ivan Petrovich Belkin*, or Odoevsky's *Motley Tales*; in others, tales structured as a cycle, with one of the tales serving as a frame." Eikhenbaum, "*Geroi nashego vremeni*," 250.

5. Ibid., 249.

6. Shklovskii, *Razvertyvanie siuzheta*, 15.

7. Donovan, *Women and the Rise of the Novel, 1405–1726*, 29.

8. Ibid. Donovan defines the framed-novelle as "short stories that are linked by a frame narrative, usually that of the social interaction among the story tellers" (ibid.). Another term commonly used for the prose cycle is "frame-tale."

9. Shklovskii, *Razvertyvanie siuzheta*, 49.

10. Ibid., 22.

11. Donovan, *Women and the Rise of the Novel, 1405–1726*, 31–32.

12. Of course, *Canterbury Tales* is not an example of the prose cycle; all but two inset tales are composed in verse. But as the focus here is on the relationship between frame and embedded tales within the cyclical narrative, the poetry/prose distinction can be bracketed.

13. Cannon, "Introduction," xiv.

14. Despite the unfinished state of *Canterbury Tales* and substantial uncertainty as to the tales' order, discussion of its mechanisms of coherency remains a

fruitful area in Chaucer scholarship. My emphasis on these mechanisms, moreover, is by no means intended to disregard the aspects of discontinuity in either Boccaccio or Chaucer; I mean, rather, to highlight the qualitatively different scale and scope of dissolution of the thematic and structural linkages in the Russian cyclical narratives of the 1820s–30s.

15. Donovan, *Women and the Rise of the Novel, 1405–1726*, 39.

16. For instance, Donovan observes (ibid.) that in de Navarre's *Heptameron*, "the frame characters—five women and five men—are distinct (psychologically and ideologically consistent) individuals. . . . Each character in the frame has a consistent position in the *querelle des femmes*, which is the issue that dominates the discussions, providing the text's hypotaxis."

17. Of course, the search for unifying elements (structural, thematic, stylistic, etc.) is a prominent feature of scholarly studies devoted to these Russian cycles. Intending no disregard for the valuable discoveries made in this area, I emphasize here the absence of *explicit* linkages within the embedding narrative, between the embedding and embedded tales, and among the tales themselves—an absence that, as discussed above, contrasts sharply with the organization of cyclical narratives of the earlier western European tradition. This very absence can be said to encourage and intensify interpreters' search for the Russian cycles' unifying principles; see, for instance, Gregg, "A Scapegoat for All Seasons: The Unity and Shape of *The Tales of Belkin*"; and Bethea and Davydov, "Pushkin's Saturnine Cupid: The Poetics of Parody in *The Tales of Belkin*."

18. The entire footnote reads: "'The Stationmaster' was told to him by Titular Councilor A. G. N., 'The Shot' by Lieutenant Colonel I. L. P., 'The Coffin-Maker' by Steward B. V., 'The Blizzard' and 'Lady-Peasant' by the maiden [*devitsa*] K. I. T." Pushkin, *Povesti pokoinogo Ivana Petrovicha Belkina, 48.*

19. Gogol', *Vechera na khutore bliz Dikan'ki*, 149.

20. As Neil Cornwell notes ("V. F. Odoevsky and his *Pestrye skazki*," 138), the full title of the cycle is "one of the longest in Russian literature": *Pestrye skazki s krasnym slovtsom, sobrannye Irineem Modestovichem Gomozeikoiu, magistrom filosofii i chlenom raznykh uchenykh obshchestv, izdannye V. Bezglasnym.*

21. Pushkin, *Povesti pokoinogo Ivana Petrovicha Belkina*, 48.

22. The exception is "Ivan Fedorovich Shpon'ka and His Auntie" ("Ivan Fedorovich Shpon'ka i ego tetushka"), written down, at Pan'ko's request, by the narrator Stepan Ivanovich Kurochka himself.

23. Vickie Ziegler argues that the organization of the frame narrative offered by *Decameron* and *Canterbury Tales* "remained the same until the German writers reintroduced it in the late eighteenth century" (*Bending the Frame in the German Cyclical Narrative: Achim von Arnim's "Der Wintergarten" and E. T. A. Hoffmann's "Die Serapionsbrüder,"* 1). She observes that the German cyclical narratives preserve a number of features from the earlier tradition: the isolation of the group of people, the telling of a story by each individual, the di-

vision of stories into thematic groups, and more. Ziegler's analysis of Goethe's *Unterhaltungen*, von Arnim's *Der Wintergarten*, and Hoffmann's *Die Searpionbrüder* posits the deepening, as compared with the earlier tradition, of the interaction between frame and inset stories as the prime characteristic of the German cyclical narratives (ibid., 21). In this light, the Russian cyclical tradition, which features the strengthening of the boundaries between the cycle's constituents, develops in the opposite direction. The collector's prominent role in organizing cyclical narrative may or may not be exclusive to Russian prose; further examination of cyclization in different literary traditions would be necessary to clarify this. Nonetheless, a glance at a much later stage of the cyclical tradition is interesting in this regard: Richard Shryok's *Tales of Storytelling: Embedded Narrative in Modern French Fiction* focuses on the complex reciprocal relationships between frame and inset stories, namely, the motivations for embedded narrators and the stories' effect on embedded narratees. It is precisely the absence of such relationships—an omission foregrounding the persona of tale collector—that characterizes the Russian prose cycle of the 1820s–30s and appears to differentiate it from both earlier and later cyclical traditions.

24. Nelles, *Frameworks: Narrative Levels and Embedded Narrative*, 2. Nelles's study, devoted entirely to narrative embedding, is a fine example of the narratological approach to the problem.

25. Gogol', *Vechera na khutore bliz Dikan'ki*, 146.

26. Jenny Mander observes that the textual mystification strategy of the "found manuscript" had already become easily identifiable and manifestly parodied "by the mid-1730s, [when] French readers had encountered endless variants of this particular topos of the discovered manuscript, given such playful treatment by Cervantes over one hundred years earlier in the *Quixote*. Prefaces talked of manuscripts found in cupboards, beside corpses, in libraries or even between the printed lines of other texts" (*Remapping the Rise of the European Novel*, 2). For a discussion of European, American, and Russian writers' engagement with the "found manuscript" device, and specifically Pushkin's employment of it in the *Tales of Belkin*, see Navas, "Reading Pushkin's *Tales of Belkin* through Sainte-Beuve's *Vie, Poésies et Pensées de Joseph Delorme*."

27. Navas, "Reading Pushkin's *Tales of Belkin* through Sainte-Beuve's *Vie, Poésies et Pensées de Joseph Delorme*," 94.

28. *Motley Tales* in fact features two prefaces: one from the publisher, the other from the collector Gomozeiko.

29. Zhukova, *Vechera na Karpovke*, 10.

30. Zagoskin, *Askol'dova mogila: Romany, povesti*, 545.

31. Iakubovich, "Predislovie k 'Povestiam Belkina' i povestvovatel'nye priemy Val'tera Skotta."

32. Cited ibid., 170.

33. Hoisington, "Pushkin's Belkin and the Mystifications of Sir Walter Scott," 354.

34. Ibid., 348.

35. Ibid., 353. For her part, Melissa Frazier eschews both such analytical routes: she associates Russian writers' anonymous, pseudonymous, and fictitious personae of the 1820s–30s—narrators, editors, publishers, critics—with those of Walter Scott, but ties the emergence of this trend in both western European and Russian literature to the "normal conditions" of romantic authorship, under which the writer's "'originality' lay in his apparent ability to appropriate other people's stories" (*Romantic Encounters: Writers, Readers, and the Library for Reading*, 63, 65).

36. Hoisington, "Pushkin's Belkin and the Mystifications of Sir Walter Scott," 357.

37. Ibid., 351.

38. Ibid., 354.

39. Cited in Iakubovich, "Predislovie k 'Povestiam Belkina' i povestvovatel'nye priemy Val'tera Skotta," 178.

40. Hoisington, "Pushkin's Belkin and the Mystifications of Sir Walter Scott," 354.

41. Iakubovich, "Predislovie k 'Povestiam Belkina' i povestvovatel'nye priemy Val'tera Skotta," 163.

42. Ibid., 187.

43. Ibid., 170.

44. Ibid., 177.

45. The first novel in the series, *Waverley* (1814), was published anonymously, with *Rob Roy* (1817–18) then attributed to the "author of *Waverley*." For a complete list of authorial personae at work in the Waverley series and a description of the prefatory material of each novel, see Gaston, *Prefacing the Waverley Prefaces: A Reading of Sir Walter Scott's Prefaces to the Waverley Novels*, 23–24. There undoubtedly exist thematic parallels between Pushkin's Belkin and Scott's other fictitious personae; for instance, both Iakubovich and Hoisington discuss similarities between Belkin and *Tales of My Landlord* editor Jedediah Cleishbotham, and between Belkin and *Monastery* editor Captain Clutterbuck. Iakubovich speaks of Pushkin's "powerful, condensed synthesis of a device scattered throughout all Scott's works, at times with stunningly coinciding details" ("Predislovie k 'Povestiam Belkina' i povestvovatel'nye priemy Val'tera Skotta," 172). At the same time, Belkin's status as tale collector, central to the narrative organization of the *Tales of Belkin*, ties him firmly to the only collector in the Waverley novels, the deceased schoolteacher Peter Pattieson.

46. Patricia Gaston discusses numerous instances of manuscript discoveries in Scott's Waverley novels; among these, only the "found manuscript" of *Tales of My Landlord* represents a collection of tales. Gaston, *Prefacing the Waverley Prefaces: A Reading of Sir Walter Scott's Prefaces to the Waverley Novels*, 81–103.

47. Iakubovich, "Predislovie k 'Povestiam Belkina' i povestvovatel'nye priemy Val'tera Skotta," 177.

48. Ibid., 170.

49. Iakubovich himself does not dwell on the specifics of the collector "step" in the "staircase device"; for him, it represents only an additional degree of authorial removal. Both Hoisington and Navas emphasize Belkin's collector status; for them, however, collecting stands in opposition to creativity and original authorship. As discussed above, Hoisington contrasts Belkin's lack of investigative spirit to Pattieson's historiographic pursuits; Navas opposes Belkin's mere collecting to the creativity of the poet Joseph Delorme, fictitious author of Sainte-Beuve's *Vie, poésis et pensées de Joseph Delorme*: "Characteristically, Pushkin took Sainte-Beuve's key innovation and turned it on its head. His surrogate author, Belkin, may or may not have been a great literary artist; but to us he is merely a 'writer' in the most literal sense, a compiler rather than a composer of tales" ("Reading Pushkin's *Tales of Belkin* through Sainte-Beuve's *Vie, Poésies et Pensées de Joseph Delorme*," 94). Notably, both scholars use the word "compiler" rather than "collector," which former term, implying the mere organization of an existing text, downplays the actively solicitous nature of the collector's initiative.

50. Hoisington, "Pushkin's Belkin and the Mystifications of Sir Walter Scott," 344. David Kropf, who also invokes Scott as a poet embarking on writing prose, theorizes along similar lines: "I would argue that one reason Pushkin chose the pseudonym Belkin was to isolate the attempts at prose from the author that was constituted primarily in terms of poetry" (*Authorship as Alchemy: Subversive Writing in Pushkin, Scott, Hoffman*, 75). Both writers left their first attempts at literary prose unfinished. Scott's first experiments with fiction, the two fragments *Thomas the Rhymer* and *The Lord of Ennerdale*, date from the turn of the nineteenth century; neither was carried beyond a first chapter. Pushkin's most important unfinished pieces include "Guests Were Arriving at the Dacha" ("Gosti s''ezzhalis' na dachu"), "On the Corner of a Small Square" ("Na uglu malen'koi ploshchadi"), and *A Novel in Letters* (*Roman v pis'makh*). For a discussion of Scott as editor and poet, and of the connections between his editing, poetry, and fiction, see Millgate, *Walter Scott: The Making of the Novelist*, chapters 1 and 2. Millgate emphasizes (ix) Scott's status as an accomplished editor and poet: "In 1814, the career of Walter Scott was already at mid-point. When *Waverley* appeared Scott was on the eve of his forty-third birthday and not only firmly established in his legal position as Clerk to the Court of Session but famous as a poet and editor."

51. Eikhenbaum, "Put' Pushkina k proze," 225.

52. Cited ibid., 225–26.

53. Ibid., 221.

54. Ibid., 220. Wolf Schmid takes an opposite approach in his analysis of the relationship between prose and poetry in Pushkin's oeuvre, positing particularly with regard to the *Tales of Belkin* a "criss-crossing of prosaic and poetic tendencies" ("Pushkin's 'Descent' to Prose," 210).

55. Not published until the 1970s.

56. Bakhtin, *The Dialogic Imagination: Four Essays*, 293–94.

57. Ibid., 272.

58. Bocharov, "Pushkin i Belkin," 142–43. (Quotes from the *Tales of Belkin* cited from Pushkin, *Tales of the Late Ivan Petrovich Belkin*, 5–6.) Bocharov draws on the observations of other influential Pushkin scholars, including the nineteenth-century literary critic Apollon Grigor'ev, the first to "shift" attention from the tales to the figure of Belkin himself: "[Grigor'ev's] concept (as a totality of thoughts dispersed throughout various articles) subsequently gave impulse to scholarly discussion of the issue of the role of Belkin" (Bocharov, "Pushkin i Belkin," 133).

59. Critical discussions of the "Belkin question" are suffused with intuitions of absence and indefiniteness. Schmid defines Belkin as "a null figure, indeterminacy personified" ("Pushkin's 'Descent' to Prose," 231). Compare Bocharov: "Belkin's determinacy is equal to his indeterminacy, and the portrait of his personality [or face, *litso*] depicts impersonality [or facelessness, *bezlichnost'*]" ("Pushkin i Belkin," 143). Bocharov traces this indeterminacy directly to Belkin's lack of narrative voice: "Belkin's presence in the text as author and narrator is in no way localized nor objectified by his own 'Belkinian' discourse/word. At the same time, he is involved in both narrative levels. The sounding world of Pushkin's tales are gathered together by the *silent* figure of Belkin" (ibid., 146; emphasis in original). I concur with the overall trajectory of Bocharov's argument, but would add that Belkin's "facelessness" and "indeterminacy" acquire distinctly positive content when Belkin is understood as tale collector—a narrative agent with a unique "face" and clear "determinacy." Jan Meijer, who similarly posits as decisive the role played by Belkin in Pushkin's search for the narrative organization of artistic prose, situates Belkin between "author figure" and character: "Belkin is . . . as much a character as he is an author figure, he is in fact, the former in the guise of the latter" ("The Sixth Tale of Belkin," 133). Meijer sees Belkin as a "gathering place" (ibid., 134) of the tales' narrators, but draws no qualitative distinction between these two narrative stances: "The narrators as well as Belkin have stylistic functions, but within the space thus created their roles cannot be fully separated. . . . A foreword on any of the other narrators would not have revealed essential differences in the outlook" (ibid., 126–27). Meijer's analysis omits consideration of the collector's "surplus" vis-à-vis all other narrative perspectives in the cycle, as do examinations of Russian cyclical narratives generally. For instance, Hoisington defines Gogol's Pan'ko as "the alleged editor" of the *Dikan'ka Tales* ("Pushkin's Belkin and the Mystifications of Sir Walter Scott," 355) and, following Vinogradov, as "the Russian offspring of Jedediah Cleishbotham" (ibid.). However, all similarities between Pan'ko and Cleishbotham notwithstanding, the key distinction is that Pan'ko is also (or primarily) the collector of the tales that make up the *Dikan'ka* cycle. Though both Belkin and Pan'ko can

certainly be considered "members of the Cleishbotham family" (ibid., 357), their principal narrative stance as collectors sets them apart.

60. Gogol, *The Complete Tales*, 1: 89, 91.

61. Odoevskii, *Pestrye skazki*, 23.

62. Ibid., 23–24.

63. Ibid., 24.

64. Unlike Pushkin with his Belkin, Odoevsky had further plans for the figure of Irinei Gomozeiko, envisioning for him an autobiography and a cycle of his adventures throughout Russia. Notably, however, these plans were never realized. See Cornwell, "V. F. Odoevsky and his *Pestrye skazki*," 138–39. Gomozeiko's only reappearance in a completed work comes in the novella *The Apparition* (on which see chapter 1).

65. Zhukova, *Vechera na Karpovke*, 6.

66. Zagoskin, *Askol'dova mogila. Romany, povesti*, 531.

67. Ibid., 537.

68. Ibid., 531.

69. Vinogradov, "Etiudy o stile Gogolia," 264.

70. In his integrative approach to Pushkin's *Tales of Belkin*, Richard Gregg stresses the short-lived Belkin's lot as that of experiencer of failures both personal and professional: "The story of this guileless and unlucky young man is, then, the story of yet another of life's victims, who is not only the inventor of but also the prototype for his hard-luck heroes" ("A Scapegoat for All Seasons: The Unity and Shape of *The Tales of Belkin*," 761). This conclusion would be justified were Belkin indeed an author ("inventor") or character of some "sixth tale of Belkin," as Meijer defines the preface. But Belkin is neither author nor character, but first and foremost a tale collector; his "failures," and ultimately his "death," are best understood not thematically, but as textual effects of the collector's discursive stance: that is, the collector's abdication of his or her own word results in this narrative persona's fundamental non-participation in any and all worldly pursuits.

71. Bakhtin, "Slovo v romane," 127.

72. Bakhtin, *The Dialogic Imagination: Four Essays*, 313.

73. Ibid., 327.

74. Pushkin, *Tales of the Late Ivan Petrovich Belkin*, 5.

75. Substantiation of Belkin's distinct narrative stance would also broaden, I believe, the analytical perspective from which to examine the pieces making up the *Tales of Belkin* themselves. Bocharov concludes his discussion of Belkin thus: "Within the cycle, the tales encompassed by Belkin's authorship maintain a free existence. They may be read separately; to a certain extent, they may be read 'without Belkin'; but only to a certain extent. Readers and scholars who read without Belkin, removing him completely from consideration, invariably read with a certain loss of meaning" ("Pushkin i Belkin," 145). Still, though Belkin's

significance for the poetics of Pushkin's cycle is acknowledged, some of the best analyses of the tales are performed entirely "without Belkin"; in Bocharov's own subtle examination "O smysle 'Grobovshchika,'" for instance, Belkin's presence in the cycle has no bearing on the scholar's conclusions. For an insightful reading of Pushkin's cycle that takes the tale collector into account, see Prostsevichus, "Samorazvitie literaturnogo proizvedeniia," 97–104.

76. While the conflict between "one's own" and "someone else's" word is inherent in speech production and perception, it is only in artistic prose that this standoff is definitively resolved in favor of the intentions and accents of the latter. The tale collector's orientation toward the word has a distinctly aesthetic foundation. Meijer notes that it was the transition to fictional narrative that posed a challenge to Pushkin: "That Pushkin was able to present his thoughts adequately in prose is clear enough, e.g., from his letters. But when in *Eugene Onegin* he foresaw the possibility that he would come down to writing prose, he had in mind something he had not yet been doing; he meant artistic prose" ("The Sixth Tale of Belkin," 128).

CHAPTER THREE

1. For a detailed overview of the genre, see Iezuitova, "Svetskaia povest'." Neil Cornwell provides a concise and informative outline of the historical and generic parameters of the society tale in his introduction to Cornwell, *The Society Tale in Russian Literature: From Odoevskii to Tolstoi*, 1–7.

2. See Eikhenbaum, *Lev Tolstoi: Semidesiatye gody*, 147–60; and Sloane, "Pushkin's Legacy in *Anna Karenina*." Moreover, Ivan Goncharov's first novel, *An Ordinary Story* (*Obyknovennaia istoriia*, 1847), was based on his earlier work *A Lucky Mistake* (*Schastlivaia oshibka*, 1839), a typical society tale. Scholars have also discussed the society tale's contribution to the works of Turgenev and Dostoevsky. On these and other examples of the society tale's impact on the nineteenth-century novel, and on the ways in which society tale themes, character types, settings, and plots were modified and reworked in subsequent Russian prose, see Matveyev, "From the Society Tale to the Novel: A Model of Genre Development."

3. Shepard, "The Society Tale and the Innovative Argument in Russian Prose Fiction of the 1830s," 114.

4. Ibid., 123; emphasis in original.

5. Bestuzhev-Marlinskii, *Noch' na korable: Povesti i rasskazy*, 4–5.

6. Ibid., 177, 179.

7. This narrative situation occurs in Vel'tman's novella *Radoi* (discussed in chapter 1), when the narrator, upon acquiring an anonymous manuscript, does not allow himself to simply assume that it is a real-life journal, but suspects it may well be a work of fiction intended for publication; the narrator is assured of

the manuscript's authenticity when the events related therein are corroborated independently. In Bestuzhev's *A Night on a Ship*, the narrator takes a different tack, justifying the credibility of the source of narration (the sincerity of the interpolated storyteller) rather than that of narrated events themselves.

8. Shepard, "The Society Tale and the Innovative Argument in Russian Prose Fiction of the 1830s," 135.

9. Ibid., 120.

10. "The sense of propriety depends on upbringing and other circumstances. People of high society have their own manner of thinking, their own prejudices incomprehensible to another caste. How would you explain to a peaceable Aleutian a duel between two French officers?" "O stat'iakh kn. Viazemskogo," in Pushkin, *Sobranie sochinenii v desiati tomakh*, 6: 60.

11. Bestuzhev-Marlinskii, *Noch' na korable: Povesti i rasklazy*, 230.

12. Ibid., 235.

13. Ibid.

14. Cited in Shepard, "The Society Tale and the Innovative Argument in Russian Prose Fiction of the 1830s," 130.

15. Todd, *Fiction and Society in the Age of Pushkin: Ideology, Institutions, and Narrative*, 148.

16. Reyfman, "Alexander Bestuzhev-Marlinsky: *Bretteur* and Apologist of the Duel," 251.

17. See, for instance, Susan Layton's examination of Aleksandr Druzhinin's tales of the Caucasus, particularly of how his representation of inhabitants of this region contrasts with poetic fantasies of the Caucasus in earlier romantic literature. According to Layton, who emphasizes the context of Russian colonization, "in Druzhinin's writings . . . the Caucasus has for the most part made a chronotopic shift from wild frontier to disagreeably tame colony" ("Colonial Mimicry and Disenchantment in Alexander Druzhinin's 'A Russian Circassian' and Other Stories," 66).

18. Reid, "*Princess Ligovskaia* and *Princess Mary*: The Society Tale Goes to the Caucasus," 41.

19. In her article devoted to *Princess Ligovskaia*, Helena Goscilo remarks that the narrator "staggers between omniscience and partial knowledge" ("The First Pechorin En Route to *A Hero*: Lermontov's *Princess Ligovskaia*," 158). Victor Vinogradov similarly emphasizes ("Stil' prozy Lermontova") the instability of the authorial point of view in *Princess Ligovskaia*. I propose that Lermontov's narrator does not vacillate between the two (omniscient and otherwise) vantage points, but rather consistently adheres to the position of ubiquitous invisible observer, with the only "part" definitively absent from his competency being the characters' inner life.

20. Bestuzhev-Marlinskii, *Noch' na korable: Povesti i rasskazy*, 163.

21. Lermontov, *Sochineniia*, 2: 405.

22. Ibid., 380.
23. Ibid., 402.
24. Ibid., 384.
25. Ibid., 396.
26. Ibid., 382.
27. Ibid., 409.
28. Ibid., 406.
29. Ibid., 421.
30. Ibid., 403.
31. Ibid., 393.
32. Ibid., 383.
33. Bestuzhev-Marlinskii, *Noch' na korable: Povesti i rasskazy*, 177.
34. Lermontov, *Sochineniia*, 2: 405.
35. Ibid., 407.
36. Ibid., 395.
37. Ibid., 380.
38. Ibid., 404.

39. Goscilo discusses the significant role played in the representation of characters in *Princess Ligovskaia* by the generic parameters of the physiological sketch; even the main character Pechorin, she notes, appears as "the specific example substantiating a general rule. As a social animal, he comes under the jurisdiction of the universal human laws that regulate all behavior" ("The First Pechorin En Route to *A Hero*: Lermontov's *Princess Ligovskaia*," 151). The physiological sketch, a major genre in Russian prose of the 1840s, will be discussed in chapter 4.

40. Shepard, "The Society Tale and the Innovative Argument in Russian Prose Fiction of the 1830s," 120.

41. Eikhenbaum notes that in the first chapters of *Princess Ligovskaia*, Lermontov introduces a large number of characters but "evidently hesitates in regards to the hero," which retards the plot: "Pechorin and the clerk Krasinsky compete for the status of hero; the narration advances with difficulty; the *fabula* gets complicated, the plot does not take shape" (*Lermontov: Opyt istoriko-literaturnoi otsenki*, 146).

42. Lermontov "insists upon Pechorin's superiority . . . *ad nauseam*, even though we see little of it in action." Goscilo, "The First Pechorin En Route to *A Hero*: Lermontov's *Princess Ligovskaia*," 155.

43. Heier, *Literary Portraiture in Nineteenth-Century Russian Prose*, 87. According to Heier, the physiognomic method consists in "an initial detailed description of the physical side of the hero, followed by a judgment and interpretation of the facial and bodily appearance from which the character's traits, the moral and psychological make-up, are deduced" (ibid.); on this subject see also Goscilo, "Lermontov's Debt to Lavater and Gall." For a thorough examina-

tion of French subtexts in *A Hero of Our Time*, see Meyer, *How the Russians Read the French: Lermontov, Dostoevsky, Tolstoy*, 34–88; Meyer discusses an explicit reference to Balzac's story "A Woman of Thirty," later incorporated into *Scenes from Private Life*; and stresses Balzac's physical ("physiological") description of characters (55). See also Tomashevskii, "Proza Lermontova i zapadnoevropeiskaia literaturnaia traditsiia," 43–44. The only extensive study devoted exclusively to Balzac's influence on Lermontov is "Lermontov and Balzac" by John Mersereau, who concludes: "More than just a spiritual godfather to Lermontov's prose art, Balzac deserves a place in his artistic genealogy which is closer than that of Chateaubriand or Scott and hardly more distant than that of Byron or Puškin" (257).

44. Heier, *Literary Portraiture in Nineteenth-Century Russian Prose*, 94. Particularly with regard to *Princess Ligovskaia*, Heier asserts that Lermontov's "use of Lavater's physiognomy in the Balzacian manner is too vivid to deny. . . . Throughout the novel there is a great concern with the art of reading thought or character. . . . In such cases, the essential element for physiognomic characterization is the face. . . . The constant references to facial expression and the ensuing interpretation reveal a conscious effort by Lermontov to read character traits via the physical expression" (ibid., 92–93). Goscilo, too, notes that "Lavater's theories of physiognomy . . . inform much of *Kniaginia Ligovskaia*. Clues to all the reality of the dramatis personae are contained in their physical appearance. . . . Throughout the work every play in facial expression is a signal of an emotional reaction or shift. Moods are gauged by pallor, blushes, trembling, twitches, and so forth" ("The First Pechorin En Route to *A Hero*: Lermontov's *Princess Ligovskaia*," 153–54). My analysis of *Princess Ligovskaia* shows that the narrator's expert attempts to proceed from face- to mind-reading through the use of physiognomy ultimately lead to his admission of the impassability of this route.

45. Cited in Shepard, "The Society Tale and the Innovative Argument in Russian Prose Fiction of the 1830s," 124. Shepard concludes: "During the early 1830s Balzac had delved into the private life of high society in a body of works which was of sufficient size, distinctiveness, and popularity to invite imitation, and had also repeatedly called attention to the theoretical premises on which those works rested and the devices employed in them, a practice which greatly enhanced their value as fictional prototypes" (124).

46. Jameson, *The Political Unconscious*, 166.

47. Ibid., 171.

48. Ibid., 167.

49. Ibid., 181.

50. In another conceptualization of Balzacian excess vis-à-vis the analytical method, Peter Brooks offers the epistemophilic paradigm, by which Balzac's characters' and narrators' pursuit of knowledge is not an interpretive exercise but a passion, a "lust to know," at the root of which, as in the Freudian scenario

of infantile development cited by Brooks, lies the eroticized search for the imaginary object (Brooks, "Balzac: Epistemophilia and the Collapse of the Restoration," 120.) Addressing Balzacian excess from a different angle entirely, Göran Blic questions the persistent view of Balzac as unparalleled observer, grounding the novelist's representational practice not in Lavater's physiognomy but in Mesmer's doctrine of animal magnetism; Blic argues that "within Balzac's mesmerist metaphysics the visible and observable world is a function of occult magnetic forces" (Blic, "The Occult Forces of Realism: Balzac, Mesmer, and Second Sight," 262). For her part, Andrea Goulet ("'Tomber dans le phénomène': Balzac's Optics of Narration") sees in Balzac the twin competing representational modes of observation and revelation.

51. Jameson, *The Political Unconscious*, 174–75.

52. Ibid., 183.

53. Ibid.

54. Lukács, "Balzac: Lost Illusions," 59–60.

55. Jameson, *The Political Unconscious*, 183.

56. Ibid.

57. Miller, "Balzac's Illusions Lost and Found," 170.

58. Ibid.

59. Ibid., 180.

60. Ibid., 172.

61. Ibid.

62. Ibid., 181.

63. Jameson, "*La Cousine Bette* and Allegorical Realism," 244.

64. Ibid.

65. "In *La Cousine Bette* . . . sexual energy which had previously been portrayed only indirectly, as it was invested in external symbolic objects such as money, furniture, or position, or by displacement, in the form of the various perversions, is for the first time treated directly in its primary manifestation." Ibid., 251.

66. Eikhenbaum, *Lermontov: opyt istoriko-literaturnoi otsenki*, 147.

67. See Todd, *Fiction and Society in the Age of Pushkin: Ideology, Institutions, and Narrative*, particularly chapter 4 (137–63), "*A Hero of Our Time*: The Caucasus as 'Amphitheater'"; and Cox, "Dramatic Genre as a Tool of Characterization in Lermontov's *A Hero of Our Time*." Goscilo directly links Pechorin's superb acting/directing abilities with his face-reading prowess: "His skill is so sophisticated that he can discriminate between Princess Mary's *assumed* coldness and her genuine pique when he rudely ignores her singing, and moreover, he himself can stimulate the passion so expertly that he dupes her utterly for as long as it suits his designs. . . . Pechorin is the most accomplished physiological psychologist in the novel, and that advantage is what gives him the upper hand in all his encounters" ("Lermontov's Debt to Lavater and Gall," 513).

68. Todd, *Fiction and Society in the Age of Pushkin: Ideology, Institutions, and Narrative*, 150.

69. Ibid., 149–50.

70. Ibid., 150, 151.

71. Frazier, *Romantic Encounters: Writers, Readers, and the Library for Reading*, 61.

72. Studies of *A Hero of Our Time*, particularly those considering it within the framework of irony, often underscore the reader's experience of suspension of cognitive and ethical certainty. For instance, Marie Gilroy speaks of the "demoralization of the reader" (*The Ironic Vision in Lermontov's "A Hero of Our Time,"* 36), and David Powelstock of the "seduction of the reader," a process wherein readerly expectations and desires for closure are evoked and then rejected (*Becoming Mikhail Lermontov: The Ironies of Romantic Individualism in Nicholas I's Russia*, 332–43). Both scholars discuss the significance of the work's structure for readerly activity thus configured. Complementing such irony-foregrounding examinations of the suspension of the search for meaning and morals in *A Hero of Our Time*, my analysis highlights the reader's release from spatiotemporal diversity, enabled by the work's narrative organization, as a necessary prerequisite of this suspension.

73. "Against the background of the traditional society tale," remarks Eikhenbaum, "it appears as a deviation or some kind of innovation that the novel is based on the paradoxical situation of 'I do not love you'" (*Lermontov: Opyt istoriko-literaturnoi otsenki*, 155).

74. Lermontov, *Sochineniia*, 2: 493.

75. Todd cites Lukács's classic formula of the incommensurability between novel hero and the world in which he moves to posit the mode of characterization in *A Hero of Our Time* as novelistic. Todd, *Fiction and Society in the Age of Pushkin: Ideology, Institutions, and Narrative*, 163.

76. Lermontov, *Sochineniia*, 2: 540.

CHAPTER FOUR

1. For a discussion of anti-romanticism as a thematic and structural principle in literature of the 1840s, see Mann, "Filosofiia i poetika 'natural'noi shkoly.'"

2. See, for instance, the three consecutive chapters on romanticism, the natural school, and the "age of realism" in Moser, *The Cambridge History of Russian Literature*, 136–332.

3. Given its focus on two distinct genres of 1830s–50s romantic and naturalist prose (the supernatural tale and the physiological sketch), the chapter does not address the historical and generic shifts within the Russian romantic movement as a whole. Likewise, discussion of Russian naturalism of the later nineteenth century, when this school was associated especially with the fiction of Émile Zola, exceeds the chapter's scope and critical concerns.

4. Watt, *The Rise of the Novel: Studies in Defoe, Richardson, and Fielding*, 31.

5. For instance, Andrew Hadfield, questioning the idea that the novel arose in response to modernity, examines earlier English prose fiction, particularly William Baldwin's *Beware the Cat* (1550s), and concludes that "the work makes an attempt to explore more general aspects of human behaviour than are strictly required by a religious allegory, that it does show an interest in the characters themselves [and] even . . . demonstrates aspects of 'formal realism' in its descriptions" (Hadfield, "What Was the First English Novel and What Does It Tell Us?" 30).

6. Baker, *Realism's Empire: Empiricism and Enchantment in the Nineteenth-Century Novel*, 13.

7. Ibid., 206.

8. Ibid., 208.

9. Cited ibid., 14.

10. Ibid., 205.

11. In his excellent analysis of the realist novel's character system, Alex Woloch explicates the formal problem inherent in Watt's "redundant profusion of 'particulars,'" a problem central, in Woloch's view, to the genre: "Once you are committed to 'particularity,' how do you curtail it?" (*The One vs. the Many: Minor Characters and the Space of the Protagonist in the Novel*, 19.) At the same time, Woloch does not deny that realism is possessed of "mimetic ambitions" and "empiricist aesthetics" (ibid., 20, 19); nor does he question the "achieved omniscient universe" of the realist novel (ibid., 246). Woloch speaks of the novel's own awareness of the tension between social inclusiveness and commitment to "particularity"; as a result, formal challenges of realism "are continuously manifested as themes, concerns, and 'stories' of the novels themselves" (ibid., 20). George Levine similarly emphasizes realism's heightened self-consciousness of the limitations of its own mimetic claims; but similarly forgoes any contestation of the notion that mimetic aspirations are central to realism's aesthetics. See Levine, *Realism, Ethics, and Secularism: Essays on Victorian Literature and Science*, chapter 7, "Realism," 185–209.

12. For a concise overview of contemporary conceptualizations of narrative realism, see Novak, *Realism, Photography, and Nineteenth-Century Fiction*, 154–55. Invoking a common critical distinction between realism's theory, or "project," and its practice, Novak observes that even the most recent studies of realism define this "project" as "devoted to representing the 'real' world outside of and unmediated by language" (ibid., 154); some of these studies examine the productive paradoxes that such a project entails, while others reject it as unfulfillable. Novak's own fascinating examination of the Victorian "photographic realism" redefines the "real" in both photography and fiction of the time as the "effacement of particularity" (ibid., 30). However, it is apparent that representation of consciousness is alien to photographic—or any visual arts—aesthetics,

even if one defines this aesthetics, as does Novak, in terms of anonymity and abstraction.

13. See Hamburger, *The Logic of Literature*; Banfield, *Unspeakable Sentences: Narration and Representation in the Language of Fiction*; and Banfield, "Where Epistemology, Style, and Grammar Meet Literary History." For an overview and concise critique of the author concept in contemporary literary theory, see the section "Signposts of Fictionality" in Cohn, *The Distinction of Fiction*, 123–31.

14. Cohn, *The Distinction of Fiction*, 125–26.

15. Bakhtin, *Art and Answerability: Early Philosophical Essays*, 14.

16. Nekrasov, *Fiziologiia Peterburga*, 132–33.

17. For a study of Butkov's works, see Hodgson, *From Gogol to Dostoevsky: Jakov Butkov, a Reluctant Naturalist in the 1840s*.

18. Butkov, *Peterburgskie vershiny*, 221.

19. In a feuilleton published in *Severnaia pchela*, no. 22, 1846.

20. Ibid., no. 34, 1847.

21. Ibid., no. 269, 1846.

22. Belinskii, *Polnoe sobranie sochinenii v 13 tomakh*, 10: 297.

23. Tseitlin, *Stanovlenie realizma v russkoi literature: Russkii fiziologicheskii ocherk*, 97.

24. On the influence of French prose of the 1840s (especially the *physiologie* and *roman-feuilleton*) on Russian literature of the time, see Hodgson, *From Gogol to Dostoevsky: Jakov Butkov, a Reluctant Naturalist in the 1840s*, 49–52.

25. "The Russian naturalists attempted to russify the French *physiologie* . . . . Nonetheless the realia of these sketches often bears a striking resemblance to the garrets and basements of Paris." Ibid., 50.

26. Vinogradov, *Evoliutsiia russkogo naturalizma: Gogol' i Dostoevskii*, 304.

27. Mann, "Filosofiia i poetika 'natural'noi shkoly,'" 272–73.

28. Efebovskii, "Peterburgskie raznoschiki," 434.

29. Cited in Tseitlin, *Stanovlenie realizma v russkoi literature: Russkii fiziologicheskii ocherk*, 169.

30. *Literaturnaia gazeta* 3 (1844): 45.

31. Dal', *Sochineniia*, 6: 271.

32. Shpilevaia, "Gil-Blaz 'peterburgskikh uglov' (K voprosu o zhanre i khudozhestvennom metode romana N. A. Nekrasova 'Zhizn' i pokhozhdeniia Tikhona Trosnikova')," 103.

33. Mann, "Filosofiia i poetika 'natural'noi shkoly,'" 273.

34. Nekrasov, *Fiziologiia Peterburga*, 142.

35. Ibid., 147.

36. Ibid.

37. Tseitlin, *Stanovlenie realizma v russkoi literature: Russkii fiziologicheskii ocherk*, 220–21. Gukovskii similarly asserts: "Instead of the novella or collection

of tales, there is a chain of sketches, contemporary reviews, a journal *Révue*" ("Neizdannye povesti Nekrasova v istorii russkoi prozy 1840-kh godov," 380).

38. Todorov, *The Fantastic: A Structural Approach to a Literary Genre*, 33.

39. The quintessential example of the fantastic in Russian fiction of the time is Pushkin's *The Queen of Spades* (*Pikovaia dama*, 1834). Notably, when Dostoevsky in a letter of 1880 calls this work "the pinnacle of the art of the fantastic," he uses the term precisely as does Todorov: "At the end of the story, that is, when you're finished reading, you don't know how to decide: did this vision come from Germann's nature, or is he really one of those people who has come into contact with another world, a world of evil spirits hostile to humanity. . . . Now, that is art!" (Dostoevskii, *Pis'ma v chetyrekh tomakh*, 4: 178.) Scholarly examinations that underscore the equal validity of rational (e.g., psychological) and supernatural interpretations of *The Queen of Spades* include, among others, Slonimskii, "Zakony pushkinskoi prozy"; Vinogradov, "Stil' 'Pikovoi damy'"; Bocharov, "Pikovaia dama"; and Emerson, "'The Queen of Spades' and the Open End."

40. Basom, "The Fantastic in Gogol's Two Versions of 'Portret,'" 431.

41. In her perceptive critique of Todorov's theory, Christine Brooke-Rose notes the scarcity of actual literary-historical examples of the fantastic supplied by Todorov—only two; nor is she convinced that one of these fully fits the definition. She suggests that the "pure Fantastic" be considered "not so much as an evanescent *genre* as an evanescent *element*: the hesitation as to the supernatural can last a short or a long moment and disappear with an explanation" ("Historical Genres/Theoretical Genres: A Discussion of Todorov on the Fantastic," 151; emphasis in original). Regardless of the validity of Brooke-Rose's qualification of Todorov's definition, the Russian supernatural tale of the 1820s–30s offers numerous texts in which figural and readerly "hesitation" never resolves, and which may thus be justifiably added to Todorov's examples of the "pure fantastic" genre.

42. Mikhail Epshtein's interpretation of the celebrated "patriotic passage" in *Dead Souls* provides the most striking example of this devilish encroachment; Gogol's "painfully sweet" image of Russia, he argues, contains distinctly demonic associations that literary critics from Belinsky on have failed to recognize. See Epshtein, "The Irony of Style: The Demonic Element in Gogol's Concept of Russia," 57.

43. Gippius, *Gogol'*, 33.

44. Gippius, *Ot Pushkina do Bloka*, 64.

45. Examining the role of Ukrainian puppet-theater (*vertep*) in the *Dikan'ka* cycle, Madhu Malik comes to a similar conclusion: "The Fair at Sorochintsy" is "predominantly lower-level, light-hearted fun, but at times acquires other overtones, as in the eerily dancing women at the end of the story" ("*Vertep* and the Sacred/Profane Dichotomy in Gogol's *Dikan'ka* Stories," 338).

46. See for instance Rowe, *Through Gogol's Looking Glass: Reverse Vision,*

False Focus, and Precarious Logic, 18–20; Fanger, *The Creation of Nikolai Gogol*, 92; and Mann, *Poetika Gogolia: Variatsii k teme*, 14–17, among others.

47. See Driessen, *Gogol as a Short-Story Writer: A Study of His Technique of Composition*, 69; Vaiskopf, *Siuzhet Gogolia: Morfologiia, Ideologiia, Kontekst*, 109; and Dmitrieva, "*Vechera na khutore bliz Dikan'ki*: Kommentarii," 695–96. Christopher Putney succinctly posits the omnipresence of devilry in the tale, upon the conclusion of which "the reader is invited to consider the young couple's future: will the newlyweds soon become the grotesque version of married life that Cherevik and Khivria represent? It seems likely. Is the couple's marriage brought about as a result of only a *hoax* concerning the devil? Might we not suggest that the devil—in a larger sense—may indeed be behind this union?" (*Russian Devils and Diabolic Conditionality in Nikolai Gogol's "Evenings on a Farm near Dikanka,"* 155.)

48. Gogol, *The Complete Tales*, 1: 20–21.

49. Ibid., 23.

50. Holquist, "The Devil in Mufti: The *Märchenwelt* in Gogol's Short Stories," 353.

51. Putney, *Russian Devils and Diabolic Conditionality in Nikolai Gogol's "Evenings on a Farm near Dikanka,"* 156.

52. Similar revision is taking place with regard to another *Dikan'ka* tale, one whose subject matter was formerly considered mundane against the background of the rest of the cycle; see Putney, "Gogol's Theology of Privation and the Devil in 'Ivan Fedorovich Shpon'ka and His Auntie,'" 84.

53. Epshtein, "The Irony of Style: The Demonic Element in Gogol's Concept of Russia," 61.

54. Valentsova, "O magicheskikh funktsiiakh kolokol'chika v traditsionnoi kul'ture slavian," 284.

55. Gogol, *The Complete Tales*, 1: 24–25.

56. Consequently, Putney's question cited above—"Might we not suggest that the devil—in a larger sense—may indeed be behind this union?"—can be seen as indicative of the tale's narrative organization *only* so long as it remains unanswered.

57. According to Delbert Phillips, "probably the first native Russian production in early horrific literature was Bestuzhev's 'A Page from the Diary of a Guard Officer' dated 1821" (Phillips, *Spook or Spoof?: The Structure of the Supernatural in Russian Romantic Tales*, 5). For N. Izmailov, Russian supernatural literature commences with Pogorel'sky's cycle *The Double, or My Evenings in Little Russia* (1828), which I discuss in detail in the text; see Izmailov, "Fantasticheskaia povest'."

58. Aksakov, "Val'ter Eizenberg: Zhizn' v mechte," 360.

59. Zagoskin, *Askol'dova mogila: Romany, povesti*, 596.

60. Olin, "Strannyi bal," 339.

61. Phillips notes the correlation between supernatural phenomena and realistic source of narration in the ending of Gogol's *The Overcoat* (*Shinel'*, 1842), wherein the emergence of a ghost on Petersburg streets is "couched in the form of rumors" (*Spook or Spoof?: The Structure of the Supernatural in Russian Romantic Tales*, 108).

62. Philips discusses (ibid., 117) these two works, and "Vii," as tales in which "transnormal phenomena . . . become wholly objectified since otherworldly beings are described by an omniscient eyewitness narrator who possesses conscious and independent perception of events. Numerous supernatural beings populate these stories, and the narratives may be constructed so as to express their own independent point of view." This typology ignores, however, the fact that these tales all have time- and place-specific narrators (even if somewhat hidden in the intricacies of cyclical narrative organization): the first two tales, along with "The Fair at Sorochintsy," are part of the *Dikan'ka* cycle, while "Vii" belongs to the cycle *Mirgorod*, subtitled "tales that continue *Evenings on a Farm near Dikan'ka*" (*Povesti, sluzhashchie prodolzheniem Vecherov na khutore bliz Dikan'ki*); narrative embedding is thus carried over from Gogol's first prose cycle to the next. Basom similarly takes no account of the framing of the *Dikan'ka* tales, asserting (in concurrence with Mann) that they are set in a past belonging to the "marvelous," insofar as "the supernatural intervenes directly" ("The Fantastic in Gogol's Two Versions of 'Portret,'" 432).

63. Pogorelsky, *The Double, or My Evenings in Little Russia*, 22.

64. Ibid., 20.

65. Ibid., 69–70.

66. For an insightful study of madness in *The Queen of Spades* in accordance with fantastic readings of Pushkin's novella, see Rosenshield, "Choosing the Right Card: Madness, Gambling, and Imagination in Pushkin's 'The Queen of Spades.'"

67. Greenleaf, *Pushkin and Romantic Fashion: Fragment, Elegy, Orient, Irony*, 46

68. Ibid., 45.

69. Frazier, *Romantic Encounters: Writers, Readers, and the Library for Reading*, 69.

70. Ibid., 10.

71. Ibid.

72. Frazier places at the center of her study of Russian romanticism Osip Senkovsky's literary periodical *Library for Reading*, envisioned as a "quintessentially Romantic form" (ibid., 2): "The library of the *Library for Reading* is first of all a literary genre. As an 'encyclopedic' journal, each issue of the *Library for Reading* gathered within its covers a great variety of printed material, including not just works of literature but also articles on science, industry, and agriculture. . . . The diversity that characterized the *Library for Reading* can . . . be

understood in entirely Romantic terms. Romanticism was largely driven by the search for a certain kind of literary genre, one marked by heterogeneity, fragmentariness, and infinite incompletion" (ibid., 125–26).

73. Greenleaf, *Pushkin and Romantic Fashion: Fragment, Elegy, Orient, Irony*, 343.

74. Ibid., 346.

75. Pogorelsky, *The Double, or My Evenings in Little Russia*, 20. The paradox of the peasant girls' "reveling" via "dejected" songs is unresolved in the text; but *unynie* (dejection) and nighttime *vesel'e* (revelry) may both be seen as effects, like the hero's boredom or his double's disregard for watches, of the arrest of narrated time.

76. Ibid., 26.

77. Some of the recent studies of realism question the "purity" of its adherence to spatiotemporal particularity, and foreground the presence of the fantastic within realist aesthetics. Ilya Vinitsky demonstrates Russian realist writers' interest in mysticism and spiritualism, contending that, despite these authors' denunciation of the phantoms of romanticism, such apparitions "did not disappear as the result of this realist exorcism; rather, they were tamed, absorbed by positivist rationalism, or they were 'hidden' in the depths of the work" (*Ghostly Paradoxes: Modern Spiritualism and Russian Culture in the Age of Realism*, xv). Vinitsky cites other examinations of the fantastic in realism, in particular, Nancy Trail's conclusion (*Possible Worlds of the Fantastic: The Rise of the Paranormal in Fiction*) that in realism, the fantastic is transformed into the paranormal; Terry Castle's thesis that the "aggressively rationalist imperatives" of the Enlightenment engendered the uncanny (*The Female Thermometer: The Eighteenth-Century Culture and the Invention of the Uncanny*, 8); and Michael Holquist's analogy between behind-the-scenes social forces of realism and the romantic supernatural ("The Supernatural as Social Force in *Anna Karenina*"). These studies, however, are primarily concerned with the depth and complexity of the realist story, or narrated events, rather than the discursive status of the realist novel's author, which is, I believe, where the realist novel's *own* fantastic is to be sought.

CHAPTER FIVE

1. Cohn, *Transparent Minds: Narrative Modes for Presenting Consciousness in Fiction*, 9.

2. Ibid., 8. Here Cohn cites other historians of the novel, particularly Erich Kahler and his positing of an "inward turn" in the genre's development.

3. Ibid.

4. For a different explication of Cohn's literary-historical insights, see McHale, "Islands in the Stream of Consciousness," 184–85.

5. Cohn, *Transparent Minds: Narrative Modes for Presenting Consciousness in Fiction*, 6.

6. Ibid., 22.

7. Ibid., 21–22.

8. Ibid., 59, 58.

9. Ibid., 60.

10. Ibid., 60.

11. Ibid., 26.

12. Ibid., 25–26.

13. Zunshine, *Why We Read Fiction: Theory of Mind and the Novel*, 4; emphasis in original.

14. Ibid., 6.

15. For another concise account of the humanities' "cognitive turn," see Palmer, "Social Minds in Fiction and Criticism," 199–201. Palmer formulates (200) the basic assumption of cognitive approaches to fictional minds thus: "If [the] real-mind disciplines can assist our study of fictional minds, then that is fine; if they cannot, then there is no reason to use them. However, it has been my experience that we understand fictional minds much better when we apply to them some of the work done on real minds by psychologists, philosophers, and cognitive scientists."

16. Ibid., 211.

17. Palmer, "The Construction of Fictional Minds," 29. Zunshine similarly remarks that one of the "pleasure[s] afforded by fictional narratives" is the "respite" that its "successful testing of our mind-reading adaptations . . . offers us from our everyday mind-reading uncertainties" (*Why We Read Fiction: Theory of Mind and the Novel*, 20); but at the same time, her argument is concerned with the ways in which "the joys of reading fictional minds are subject to some of the same instabilities that render our real-life mind-reading both exciting and exasperating" (ibid.).

18. Palmer, "The Construction of Fictional Minds," 30.

19. Palmer's "Social Minds in Fiction and Criticism" is based largely on his book *Social Minds in the Novel* (Columbus: Ohio State University Press, 2010), and was published in *Style* as a target essay along with responses from other scholars and a concluding rejoinder from the author.

20. Cohn, *Transparent Minds: Narrative Modes for Presenting Consciousness in Fiction*, 8.

21. Ibid., 22. Turgenev scholars emphasize his restraint in presenting interiority, his allegiance rather to the visible and audible manifestations of it not only in his early works, but in mature prose as well. For instance, Donna Orwin, referring to Henry James's formulation that, in reading Turgenev, "we are always looking and listening," speaks of Turgenev's concern to "protect [subjectivity]," his assumption of the "stance of an observer who never describes the inner life

of his characters in detail or precisely," allowing instead for the "reality of subjectivity [to disclose] itself in dress, in gestures, in settings, as well as in word and action" (*Consequences of Consciousness: Turgenev, Dostoevsky, and Tolstoy*, 41–42). Indeed, according to Willem Weststeijn ("The Description of the Appearance of Characters in Turgenev's Novels [in particular, *Fathers and Sons*]"), the highly detailed descriptions of characters' appearances in Turgenev's novels attest to the influence of Lavater's physiognomic principles. For more on the opacity of interiority in Turgenev, see Costlow, *Worlds within Worlds: The Novels of Ivan Turgenev*, particularly chapter 1, "Rhetoric and Sincerity: Turgenev and the Poetics of Silence." My examination, on the contrary, focuses precisely on Turgenev's instances of unmediated consciousness presentation, the paucity of which render them all the more significant for elucidating moments of transition from one narrative mode to another.

22. On the narrative organization of *A Sportsman's Sketches* and, specifically, the persona of the narrator, see Grossman, "Rannii zhanr Turgeneva"; Reid, "*A Hunter's Sketches*: A Peircean Perspective"; Masing-Delic, "Hidden Spaces in Turgenev's Short Prose: What They Conceal and What They Show"; and Orwin, *Consequences of Consciousness: Turgenev, Dostoevsky, and Tolstoy*, 34–45.

23. Frost, "Turgenev's 'Mumu' and the Absence of Love," 51. Other interpretations of Gerasim's fate as that of defeat include, for instance, Seeley, *Turgenev: A Reading of His Fiction*, 122–23.

24. Frost, "Turgenev's 'Mumu' and the Absence of Love," 53.

25. Zimovets, *Molchanie Gerasima: Psikhoanaliticheskie i filosofskie esse o russkoi kul'ture*, 15.

26. Turgenev, *The Novels of Ivan Turgenev*, 11: 403.

27. Ibid., 357

28. Ibid., 403.

29. See Zhitova, *Vospominaniia o sem'e I. S. Turgeneva*, 76–82.

30. See, for instance, Marantsman, "Povest' I. S. Turgeneva 'Mumu' v chitatel'skom vospriiatii shkol'nikov."

31. For instance: "It was a tragic day when Gerasim and Mumu sailed away in the boat. Eroshka, who had been following them, ran off in order to tell everyone about the death of the dog. But Gerasim was not going to drown Mumu. They sailed until they reached the shore. *No one suspected that the two friends escaped.* When the people on the estate learned that the serf had run away, the mistress had a stroke and died. At the outskirts of the village, Gerasim and Mumu lived happily ever after." Ekaterina Siniavskaia, website of the *Mumu* project of Chekhov Gymnasium #2 (Taganrog, Rostov region), http://gimnazia.narod.ru/tvorim/mumu.htm; emphasis mine.

32. Which interpretation reaches its apex in the following passage from a student's essay: "The peasant let the mistress know (by signs) that he was leaving,

that even should he be threatened with death, he was going home. The old lady understood it this way: 'I am leaving despite serfdom. If you have even a drop of conscience, let me go.' The mistress started to cry and couldn't help but let him leave" (Aleksandra Kriulenko, website of the *Mumu* project of Chekhov Gymnasium #2). Such imagined scenarios demonstrate the insufficiency of the interpretation of Gerasim as rebel, the considerable modifications Turgenev's story would need to undergo in order for such a reading to work.

33. Noting this detail as well, the children recasting Gerasim as a rebel move it to its "proper" place in the narrative (citing from the website of the *Mumu* project of Chekhov Gymnasium #2): "When the mistress ordered him to kill Mumu, Gerasim had been thinking a lot about what to do. He decided that no matter what, he would take Mumu and leave the mistress. *He packed his belongings*, called Mumu, and left for his native village" (Nadezhda Shirokobokova; emphasis mine). Or: "Then the mistress ordered him to kill Mumu. When Gerasim learned about this, he decided to run away with Mumu. Night came. *Gerasim packed his belongings*, put Mumu in his bosom. They quickly left the house and headed toward the village" (Iana Boltenkova; emphasis mine).

34. Seeley notes that Gerasim "suffers perforce in silence: we can only guess what he feels, we can hardly guess what he thinks" (*Turgenev: A Reading of His Fiction*, 123), but does not further develop this observation on the character's incomprehensibility.

35. Turgenev, *The Novels of Ivan Turgenev*, 11: 389.

36. Ibid., 376.

37. Ibid., 356.

38. Frost, "Turgenev's 'Mumu' and the Absence of Love," 41.

39. Ibid.

40. Turgenev, *The Novels of Ivan Turgenev*, 11: 379.

41. Kolotaev, *Poetika destruktivnogo erosa*, 351.

42. In this light, *Moo-moo*, rather than the currently accepted *Mumu*, would more properly render Turgenev's title in English, preserving the Russian original's complete phonetic and orthographic identity between Gerasim's bovine pronouncement and the dog's name.

43. Turgenev, *The Novels of Ivan Turgenev*, 11: 379.

44. Ibid., 363.

45. Ibid., 389.

46. Ibid., 403.

47. Ibid., 406.

48. Indeed, *zhivet . . . bobylem* could also be translated, without the disconsolate tinge of "a lonely man," via the literal rendering of "is living as a solitary or landless peasant."

49. Turgenev, *A Hunter's Sketches*, 216.

50. "It was two years after my visit that Pantelei Eremeich's troubles

began—his real troubles. Disappointments, disasters, even misfortunes he had had before that time, but he had paid no attention to them and had risen superior to them in former days" (ibid., 218).

51. Paraphrase of the narrator's statement in "Chertopkhanov and Nedopiuskin" (*Zapiski okhotnika*, 300) that he "began to gather information" (*nachal navodit' spravki*); the narrator frequently uses such wording (*sobirat', navodit' spravki*) in other tales as well.

52. Turgenev, *A Hunter's Sketches*, 218.

53. Ibid., 220.

54. Ibid., 223.

55. Ibid., 241–42.

56. Cohn, *Transparent Minds: Narrative Modes for Presenting Consciousness in Fiction*, 59–60.

57. Turgenev, *A Hunter's Sketches*, 222.

58. Ibid., 223.

59. Ibid., 241–42.

60. Ibid., 222.

61. Ibid., 228.

62. Ibid., 238–39.

63. Peterson, "The Completion of *A Sportsman's Sketches*: Turgenev's Parting Word," 54.

64. Delaney, "Turgenev's Sportsman: Experiment in Unity," 20.

65. Grossman, "Turgenev's Early Genre," 69.

66. Ibid., 69. For a recent examination of the significance of the dramatic generic mode and narrative techniques in Turgenev, see Wiggins, "The Drama in Disguise: Dramatic Modes of Narration and Textual Structure in the Mid-Nineteenth-Century Russian Novel."

67. Grossman, "Rannii zhanr Turgeneva," 249. Specifically, "the aging Turgenev learned to construct a short story after the long experience of his novels and stories, after many years of great attention to the development of the European novella, after friendship, conversations, and correspondence with the 'infallible' Flaubert." Cited from a translated excerpt from this work: Grossman, "Turgenev's Early Genre," 69.

68. Letter to Stasiulevich, September 20/October 2, 1872, in Grishunin, Dolotova, and Smirnova, "*Zapiski okhotnika*: *Primechaniia*," 600.

69. Ibid.

70. Ibid.

71. Ibid.

72. *Russkoe obozrenie* no. 5 (1898): 23.

73. Letter to Pavel Annenkov, October 25/November 6, 1872; Grishunin, Dolotova, and Smirnova, "*Zapiski okhotnika*: *Primechaniia*," 602. For a detailed publication history of "The End of Chertopkhanov," see ibid., 599–602.

For more on Annenkov's evaluation of *Sketches* and "The End's" place therein, see Orwin, *Consequences of Consciousness: Turgenev, Dostoevsky, and Tolstoy*, 35–36.

74. Turgenev, *A Hunter's Sketches*, 209.

75. Grossman remarks ("Turgenev's Early Genre," 69) that the "whole composition of the story is built . . . on a chain of disasters."

76. Turgenev, *A Hunter's Sketches*, 228.

77. Ibid., 236–37.

78. Ibid., 242.

79. Ibid., 243–44.

80. Cohn, *Transparent Minds: Narrative Modes for Presenting Consciousness in Fiction*, 100.

CHAPTER SIX

1. Ehre, *Oblomov and His Creator: The Life and Art of Ivan Goncharov*, 87. For a detailed history of the novel's creation and publication, see ibid., 86–90; and Geiro, "Istoriia sozdaniia i publikatsii romana *Oblomov*." Goncharov himself gives a brief summary of this history in a letter to Vladimir Stasov of October 27, 1888; in other letters, he elaborates on various stages of the writing process. See Goncharov, "Correspondence Related to *Oblomov*," 159.

2. Ehre, *Oblomov and His Creator: The Life and Art of Ivan Goncharov*, 162.

3. Ibid., 155.

4. Peace, *Oblomov: A Critical Examination of Goncharov's Novel*, 6. See also Wiggins's chapter on Oblomov in "The Drama in Disguise: Dramatic Modes of Narration and Textual Structure in the Mid-Nineteenth-Century Russian Novel."

5. Dobroliubov, "Chto takoe oblomovshchina?" 47. The critic emphasized, however, that his purported review of Goncharov's novel was intended to be "not about Oblomov, but only on the subject of Oblomov" (*ne ob Oblomove, a tol'ko po povodu Oblomova*) (ibid., 35); he did not set for himself the task of explicating the work's aesthetic complexity, but rather the sociohistorical issues it evoked.

6. Tseitlin, *Stanovlenie realizma v russkoi literature: Russkii fiziologicheskii ocherk*, 113.

7. Goncharov, *Oblomov*, 78.

8. Peace, *Oblomov: A Critical Examination of Goncharov's Novel*, 29.

9. Goncharov, *Oblomov*, 16.

10. Ingrid Kleespies discusses the role of travel in *Oblomov* and analyzes Goncharov's aborted plan to send Oblomov on a voyage abroad in *A Nation Astray: Nomadism and National Identity in Russian Literature*, chapter 4 (113–43).

11. Goncharov, "Correspondence Related to *Oblomov*," 147–48. Diment notes that although "Oblomov's Dream" was the first segment of the work to be published, "Goncharov's memoirs suggest that several initial chapters of the novel were written before the completion of the dream" ("The Precocious Talent of Ivan Goncharov," 44).

12. One of the key figures of Russian literary life of the 1850s, Aleksandr Druzhinin, remarks on this incongruence in his 1859 review of *Oblomov*, published in the *Library for Reading*: "Between the Oblomov who mercilessly torments his Zakhar and the Oblomov in love with Olga . . . there is a whole chasm. . . . Having worked, and worked hard, on an impossible task, Mr. Goncharov was finally convinced that . . . he would be unable to fill the chasm between the two Oblomovs. . . . Convinced of this, the novel's author gave up the matter as hopeless [*makhnul rukoi*] and inscribed under the first part of the novel the all-explaining number 1849" ("*Oblomov*: Roman I. A. Goncharova," 113–14). Indeed, when publishing *Oblomov* in *Notes of the Fatherland*, Goncharov marked part 1 with the date 1849; parts 2 and 3 with 1857; and part 4 with 1857–58; see Nedzvetskii, *Roman Goncharova* Oblomov: *Putevoditel' po tekstu*, 14. Notably, according to Druzhinin, the "first" Oblomov of 1849 is present "do samogo 'Sna,'" that is, "right up to" the dream narrative of chapter 9 ("*Oblomov*: Roman I. A. Goncharova," 114).

13. Goncharov, *Oblomov*, 161.

14. For a detailed examination of Goncharov's revisions of part 1, see Geiro, "Istoriia sozdaniia i publikatsii romana *Oblomov*"; in particular, Geiro notes that Goncharov significantly reduced some of the most glaring features of naturalist discourse, for instance, detailed physiological descriptions of Tarant'ev, Zakhar, Alekseev, and Oblomov himself.

15. For a concise summary of critical approaches taken toward the dream narrative in *Oblomov*, see Klein, "Zur Interpretation von Gončarovs *Oblomov*: Der Traum und das Unbewußte," 136–37. Most of the studies cited are concerned with this narrative's thematic and stylistic components. For his part, Klein convincingly argues that the dream introduces the hero's childhood not merely in order to establish the earliest factors determining his development and way of life (such groundwork-laying, a feature of naturalist poetics, in and of itself would not require a dream format); instead, according to Klein, the dream narrative grants the hero a psychological substratum, namely, that of the unconscious (144–45).

16. Pearl trans. of *Oblomov*, 81.

17. States, *Dreaming and Storytelling*, 43–44.

18. For a discussion of the Russian supernatural tale of the 1820–30s and the problem of the fantastic in fiction of the period, see chapter 4.

19. Goncharov, *Oblomov*, 79.

20. For a meticulous analysis of the "exceptional moment of uninhibited lyr-

icism and rhetorical expansiveness without deflating irony" at the beginning of "Oblomov's Dream," see Ehre, *Oblomov and His Creator: The Life and Art of Ivan Goncharov*, 173–74.

21. States, *Dreaming and Storytelling*, 56.

22. Ibid., 89.

23. For a concise discussion of the subject of the dream experience, see Paperno, *Stories of the Soviet Experience: Memoirs, Diaries, Dreams*, 163; in particular, Paperno cites Jung's conceptualization of dream figures as "personified features of the dreamer's own personality" and his definition of dreaming as "a theater in which the dreamer is the scene, the player, the prompter, the producer, the author, the public, and the critic."

24. Galya Diment reaches a similar conclusion with regard to the narrative perspective in "Oblomov's Dream": "If the sentiments expressed in the opening of the dream are so much like Oblomov's own (and, sometimes, even couched in strikingly Oblomovian language), and if it is, after all, *his* dream, as seen through *his* dormant eyes, would it not be logical to assume that the narrator here may be Oblomov himself or, at the very least, that it is Oblomov's point of view that is being reflected?" ("The Precocious Talent of Ivan Goncharov," 21–22; emphasis in original.) In the elevated style of the beginning of "Oblomov's Dream," Diment perceives elements of the character's speech, of Oblomov's "tendency to ask himself repeated, often rhetorical, questions and his penchant for exclamations" (ibid., 44). Ehre, too, speaks of the narrator's "relinquish[ing] 'point of view' to the mind of the dreaming hero" (*Oblomov and His Creator: The Life and Art of Ivan Goncharov*, 209). I view this convergence with the character's perspective as in effect "required" of the narrator by the architectonics of dream narration, namely, its single-option discursive stance.

25. Paperno addresses the question of the analogy between dream and fiction in *Stories of the Soviet Experience*, 162–64; some aspects of correspondence include "the use of images to symbolize thoughts, feelings, and situations; the transformation of one image into an expression for another; the creation of sequential narrative by fusing concordance and discordance; and for probing the reality of our lives" (162). My own interest in this analogy concerns the discursive perspective of the fictional dream's narration. I emphasize that this perspective enables the convergence of the narrator's and dreamer's viewpoints on dream-events, and it is in this convergence that dream narration and fiction (specifically, novelistic discourse) are particularly akin.

26. Lounsbery, "The World on the Back of a Fish: Mobility, Immobility, and Economics in *Oblomov*," 43.

27. Ehre, *Oblomov and His Creator: The Life and Art of Ivan Goncharov*, 163.

28. States, "Bizarreness in Dreams and Other Fictions," 14.

29. Cited ibid.

30. Nerval, "Aurélia, or Dream and Life," 265.

31. Pearl trans. of *Oblomov*, 81–82.

32. Ibid., 309.

33. Ibid., 235. Holmgren remarks ("Questions of Heroism in Goncharov's *Oblomov*," 85) that Olga "reverses and revises male-female roles in playing Pygmalion to Oblomov's unprepossessing Galatea."

34. Pearl trans. of *Oblomov*, 323–24.

35. Holmgren, "Questions of Heroism in Goncharov's *Oblomov*," 84.

36. Ehre, "Goncharov," 179.

37. Givens, "Wombs, Tombs, and Mother Love: A Freudian Reading of Goncharov's *Oblomov*," 101. According to Holmgren, Goncharov "draw[s] Olga's character schematically, although without Stolz's obvious and unerring syntheses. She is present more as potential than solution" ("Questions of Heroism in Goncharov's *Oblomov*," 85).

38. Pearl trans. of *Oblomov*, 328.

39. Ibid., 327.

40. Ibid., 426.

41. Christine Borowec singles out two opposing patterns of temporality in the novel: one, associated with Oblomov, is cyclical or repetitive; the other, associated with Stolz and Olga, linear or progressive. See Borowec, "Time after Time: The Temporal Ideology of *Oblomov*."

42. Diment, "The Precocious Talent of Ivan Goncharov," 3.

43. Dobroliubov, "Chto takoe oblomovshchina?" 47.

44. For a summary of such readings, see Givens, "Wombs, Tombs, and Mother Love: A Freudian Reading of Goncharov's *Oblomov*"; and LeBlanc, "Oblomov's Consuming Passion: Food, Eating, and the Search for Communion."

45. Lounsbery, "The World on the Back of a Fish: Mobility, Immobility, and Economics in *Oblomov*," 50.

46. Ibid. One prominent representative of this line of thought is Apollon Grigor'ev. Though Grigor'ev never devoted an essay exclusively to *Oblomov*, such critical works of his as "I. S. Turgenev and His Work: On the Novel *A Nest of the Gentry*" ("I. S. Turgenev i ego deiatel'nost: Po povodu romana 'Dvorianskoe gnezdo,'" 1859) and "After Ostrovsky's *Storm*" ("Posle 'Grozy' Ostrovskogo," 1860) contain a number of passages that discuss Goncharov's novel.

47. Lounsbery, "The World on the Back of a Fish: Mobility, Immobility, and Economics in *Oblomov*," 64.

48. Here I refer to another (along with Dobroliubov's "What Is Oblomovism?") influential piece of radical literary criticism, Nikolai Chernyshevsky's "The Russian at a Rendezvous: Reflections on Reading Mr. Turgenev's Novella *Asia*" ("Russkii Chelovek na Rendez-vous: Razmyshleniia po prochteniiu povesti g. Turgeneva 'Asia'"), published in the literary journal *Atheneum* in 1858. Though the essay is devoted specifically to a Turgenev protagonist, Chernyshevsky makes

clear that such individuals' key traits, especially their inability to bridge the gap between their armchair exalted ideals and the risk- and decisiveness-requiring world of reality makes them representative of whole groups of characters portrayed in contemporaneous fiction, some of whom he cites. On the level of plot development, the character under discussion reveals his moral weakness and cowardice when he fails the woman he loves, unable to respond in kind to her fervor and devotion. Goncharov's novel was published a year after Chernyshevsky's essay, but there is no doubt that the critic would have included Oblomov in this group.

49. Ehre, *Oblomov and His Creator: The Life and Art of Ivan Goncharov*, 160.

50. Pearl trans. of *Oblomov*, 54.

51. Ibid., 54.

52. Ibid., 62.

53. Ibid., 418.

54. Givens's and LeBlanc's overviews of psychoanalytic readings of the novel, specifically of the Oblomov-Agaf'ia relationship, have already been mentioned. According to Givens, Agaf'ia represents a "forbidden mother" whom the hero marries to "complete his regression and fulfill his Oedipal wish" ("Wombs, Tombs, and Mother Love: A Freudian Reading of Goncharov's *Oblomov*," 101). LeBlanc examines food imagery in the novel and argues that in his attraction to Agaf'ia, Oblomov strives to recapture the oral stage of his infantile past; his new wife "becomes at once his surrogate mother and nanny substitute" ("Oblomov's Consuming Passion: Food, Eating, and the Search for Communion," 129).

55. Pearl trans. of *Oblomov*, 337.

56. Ibid.

57. Aikhenval'd, *Siluety russkikh pisatelei*, 135. One of the first critics to liken Goncharov to a Flemish master was Aleksandr Druzhinin ("*Oblomov*: Roman I. A. Goncharova," 112). Comparing Gogol's and Goncharov's "concern with the pettiness of so many people's lives," Vsevolod Setchkarev states that the crucial difference between the two writers is that "Gogol regards the myriad of petty cares plaguing man as machinations of the devil, whereas Goncharov sees the possibility of attaching positive value to them" (*Ivan Goncharov: His Life and His Works*, 156). For his part, Ehre notes that "a lyrical apprehension of the things of domesticity is pervasive" in *Oblomov* (*Oblomov and His Creator: The Life and Art of Ivan Goncharov*, 215).

58. Lounsbery, "The World on the Back of a Fish: Mobility, Immobility, and Economics in *Oblomov*," 63; emphasis in original.

59. Pearl trans. of *Oblomov*, 68.

60. Ibid., 429.

61. Givens, "Wombs, Tombs, and Mother Love: A Freudian Reading of Goncharov's *Oblomov*," 102.

62. Kleespies, *A Nation Astray: Nomadism and National Identity in Russian Literature*, 142.

63. Ibid.

64. Pearl trans. of *Oblomov*, 427. Oblomov's uttering "quietly" here may convey, in English, too strictly a physical meaning of *pokoino*, which original especially emphasizes the speaker's tranquil inner state.

65. Ibid., 432.

66. Ibid., 429.

67. Ibid., 433.

68. Goncharov, *Oblomov*, 380.

69. Pearl trans. of *Oblomov*, 433.

70. Goncharov, *Oblomov*, 380.

71. Pearl trans. of *Oblomov*, 435.

72. Peace states that the description of the littérateur is a "thinly disguised authorial portrait" (*Oblomov: A Critical Examination of Goncharov's Novel*, 7). Diment notes that "this description fits Oblomov as well" ("The Precocious Talent of Ivan Goncharov," 21).

73. Pearl trans. of *Oblomov*, 436.

AFTERWORD AND AFTERWARD

1. In Shklovsky's formulation: "The devices by which Tolstoi estranges his material may be boiled down to the following: he does not call a thing by its name, that is, he describes it as if it were perceived for the first time, while the incident is described as if it were happening for the first time. In addition, he foregoes the conventional names of the various parts of a thing, replacing them instead with the names of corresponding parts in other things" ("Art as Device," 6). While arguing that estranged perception plays a crucial role in aesthetic experience generally, Shklovsky also posits this "device" as central to Tolstoy's poetics, adducing most of his illustrations of the concept from Tolstoy's works.

2. Tolstoy, *War and Peace*, 498.

3. Ibid., 244.

4. Shklovsky, "Art as Device," 5.

5. Shklovskii, *Material i stil' v proizvedeniiakh L'va Tolstogo*, 119–20.

6. Ginzburg, "Making Things Strange: The Prehistory of a Literary Device," 18. In Edward Wasiolek's interpretation of the opera episode, estrangement is understood as a way of exposing the hypocrisy of societal conventions that occlude Natasha's moral integrity: "Surrounded by falseness, encouraged by example, she is led to accept what the world approves rather than what her heart approves. In the absence of the real, she is unable to recognize what is unreal" (*Tolstoy's Major Fiction*, 109). Natasha's perception of the opera is taken as a flash of truth: Wasiolek refers to the performance as "the nonsense that is going

on on the stage" (ibid., 108). Similarly, according to Gary Saul Morson, Tolstoy "describes the perspective of a naïf in a battle (or at an opera) as the most accurate one" (*Hidden in Plain View: Narrative and Creative Potentials in "War and Peace,"* 166).

7. Several recent studies examine the broader contexts of Shklovskian estrangement. For instance, in a special issue of *Poetics Today* devoted to "Estrangement Revisited" (its subtitle), Michael Holquist and Ilya Kliger situate the concept within the post-Kantian philosophical debate on the role of language in epistemology ("Minding the Gap: Toward a Historical Poetics of Estrangement"); and in "Shklovsky's *ostranenie*, Bakhtin's *vnenakhodimost'* (How Distance Serves an Aesthetics of Arousal Differently from an Aesthetics Based on Pain)," Caryl Emerson juxtaposes Shklovsky's estrangement and Bakhtin's outsideness as two different conceptualizations of distancing in aesthetic activity. Douglas Robinson's book-length study (*Estrangement and the Somatics of Literature: Tolstoy, Shklovsky, Brecht*) presents a comparative analysis of the notions of estrangement and alienation in Russian and German aesthetic theories.

8. Tolstoy, *War and Peace*, 244.

9. Tolstoi, *Sobranie sochinenii v dvadtsati tomakh*, 5: 176–77.

10. Tolstoy, *War and Peace*, 502–3.

11. Ibid., 244.

12. Ibid., 499.

13. See, for instance, Patricia Garden's reading: "For Andrei the sky represents an emptying of self. Only by turning away to the eternal can he empty himself of the worldly dreams of glory that stand in the way of the development of his inner man" ("The Expressive Self in *War and Peace*," 529). According to Morson's analysis of this "crucial and famous scene," the relationship between Prince Andrei's estranged perception of the soldiers' struggle and his vision of the lofty heavens is one of contrast: "an interrupted narrative followed by a timeless lesson, a lesson on the pettiness and falsity of everything that might be narrated" (*Hidden in Plain View: Narrative and Creative Potentials in "War and Peace,"* 163).

14. Tolstoy, *War and Peace*, 244.

15. Ibid.

16. Ibid., 236.

17. Ibid., 242.

18. Ibid., 252.

19. Ibid., 504.

20. Ibid., 514.

21. Ibid., 244.

22. Tolstoi, *Sobranie sochinenii v dvadtsati tomakh*, 4: 379.

23. Tolstoy, *War and Peace*, 513.

24. Tolstoi, *Sobranie sochinenii v dvadtsati tomakh*, 5: 384.

25. Melissa Frazier notes that a number of prominent Tolstoy scholars—from Chernyshevsky to Eikhenbaum to Ginzburg—emphasize that Tolstoy is interested not so much in the content of his characters' psychological states, but rather the process of changes therein, the "mechanism" that brings about "a hundred-and-eighty degree turn from" a previous outlook ("De-Familiarizing the Tolstoy of Formalism," 153). Frazier also identifies the affinities between Tolstoy's and the formalists' views on the philosophy of history, whether personal, social, or universal: "Both Tolstoy and Formalism present history as an unceasing flow which under closer scrutiny reveals itself to be an infinite succession of antithetical states. . . . This history is apparently chaotic, but is yet not entirely inexplicable or unpredictable; there are laws to its succession of states, and it is these laws which both Tolstoy and Formalism set out to find" (ibid., 148). My analysis of sequences of antithetical states in *War and Peace* suggests that in the pattern of these states' succession, an important role is played by estrangement—understood as a two-sided process of (de-)symbolization, rather than a device of delegitimization or of sensitizing habitual perception.

26. Vadim Rudnev emphasizes the instrumentality of estrangement, demonstrating that it could have been applied, for instance, to Natasha's first ball (in the novel as written, perceived by Natasha as magical, that is, in the same terms broadly accepted for such an institution): "Women in white long dresses and men in pantaloons approached one another, then started to spin around one another, bow and bounce to the music, and so on" ("Depersonalizatsiia, ili psikhicheskaia anestiziia (L. N. Tolstoi i V. B. Shklovskii)," 60).

27. In his reading of *After the Ball*, Justin Weir points out that the story "comes after the major realist fiction, a kind of metafictional commentary on its goals and methods" (*Leo Tolstoy and the Alibi of Narrative*, 174).

28. Tolstoy, "After the Ball," 271.

29. Ibid., 274.

30. Ibid., 279.

31. Ibid., 271.

32. Ibid., 275.

33. Ibid., 276 (trans. of first sentence is mine; missing in *Tolstoy's Short Fiction*).

34. Ibid.

35. Ibid.

36. Ibid., 277.

37. Ibid., 277–78.

38. Ibid., 277, 279.

39. Ibid., 279. For a different interpretation of the protagonist's "excess of love quantity" and its textual consequences, see Zholkovsky, "Before and After 'After the Ball.'"

40. Tolstoy, "After the Ball," 279.

41. Ibid.
42. Ibid.
43. Ibid., 271.
44. Ibid., 279.
45. Bakhtin, *Art and Answerability: Early Philosophical Essays*, 14.

Works Cited

Aikhenval'd, Iulii. *Siluety russkikh pisatelei*. Berlin: Slovo, 1923.

Aksakov, Konstantin. "Val'ter Eizenberg: zhizn' v mechte." In *Russkaia romanticheskaia povest' pisatelei 20–40 godov XIX veka*, edited by V. I. Sakharov, 343–62. Moscow: Pressa, 1992.

Alber, Jan, Stefan Iversen, Henrik Skov Nielsen, and Brian Richardson. "Unnatural Narratives, Unnatural Narratology: Beyond Mimetic Models." *Narrative* 18, no. 2 (May 2010): 113–36.

Alter, Robert. *Fielding and the Nature of the Novel*. Cambridge, Mass.: Harvard University Press, 1968.

———. *Partial Magic: The Novel as a Self-Conscious Genre*. Berkeley: University of California Press, 1975.

Baker, Geoffrey. *Realism's Empire: Empiricism and Enchantment in the Nineteenth-Century Novel*. Columbus: Ohio University Press, 2009.

Bakhtin, Mikhail. *Art and Answerability: Early Philosophical Essays*. Edited by Michael Holquist and Vadim Liapunov. Translated by Vadim Liapunov. Austin: University of Texas Press, 1990.

———. *The Dialogic Imagination: Four Essays*. Edited by Michael Holquist. Translated by Caryl Emerson and Michael Holquist. Austin: University of Texas Press, 1981.

———. "Slovo v romane." In *Voprosy literatury i estetiki*, by Mikhail Bakhtin, 72–233. Moscow: Khudozhestvennaia literatura, 1975.

Banfield, Ann. *Unspeakable Sentences: Narration and Representation in the Language of Fiction*. London: Routledge and Kegan Paul, 1982.

———. "Where Epistemology, Style, and Grammar Meet Literary History." *New Literary History* 9, no. 3 (1978): 415–54.

Barthes, Roland. *The Pleasure of the Text*. Translated by Richard Miller. New York: Hill and Wang, 1975.

Basom, Anne Marie. "The Fantastic in Gogol's Two Versions of 'Portret.'" *Slavic and East European Journal* 38, no. 3 (1994): 419–37.

Belinskii, Vissarion. *Polnoe sobranie sochinenii v 13 tomakh*. Moscow: AN SSSR, 1953–59.

Bender, John. "Making the World Safe for Narratology: A Reply to Dorrit Cohn." *New Literary History* 26, no. 1 (1995): 29–33.

Bestuzhev-Marlinskii, Aleksandr. *Noch' na korable: Povesti i rasskazy*. Moscow: Khudozhestvennaia literatura, 1988.

———. *Sochineniia v dvukh tomakh*. Moscow: Khudozhestvennaia literatura, 1958.

Bethea, David M., and Sergei Davydov. "Pushkin's Saturnine Cupid: The Poetics of Parody in *The Tales of Belkin*." *PMLA* 96, no. 1 (January 1981): 8–21.

Blic, Göran. "The Occult Forces of Realism: Balzac, Mesmer, and Second Sight." *Studies in Eighteenth Century Culture* 36 (2007): 261–80.

Bocharov, Sergei. "O smysle 'Grobovshchika.'" In *Kontekst 1973*, edited by G. Velikovskaia, 196–228. Moscow: Nauka, 1974.

———. "Pikovaia dama." In *Poetika Pushkina*, by Sergei Bocharov, 186–204. Moscow: Nauka, 1974.

———. "Pushkin i Belkin." In *Poetika Pushkina*, by Sergei Bocharov, 127–87. Moscow: Nauka, 1974.

Booth, Wayne C. *The Rhetoric of Fiction*. Chicago: University of Chicago Press, 1983.

Borowec, Christine. "Time after Time: The Temporal Ideology of *Oblomov*." *Slavic and East European Journal* 38, no. 4 (1994): 561–73.

Brooke-Rose, Christine. "Historical Genres/Theoretical Genres: A Discussion of Todorov on the Fantastic." *New Literary History* 8, no. 1 (1976): 145–58.

Brooks, Peter. "Balzac: Epistemophilia and the Collapse of the Restoration." *Yale French Studies*, no. 101 (2001): 119–31.

———. "The Novel and the Guillotine, or Fathers and Sons in *Le Rouge et le noir*." *PMLA* 97, no. 3 (1982): 348–62.

Budgen, David. "Fedor Emin and the Beginnings of the Russian Novel." In *Russian Literature in the Age of Catherine the Great*, edited by A. G. Cross, 67–94. Oxford: W. A. Meeuws, 1976.

Burling, William. Review of *Factual Fictions: The Origins of the English Novel*, by Lennard J. Davis. *Novel: A Forum on Fiction* 17, no. 3 (Spring 1984): 282–85.

Butkov, Iakov. *Peterburgskie vershiny*. In *Russkii ocherk: 40–50-e gody XIX veka*, edited by V. Kuleshov, 219–337. Moscow: Izdatel'stvo Moskovskogo universiteta, 1989.

Cannon, Christopher. "Introduction." In *The Canterbury Tales*, by Geoffrey Chaucer, x–xxvii. Oxford: Oxford University Press, 2011.

Castle, Terry. *The Female Thermometer: Eighteenth-Century Culture and the Invention of the Uncanny*. New York: Oxford University Press, 1995.

Cohen, Margaret, and Carolyn Dever, eds. *The Literary Channel: The Inter-National Invention of the Novel*. Princeton, N.J.: Princeton University Press, 2002.

Cohn, Dorrit. *The Distinction of Fiction*. Baltimore: Johns Hopkins University Press, 1999.

———. "Optics and Power in the Novel." *New Literary History* 26, no. 1 (1995): 3–20.

———. "Reply to John Bender and Mark Seltzer." *New Literary History* 26, no. 1 (1995): 35–37.

———. *Transparent Minds: Narrative Modes for Presenting Consciousness in Fiction*. Princeton, N.J.: Princeton University Press, 1978.

Cornwell, Neil, ed. *The Society Tale in Russian Literature: From Odoevskii to Tolstoi*. Amsterdam: Rodopi, 1998.

———. "V. F. Odoevsky and his *Pestrye skazki*." In *Vladimir Odoevsky and Romantic Poets: Collected Essays*, by Neil Cornwell, 136–44. Oxford: Berghahn Books, 1998.

Costlow, Jane. *Worlds within Worlds: The Novels of Ivan Turgenev*. Princeton, N.J.: Princeton University Press, 1990.

Cox, Gary. "Dramatic Genre as a Tool of Characterization in Lermontov's *A Hero of Our Time*." *Russian Literature* 11 (1982): 163–72.

Culler, Jonathan. "Fabula and Sjuzhet in the Analysis of Narrative: Some American Dimensions." *Poetics Today* 1, no. 3 (Spring 1980): 27–37.

———. "Omniscience." *Narrative* 12, no. 1 (2004): 22–34.

Dal', Vladimir. *Sochineniia*. St. Petersburg: Izdatel'stvo M. O. Vol'fa, 1861.

Davis, Lennard J. *Factual Fictions: The Origins of the English Novel*. New York: Columbia University Press, 1983.

De Armas Wilson, Diana. "Of Pilgrims and Polyglots: Heliodorus, Cervantes, and Defoe." In *Remapping the Rise of the European Novel*, edited by Jenny Mander, 47–57. Oxford: Voltaire Foundation, 2007.

Delaney, Consolata. "Turgenev's Sportsman: Experiment in Unity." *Slavic and East European Journal* 8, no. 1 (1964): 17–25.

Di Salvo, Maria. "Povest'." In *The Novel: History, Geography and Culture*, edited by Franco Moretti, 1: 283–88. Princeton, N.J.: Princeton University Press, 2006.

Diment, Galya, ed. *Goncharov's "Oblomov": A Critical Companion*. Evanston, Ill.: Northwestern University Press, 1998.

———. "The Precocious Talent of Ivan Goncharov." In *Goncharov's "Oblomov": A Critical Companion*, edited by Galya Diment, 3–47. Evanston, Ill.: Northwestern University Press, 1998.

Dmitrieva, Ekaterina. "*Vechera na khutore bliz Dikan'ki*: Kommentarii." In *Polnoe sobranie sochinenii i pisem*, by N. V. Gogol', 1: 621–850. Moscow: Nasledie, 2001.

Dobroliubov, "Chto takoe oblomovshchina?" In *Roman I. A. Goncharova "Oblomov" v russkoi kritike*, edited by M. V. Otradin, 34–67. Leningrad: Izdatel'stvo Leningradskogo universiteta, 1991.

Dolinin, Aleksandr. *Pushkin i Angliia*. Moscow: Novoe literaturnoe obozrenie, 2007.

Donovan, Josephine. *Women and the Rise of the Novel, 1405–1726*. New York: St. Martin's, 1999.

Doody, Margaret A. "The Representation of Consciousness in the Ancient Novel." In *Remapping the Rise of the European Novel*, edited by Jenny Mander, 35–45. Oxford: Voltaire Foundation, 2007.

Dostoevskii, F. M. *Pis'ma v chetyrekh tomakh*. Edited by A. S. Dolinin. Moscow: Goslitizdat, 1959.

———. *Polnoe sobranie sochinenii*. Edited by V. G. Bazanov et al. Leningrad: Nauka, 1972–90.

Driessen, Frederik. *Gogol as a Short-Story Writer: A Study of His Technique of Composition*. Translated by Ian F. Finlay. The Hague: Mouton, 1965.

Druzhinin, Aleksandr. "*Oblomov*: Roman I. A. Goncharova." In *Roman I. A. Goncharova "Oblomov" v russkoi kritike*, edited by M. V. Otradin, 106–24. Leningrad: Izdatel'stvo Leningradskogo universiteta, 1991.

Efebovskii, Pavel. "Peterburgskie raznoschiki." In *Russkii ocherk: 40–50-e gody XIX veka*, edited by V. Kuleshov, 403–35. Moscow: Izdatel'stvo Moskovskogo universiteta, 1989.

Ehre, Milton. "Goncharov." In *Handbook of Russian Literature*, edited by Victor Terras, 178–79. New Haven, Conn.: Yale University Press, 1985.

———. *Oblomov and His Creator: The Life and Art of Ivan Goncharov*. Princeton, N.J.: Princeton University Press, 1973.

Eikhenbaum, Boris. "*Geroi nashego vremeni*." In *O proze, o poezii: Sbornik statei*, by Boris Eikhenbaum, 231–305. Leningrad: Khudozhestvennaia literatura, 1969.

———. *Lermontov: Opyt istoriko-literaturnoi otsenki*. Leningrad, 1924; reprint edition: Munich: Wilhelm Fink Verlag, 1967.

———. *Lev Tolstoi: Semidesiatye gody*. Leningrad: Khudozhestvennaia literatura, 1974.

———. "Put' Pushkina k proze." In *O proze, o poezii: Sbornik statei*, by Boris Eikhenbaum, 214–30. Leningrad: Khudozhestvennaia literatura, 1969.

Eikhenbaum, Boris, and Iurii Tynianov, eds. *Russkaia proza*. The Hague: Mouton, 1963.

Emerson, Caryl. *The First Hundred Years of Mikhail Bakhtin*. Princeton, N.J.: Princeton University Press, 1997.

———. "'The Queen of Spades' and the Open End." In *Puškin Today*, edited by David Bethea, 31–37. Bloomington: Indiana University Press, 1992.

———. "Shklovsky's *ostranenie*, Bakhtin's *vnenakhodimost'* (How Distance Serves an Aesthetics of Arousal Differently from an Aesthetics Based on Pain)." *Poetics Today* 26, no. 4 (Winter 2005): 637–64.

Epshtein, Mikhail. "The Irony of Style: The Demonic Element in Gogol's Concept of Russia." In *Gogol: Exploring Absence: Negativity in 19th Century Russian Literature*, edited by Sven Spieker and Natascha Drubek-Meyer, 55–72. Bloomington, Ind.: Slavica, 1999.

Fanger, Donald. *The Creation of Nikolai Gogol*. Cambridge, Mass.: Harvard University Press, 1979.

———. *Dostoevsky and Romantic Realism: A Study of Dostoevsky in Relation to Balzac, Dickens, and Gogol*. Chicago: University of Chicago Press, 1967.

Fludernik, Monika. "Naturalizing the Unnatural: A View from Blending Theory." *Journal of Literary Semantics* 39 (2010): 1–27.

———. *Toward A Natural Narratology*. London: Routledge, 1996.

Frazier, Melissa. "De-Familiarizing the Tolstoy of Formalism." *Russian Literature* 44 (1998): 143–58.

———. *Romantic Encounters: Writers, Readers, and the Library for Reading*. Stanford, Calif.: Stanford University Press, 2007.

Freeborn, Richard. *The Rise of the Russian Novel: Studies in the Russian Novel from "Eugene Onegin" to "War and Peace."* Cambridge, Eng.: Cambridge University Press, 1973.

Frost, Edgar. "Turgenev's 'Mumu' and the Absence of Love." In *Ivan Turgenev*, edited by Harold Bloom, 39–56. Philadelphia: Chelsea House, 2003.

Gallagher, Catherine. "The Rise of Fictionality." In *The Novel: History, Geography, and Culture*, edited by Franco Moretti, 1: 336–63. Princeton, N.J.: Princeton University Press, 2006.

Garden, Patricia. "The Expressive Self in *War and Peace*." *Canadian-American Slavic Studies* 12, no. 4 (1978): 519–34.

Gasperetti, David. *The Rise of the Russian Novel: Carnival, Stylization, and Mockery of the West*. DeKalb: Northern Illinois University Press, 1996.

Gaston, Patricia Sullivan. *Prefacing the Waverley Prefaces: A Reading of Sir Walter Scott's Prefaces to the Waverley Novels*. New York: P. Lang, 1991.

Geiro, L. S. "Istoriia sozdaniia i publikatsii romana *Oblomov*." In *Oblomov*, by Ivan Goncharov, 551–646. Leningrad: Nauka, 1987.

Genette, Gerard. *Narrative Discourse: An Essay in Method*. Ithaca, N.Y.: Cornell University Press, 1980.

Gilroy, Marie. *The Ironic Vision in Lermontov's "A Hero of Our Time."* Birmingham, Eng.: University of Birmingham, 1989.

Ginzburg, Carlo. "Making Things Strange: The Prehistory of a Literary Device." *Representations* 56 (1996): 8–28.

Gippius, Vasilii. *Gogol'*. Leningrad: Mysl', 1924.

———. *Ot Pushkina do Bloka*. Moscow: Nauka, 1966.

Givens, John. "Wombs, Tombs, and Mother Love: A Freudian Reading of Goncharov's *Oblomov*." In *Goncharov's "Oblomov": A Critical Companion*, edited by Galya Diment, 90–109. Evanston, Ill.: Northwestern University Press, 1998.

Gogol, Nikolai. *The Complete Tales*. Translated by Constance Garnett. Edited by Leonard J. Kent. Chicago: University of Chicago Press, 1964.

———. *Vechera na khutore bliz Dikan'ki*. In *Sobranie sochinenii v chetyrekh tomakh*, edited by N. L. Stepanov, 1: 57–272. Moscow: Pravda, 1968.

Goncharov, Ivan. "Correspondence Related to *Oblomov*." Translated by Brian Thomas Oles. In *Goncharov's "Oblomov": A Critical Companion*, edited by Galya Diment, 139–61. Evanston, Ill.: Northwestern University Press, 1998.

———. *Oblomov*. Leningrad: Nauka, 1987.

———. *Oblomov*. Trasnlated by Stephen Pearl. New York: Bunim and Bannigan, 2006.

Goody, Jack. "From Oral to Written: An Anthropological Breakthrough in Storytelling." In *The Novel: History, Geography, and Culture*, edited by Franco Moretti, 1: 3–36. Princeton, N.J.: Princeton University Press, 2006.

Goscilo, Helena. "The First Pechorin En Route to *A Hero*: Lermontov's *Princess Ligovskaia*." *Russian Literature* 11 (1982): 129–62.

———. "Lermontov's Debt to Lavater and Gall." *Slavonic and East European Review* 59, no. 4 (1981): 500–515.

Goulet, Andrea. "'Tomber dans le phénomène': Balzac's Optics of Narration." *French Forum* 26, no. 3 (2001): 43–70.

Greenleaf, Monika. *Pushkin and Romantic Fashion: Fragment, Elegy, Orient, Irony*. Stanford, Calif.: Stanford University Press, 1997.

Gregg, Richard A. "A Scapegoat for All Seasons: The Unity and Shape of *The Tales of Belkin*." *Slavic Review* 30 (1971): 748–61.

Griffiths, Frederick, and Stanley Rabinowitz. *Novel Epics: Gogol, Dostoevsky, and National Narrative*. Evanston, Ill.: Northwestern University Press, 1990.

Grishunin, A. L., L. M. Dolotova, and L. N. Smirnova. "*Zapiski okhotnika*: Primechaniia." In *Polnoe sobranie sochinenii i pisem*, by Ivan Turgenev, 4: 489–611. Moscow: Izdatel'stvo Akademii nauk SSSR, 1963.

Grossman, Leonid. "Rannii zhanr Turgeneva." In *Ot Pushkina do Bloka: Etiudy i portrety*, by Leonid Grossman, 249–78. Moscow: Sovremennye problemy, 1926.

———. "Turgenev's Early Genre." Translated by David A. Lowe. In *Critical Essays on Ivan Turgenev*, edited by David A. Lowe, 63–73. Boston: G. K. Hall, 1989.

Gukovskii, G. "Neizdannye povesti Nekrasova v istorii russkoi prozy 1840-kh godov." In *Zhizn' i pokhozhdeniia Tikhona Trosnikova: Novonaidennaia rukopis' Nekrasova*, by Nikolai Nekrasov, edited by V. Evgen'ev-Maksimov and K. Chukovskii, 366–73. Moscow: Gosudarstvennoe izdatel'stvo khudozhestvennoi literatury, 1931.

Hadfield, Andrew. "What Was the First English Novel and What Does It Tell Us?" In *Remapping the Rise of the European Novel*, edited by Jenny Mander, 23–34. Oxford: Voltaire Foundation, 2007.

Hamburger, Käte. *The Logic of Literature*. Translated by Marilyn Rose. Bloomington: Indiana University Press, 1993.

Heier, Edmund. *Literary Portraiture in Nineteenth-Century Russian Prose*. Cologne: Böhlau, 1993.

Hodgson, Peter. *From Gogol to Dostoevsky: Jakov Butkov, a Reluctant Naturalist in the 1840s*. Munich: Wilhelm Fink, 1976.

Hoisington, Sona Stephan. "Pushkin's Belkin and the Mystifications of Sir Walter Scott." *Comparative Literature* 33 (1981): 342–57.

Holmgren, Beth. "Questions of Heroism in Goncharov's *Oblomov*." In *Goncharov's "Oblomov": A Critical Companion*, edited by Galya Diment, 77–89. Evanston, Ill.: Northwestern University Press, 1998.

Holquist, James M. "The Devil in Mufti: The *Märchenwelt* in Gogol's Short Stories." *PMLA* 82, no. 5 (1967): 352–62.

Holquist, Michael. "The Supernatural as Social Force in *Anna Karenina*." In *The Supernatural in Slavic and Baltic Literature: Essays in Honor of Victor Terras*, edited by Amy Mandelker and Roberta Reeder, 176–90. Columbus, Ohio: Slavica, 1988.

Holquist, Michael, and Ilya Kliger. "Minding the Gap: Toward a Historical Poetics of Estrangement." *Poetics Today* 26, no. 4 (Winter 2005): 613–36.

Iakubovich, Dmitrii. "Predislovie k 'Povestiam Belkina' i povestvovatel'nye priemy Val'tera Skotta." In *Pushkin v mirovoi literature*, edited by N. V. Iakovlev, 160–87. Leningrad: Gosudarstvennoe izdatel'stvo, 1926.

Iezuitova, R. V. "Puti razvitiia romanticheskoi povesti." In *Russkaia povest' 19-go veka: Istoriia i problematika zhanra*, edited by B. Meilakh, 77–107. Leningrad: Nauka, 1973.

———. "Svetskaia povest'." In *Russkaia povest' 19-go veka: istoriia i problematika zhanra*, edited by B. Meilakh, 169–99. Leningrad: Nauka, 1973.

Izmailov, N. V. "Fantasticheskaia povest'." In *Russkaia povest' 19-go veka: istoriia i problematika zhanra*, edited by B. Meilakh, 134–69. Leningrad: Nauka, 1973.

Jaffe, Audrey. *Vanishing Points: Dickens, Narrative, and the Subject of Omniscience*. Berkeley: University of California Press, 1991.

Jameson, Fredric. "*La Cousine Bette* and Allegorical Realism." *PMLA* 86, no. 2 (1971): 241–54.

———. *The Political Unconscious*. Ithaca, N.Y.: Cornell University Press, 1981.

Kahn, Andrew. "The Rise of the Russian Novel and the Problem of Romance." In *Remapping the Rise of the European Novel*, edited by Jenny Mander, 185–98. Oxford: Voltaire Foundation, 2007.

Kleespies, Ingrid. *A Nation Astray: Nomadism and National Identity in Russian Literature*. DeKalb: NIU Press, 2012.

Klein, Joachim. "Zur Interpretation von Gončarovs *Oblomov*: Der Traum und das Unbewußte." In *Res Slavica: Festschrift für Hans Rothe zum 65. Ge-*

burtstag, edited by Hans Rothe, Peter Thiergen, Ludger Udolph, and Wilfried Potthoff, 135–45. Zürich: Ferdinand Schoningh, 1994.

Kliger, Ilya. "World Literature Beyond Hegemony in Yuri M. Lotman's Cultural Semiotics." *Comparative Critical Studies* 7, nos. 2–3 (2010): 257–74.

Klioutchkine, Konstantine. "The Rise of *Crime and Punishment* from the Air of the Media." *Slavic Review* 61, no. 1 (Spring 2002): 88–108.

Kolotaev, Valentin. *Poetika destruktivnogo erosa*. Moscow: Agraf, 2001.

Kropf, David. *Authorship as Alchemy: Subversive Writing in Pushkin, Scott, Hoffman*. Stanford, Calif.: Stanford University Press, 1994.

Layton, Susan. "Colonial Mimicry and Disenchantment in Alexander Druzhinin's 'A Russian Circassian' and Other Stories." *Russian Review* 60, no. 1 (2001): 56–71.

LeBlanc, Ronald. "A la recherche du genre perdu: Fielding, Gogol, and Bakhtin's Genre Memory." In *Russian Subjects: Empire, Nation, and the Culture of the Golden Age*, edited by Monika Greenleaf and Stephen Moeller-Sally, 101–22. Evanston, Ill.: Northwestern University Press, 1998.

———. "Oblomov's Consuming Passion: Food, Eating, and the Search for Communion." In *Goncharov's "Oblomov": A Critical Companion*, edited by Galya Diment, 110–35. Evanston, Ill.: Northwestern University Press, 1998.

Lermontov, M. Iu. *Sochineniia*. Moscow: Pravda, 1990.

Levine, George. *Realism, Ethics, and Secularism: Essays on Victorian Literature and Science*. Cambridge, Eng.: Cambridge University Press, 2008.

Lodge, David. "Mimesis and Diegesis in Modern Fiction." *SPELL* 1 (1984): 89–108.

Lounsbery, Anne. *Thin Culture, High Art: Gogol, Hawthorne, and Authorship in Nineteenth-Century Russia and America*. Cambridge, Mass.: Harvard University Press, 2007.

———. "The World on the Back of a Fish: Mobility, Immobility, and Economics in *Oblomov*." *Russian Review* 70, no. 1 (2011): 43–64.

Lukács, Georg. "Balzac: Lost Illusions." In *Studies in European Realism*, by Georg Lukács, 47–64. Translated by Edith Bone. New York: Universal Library, 1964.

Malik, Madhu. "*Vertep* and the Sacred/Profane Dichotomy in Gogol's *Dikan'ka* Stories." *Slavic and East European Journal* 34, no. 3 (1990): 332–47.

Malina, Debra. *Breaking the Frame: Metalepsis and the Construction of the Subject*. Columbus: Ohio University Press, 2002.

Mander, Jenny, ed. *Remapping the Rise of the European Novel*. Oxford: Voltaire Foundation, 2007.

Mann, Iu. "Filosofiia i poetika 'natural'noi shkoly.'" In *Problemy tipologii russkogo realizma*, edited by N. L. Stepanov, 241–305. Moscow: Nauka, 1969.

———. *Poetika Gogolia: Variatsii k teme*. Moscow: Coda, 1996.

Marantsman, V. G. "Povest' I. S. Turgeneva 'Mumu' v chitatel'skom vospriiatii shkol'nikov." In *Izuchenie literatury v 5 klasse: Metodicheskie rekomendatsii*, edited by V. Marantsman. St. Petersburg, 1996.

Martínez-Bonati, Félix. *Fictive Discourse and the Structures of Literature: A Phenomenological Approach*. Translated by P. Silver. Ithaca, N.Y.: Cornell University Press, 1981.

Masing-Delic, Irene. "Hidden Spaces in Turgenev's Short Prose: What They Conceal and What They Show." In *Turgenev: Art, Ideology, and Legacy*, edited by Robert Reid and Joe Andrew, 23–40. Amsterdam: Rodopi, 2010.

Maslov, Boris. "Comparative Literature and Revolution, or the Many Arts of (Mis)reading Alexander Veselovsky." *Compar(a)ison: An International Journal of Comparative Literature* 2008 (2013) 2: 101–29.

Matveyev, Rebecca Epstein. "From the Society Tale to the Novel: A Model of Genre Development." In *The Society Tale in Russian Literature: From Odoevskii to Tolstoi*, edited by Neil Cornwell, 169–86. Amsterdam: Rodopi, 1998.

Mayer, Robert. *History and the Early English Novel: Matters of Fact from Bacon to Defoe*. New York: Cambridge University Press, 1977.

McHale, Brian. "Islands in the Stream of Consciousness." Review of *Transparent Minds*, by Dorrit Cohn. *Poetics Today* 2, no. 2 (1981): 183–91.

McKeon, Michael. "Generic Transformation and Social Change: Rethinking the Rise of the Novel." In *Theory of the Novel: A Historical Approach*, edited by Michael McKeon, 382–99. Baltimore: Johns Hopkins University Press, 2000.

———. *The Origins of the English Novel, 1600–1740*. Baltimore: Johns Hopkins University Press, 2002.

———. Review of *Factual Fictions: The Origins of the English Novel*, by Lennard J. Davis. *Modern Philology* 82, no. 1 (August 1984): 76–86.

Meijer, Jan M. "The Sixth Tale of Belkin." In *The Tales of Belkin by A.S. Puškin*, edited by Jan van der Eng, 109–33. The Hague: Mouton, 1968.

Mersereau, John. "Lermontov and Balzac." In *American Contributions to the Fifth International Congress of Slavists*, 2: 233–58. The Hague: Mouton, 1963.

Meyer, Priscilla. *How the Russians Read the French: Lermontov, Dostoevsky, Tolstoy*. Madison: University of Wisconsin Press, 2008.

Miller, D. A. "Balzac's Illusions Lost and Found." *Yale French Studies* 67 (1984): 164–81.

———. *The Novel and the Police*. Berkeley: University of California Press, 1989.

Millgate, Jane. *Walter Scott: The Making of the Novelist*. Toronto: University of Toronto Press, 1984.

Moeller-Sally, Stephen. "0000; or, The Sign of the Subject in Gogol's Petersburg." In *Russian Subjects: Empire, Nation, and the Culture of the Golden Age*, edited by Monika Greenleaf and Stephen Moeller-Sally, 325–46. Evanston, Ill.: Northwestern University Press, 1998.

Moretti, Franco, ed. *The Novel: History, Geography, and Culture*. Princeton, N.J.: Princeton University Press, 2006.

Morson, Gary Saul. *Hidden in Plain View: Narrative and Creative Potentials in "War and Peace."* Stanford, Calif.: Stanford University Press, 1987.

Moser, Charles A., ed. *The Cambridge History of Russian Literature*. Cambridge, Eng.: Cambridge University Press, 1992.

Navas, Ana Rodriguez. "Reading Pushkin's Tales of Belkin through Sainte-Beuve's *Vie, Poésies et Pensées de Joseph Delorme*." *Pushkin Review/Pushkinskii vestnik* 11 (2008): 81–101.

Nedzvetskii, V. A. *Roman Goncharova "Oblomov": Putevoditel' po tekstu*. Moscow: Izdatel'stvo Moskovskogo universiteta, 2010.

Nekrasov, Nikolai. *Fiziologiia Peterburga*. Moscow: Sovetskaia Rossiia, 1984.

———. *Zhizn' i pokhozhdeniia Tikhona Trosnikova: Novonaidennaia rukopis' Nekrasova*. Edited by V. Evgen'ev-Maksimov and K. Chukovskii. Moscow: Gosudarstvennoe izdatel'stvo khudozhestvennoi literatury, 1931.

Nelles, William. *Frameworks: Narrative Levels and Embedded Narrative*. New York: Peter Lang, 1997.

Nerval, Gérard de. "Aurélia, or Dream and Life." In *Selected Writings*, by Gérard de Nerval, 265–316. Translated by Richard Sieburth. New York: Penguin Classics, 1999.

Novak, Daniel Akiva. *Realism, Photography, and Nineteenth-Century Fiction*. Cambridge, Eng.: Cambridge University Press, 2008.

Odoevskii, V. F. *Pestrye skazki*. Edited by Neil Cornwell. Durham, Eng.: University of Durham, 1988.

———. *Sochineniia v dvukh tomakh*. Moscow: Khudozhestvennaia literatura, 1981.

Olin, Valer'ian. "Strannyi bal." In *Russkaia romanticheskaia povest' pisatelei 20–40 godov XIX veka*, edited by V. I. Sakharov, 329–42. Moscow: Pressa, 1992.

Orwin, Donna Tussing. *Consequences of Consciousness: Turgenev, Dostoevsky, and Tolstoy*. Stanford, Calif.: Stanford University Press, 2007.

Palmer, Alan. "The Construction of Fictional Minds." *Narrative* 10, no. 1 (2002): 28–46.

———. "Social Minds in Fiction and Criticism." *Style* 45, no. 2 (2011): 196–240.

Palti, Elías José. "The Problem of 'Misplaced Ideas' Revisited: Beyond the History of Ideas in Latin America." *Journal of the History of Ideas* 67, no. 1 (January 2006): 149–79.

Paperno, Irina. *Stories of the Soviet Experience: Memoirs, Diaries, Dreams*. Ithaca, N.Y.: Cornell University Press, 2009.

Pavlov, Nikolai. *Tri povesti*. Moscow: Khudozhestvennaia literatura, 1958.

Peace, Richard. *Oblomov: A Critical Examination of Goncharov's Novel*. Birmingham, Eng.: University of Birmingham, 1991.

Peterson, Dale. "The Completion of *A Sportsman's Sketches*: Turgenev's Parting

Word." In *The Poetics of Ivan Turgenev*, edited by D. Lowe, 53–62. Washington: Kennan Institute Occasional Papers, 1989.

Phillips, Delbert. *Spook or Spoof?: The Structure of the Supernatural in Russian Romantic Tales*. Washington, D.C.: University Press of America, 1982.

Pogorel'skii, Antonii. *Dvoinik: Izbrannye proizvedeniia*. Kiev: Dnipro, 1990.

Pogorelsky, Antony. *The Double, or My Evenings in Little Russia*. Translated with an introduction by Ruth Sobel. Ann Arbor, Mich.: Ardis, 1988.

Powelstock, David. *Becoming Mikhail Lermontov: The Ironies of Romantic Individualism in Nicholas I's Russia*. Evanston, Ill.: Northwestern University Press, 2005.

Prostsevichus, Vladislav. "Samorazvitie literaturnogo proizvedeniia." Ph.D. diss., Donetsk State University, 1993.

Puckett, Kent. *Bad Form: Social Mistakes and the Nineteenth-Century Novel*. Oxford: Oxford University Press, 2008.

Pushkin, Aleksandr. *Povesti pokoinogo Ivana Petrovicha Belkina*. In *Sobranie sochinenii v desiati tomakh*, edited by D. D. Blagoi, S. M. Bondi, et al., 5: 45–118. Moscow: Izdatel'stvo khudozhestvennoi literatury, 1959–62.

———. *Sobranie sochinenii v desiati tomakh*. Edited by D. D. Blagoi, S. M. Bondi, et al. Moscow: Izdatel'stvo khudozhestvennoi literatury, 1959–62.

———. *Tales of the Late Ivan Petrovich Belkin*. Translated by Alan Myers. Edited by Andrew Kahn. Oxford: Oxford World's Classics, 1999.

Putney, Christopher. "Gogol's Theology of Privation and the Devil in 'Ivan Fedorovich Shpon'ka and His Auntie.'" In *Gogol: Exploring Absence: Negativity in 19th Century Russian Literature*, edited by Sven Spieker and Natascha Drubek-Meyer, 73–84. Bloomington, Ind.: Slavica, 1999.

———. *Russian Devils and Diabolic Conditionality in Nikolai Gogol's "Evenings on a Farm near Dikanka."* New York: P. Lang, 1999.

Raven, James. "Britain, 1750–1830." In *The Novel: History, Geography, and Culture*, edited by Franco Moretti, 1: 429–54. Princeton, N.J.: Princeton University Press, 2006.

Reid, Robert. "*A Hunter's Sketches*: A Peircean Perspective." In *Turgenev and Russian Culture: Essays to Honour Richard Peace*, edited by Joe Andrew, Derek Offord, and Robert Reid, 301–32. Amsterdam: Rodopi, 2008.

———. "*Princess Ligovskaia* and *Princess Mary*: The Society Tale Goes to the Caucasus." In *The Society Tale in Russian Literature: From Odoevskii to Tolstoi*, edited by Neil Cornwell, 41–57. Amsterdam: Rodopi, 1998.

Reyfman, Irina. "Alexander Bestuzhev-Marlinsky: *Bretteur* and Apologist of the Duel." In *Russian Subjects: Empire, Nation, and the Culture of the Golden Age*, edited by Monika Greenleaf and Stephen Moeller-Sally, 243–58. Evanston, Ill.: Northwestern University Press, 1998.

Rimmon-Kenan, Shlomith. *Narrative Fiction: Contemporary Poetics*. London: Methuen, 1983.

Robinson, Douglas. *Estrangement and the Somatics of Literature: Tolstoy, Shklovsky, Brecht*. Baltimore: Johns Hopkins University Press, 2008.

Rosenshield, Gary. "Choosing the Right Card: Madness, Gambling, and Imagination in Pushkin's 'The Queen of Spades.'" *PMLA* 109, no. 5 (1994): 995–1008.

Rowe, William. *Through Gogol's Looking Glass: Reverse Vision, False Focus, and Precarious Logic*. New York: New York University Press, 1976.

Rudnev, Vadim. "Depersonalizatsiia, ili psikhicheskaia anestiziia (L. N. Tolstoi i V. B. Shklovskii)." *Logos* 11/12, no. 21 (1991): 55–63.

Sadoff, Dianne. "Storytelling and the Figure of the Father in *Little Dorrit*." *PMLA* 95, no. 2 (1980): 234–45.

Schmid, Wolf. "Pushkin's 'Descent' to Prose." In *The Pushkin Handbook*, edited by David M. Bethea, 210–40. Madison: University of Wisconsin Press, 2005.

Schwarz, Roberto. *Misplaced Ideas: Essays on Brazilian Culture*. London: Verso, 1992.

Seeley, Frank. *Turgenev: A Reading of His Fiction*. Cambridge, Eng.: Cambridge University Press, 1991.

Setchkarev, Vsevolod. *Ivan Goncharov: His Life and His Works*. Wurzburg: Jal-Verlag, 1974.

Shepard, Elizabeth. "The Society Tale and the Innovative Argument in Russian Prose Fiction of the 1830s." *Russian Literature* 10 (1981): 111–62.

Shklovskii, Viktor. "Iskusstvo kak priem." In *O teorii prozy*, by Viktor Shklovskii, 7–23. Moscow: Sovetskii pisatel', 1983.

———. *Material i stil' v proizvedeniiakh L'va Tolstogo*. Reprint edition: The Hague: Mouton, 1970.

———. *Razvertyvanie siuzheta* (1921). Reprint edition: *Russian Titles for the Specialist* no. 188. Letchworth Herts, Eng.: Prideaux, 1979.

———. *'Tristram Shendi' Sterna i teoriia romana*. Petrograd: Opoiaz, 1921.

Shklovsky, Viktor. "Art as Device." In *Theory of Prose*, by Victor Shklovsky, 1–14. Translated by Benjamin Sher. Elmwood Park, Ill.: Dalkey Archive, 1990.

Shpilevaia, Galina. "Gil-Blaz 'peterburgskikh uglov' (K voprosu o zhanre i khudozhestvennom metode romana N. A. Nekrasova 'Zhizn' i pokhozhdeniia Tikhona Trosnikova')." *Vestnik VGU* 1 (2004): 87–111.

Shryok, Richard. *Tales of Storytelling: Embedded Narrative in Modern French Fiction*. New York: Peter Lang, 1993.

Sloane, David. "Pushkin's Legacy in *Anna Karenina*." *Tolstoy Studies Journal*, no. 4 (1991): 1–23.

Slonimskii, A. L. "Zakony pushkinskoi prozy." In *Masterstvo Pushkina*, by A. L. Slonimskii, 501–25. Moscow: Gosudarstvennoe izdatel'stvo khudozhestvennoi literatury, 1959.

Smith, Barbara Herrnstein. "Narrative Versions, Narrative Theories." *Critical Inquiry* 7, no. 1 (Autumn 1980): 213–36.

Somov, O. *Byli i nebylitsy*. Moscow: Sovetskaia Rossiia, 1984.

States, Bert O. "Bizarreness in Dreams and Other Fictions." In *The Dream and the Text: Essays on Literature and Language*, edited by Carol Schreier Rupprecht, 13–31. Albany: State University of New York Press, 1993.

———. *Dreaming and Storytelling*. Ithaca, N.Y.: Cornell University Press, 1993.

Todd, William Mills. *The Familiar Letter as a Literary Genre in the Age of Pushkin*. Princeton, N.J.: Princeton University Press, 1976.

———. *Fiction and Society in the Age of Pushkin: Ideology, Institutions, and Narrative*. Cambridge, Mass.: Harvard University Press, 1986.

———. "The Ruse of the Russian Novel." In *The Novel: History, Geography, and Culture*, edited by Franco Moretti, 1: 401–23. Princeton, N.J.: Princeton University Press, 2006.

Todorov, Tzvetan. *The Fantastic: A Structural Approach to a Literary Genre*. Ithaca, N.Y.: Cornell University Press, 1975.

Tolstoi, Lev. *Sobranie sochinenii v dvadtsati tomakh*. Moscow: Gosudarstvennoe izdatel'stvo khudozhestvennoi literatury, 1960–65.

Tolstoy, Leo. "After the Ball." In *Tolstoy's Short Fiction*, translated by Aylmer Maude, edited and with revised translations by Michael Katz, 271–79. New York: Norton, 1991.

———. *War and Peace*. Translated by Aylmer and Louise Maude. Edited and revised by George Gibian. New York: Norton, 1996.

Tomashevskii, Boris. "Proza Lermontova i zapadno-evropeiskaia literaturnaia traditsiia." In *Literaturnoe nasledstvo 43–44. M. Iu. Lermontov*, edited by P. I. Lebedev-Polianskii, 469–516. Moscow: Akademiia nauk SSSR, 1941.

Tosi, Alessandra. *Waiting for Pushkin: Russian Fiction in the Reign of Alexander I (1801–1825)*. Amsterdam: Rodopi, 2006.

Trail, Nancy. *Possible Worlds of the Fantastic: The Rise of the Paranormal in Fiction*. Toronto: University of Toronto Press, 1996.

Tseitlin, Aleksandr. *Stanovlenie realizma v russkoi literature: russkii fiziologicheskii ocherk*. Moscow: Nauka, 1965.

Turgenev, Ivan. *A Hunter's Sketches*. Translated by Constance Garnett. Kessinger, 2004.

———. "Mumu." In *Polnoe sobranie sochinenii i pisem*, by Ivan Turgenev, 5: 264–92. Moscow: Izdatel'stvo Akademii nauk SSSR, 1963.

———. *The Novels of Ivan Turgenev*. Translated by Constance Garnett. New York: Macmillan, 1920.

———. *Polnoe sobranie sochinenii i pisem*. Moscow: Izdatel'stvo Akademii nauk SSSR, 1963.

———. *Zapiski okhotnika*. In *Polnoe sobranie sochinenii i pisem*, by Ivan Turgenev, 4: 7–388. Moscow: Nauka, 1963.

Vaiskopf, Mikhail. *Siuzhet Gogolia: Morfologiia, Ideologiia, Kontekst*. Moscow: Radiks, 1993.

Valentsova, M. M. "O magicheskikh funktsiiakh kolokol'chika v traditsionnoi kul'ture slavian." In *Mir zvuchashchii i molchashchii: Semiotika zvuka i rechi v traditsionnoi kul'ture slavian*, edited by S. M. Tolstaia, 283–93. Moscow: Indrik, 1999.

Vel'tman, Aleksandr. *Povesti i rasskazy*. Moscow: Sovetskaia Rossiia, 1979.

Vinitsky, Ilya. *Ghostly Paradoxes: Modern Spiritualism and Russian Culture in the Age of Realism*. Toronto: University of Toronto Press, 2009.

Vinogradov, Viktor. "Etiudy o stile Gogolia." In *Poetika russkoi literatury: Izbrannye trudy*, by Viktor Vinogradov, 230–366. Moscow: Nauka, 1976.

———. *Evoliutsiia russkogo naturalizma: Gogol' i Dostoevskii*. Leningrad: Academia, 1929.

———. *Gogol' i natural'naia shkola*. Leningrad: Obrazovanie, 1925.

———. "Stil' 'Pikovoi damy.'" *Pushkin: Vremennik Pushkinskoi komissii*, no. 2 (1936): 74–147.

———. "Stil' prozy Lermontova." In *Literaturnoe nasledstvo 43–44. M. Iu. Lermontov*, edited by P. I. Lebedev-Polianskii, 541–58. Moscow: Akademiia nauk SSSR, 1941.

———. *Zhiul' Zhanin i Gogol'*. Leningrad: Obrazovanie, 1925.

Wasiolek, Edward. *Tolstoy's Major Fiction*. Chicago: University of Chicago Press, 1978.

Watt, Ian. *The Rise of the Novel: Studies in Defoe, Richardson, and Fielding*. Berkeley: University of California Press, 1957.

Weir, Justin. *Leo Tolstoy and the Alibi of Narrative*. New Haven, Conn.: Yale University Press, 2011.

Weststeijn, Willem. "The Description of the Appearance of Characters in Turgenev's Novels (in particular, *Fathers and Sons*)." In *Turgenev: Art, Ideology, and Legacy*, edited by Robert Reid and Joe Andrew, 123–38. Amsterdam: Rodopi, 2010.

Wiggins, Cameron. "The Drama in Disguise: Dramatic Modes of Narration and Textual Structure in the Mid-Nineteenth-Century Russian Novel." Ph.D. diss., University of California-Berkeley, 2011.

Woloch, Alex. *The One vs. the Many: Minor Characters and the Space of the Protagonist in the Novel*. Princeton, N.J.: Princeton University Press, 2003.

Zagoskin, Mikhail. *Askol'dova mogila: Romany, povesti*. Moscow: Sovremennik, 1989.

Zhitova, V. N. *Vospominaniia o sem'e I. S. Turgeneva*. Tula: Tul'skoe knizhnoe izdatel'stvo, 1961.

Zholkovsky, Alexander. "Before and After 'After the Ball.'" In *Text Counter Text: Rereadings in Russian Literary History*, by Alexander Zholkovsky, 59–87. Stanford, Calif.: Stanford University Press, 1994.

Zhukova, Mariia. *Vechera na Karpovke*. Moscow: Sovetskaia Rossiia, 1986.

Ziegler, Vickie L. *Bending the Frame in the German Cyclical Narrative: Achim von Arnim's "Der Wintergarten" and E. T. A. Hoffmann's "Die Serapionsbrüder."* Washington, D.C.: Catholic University of America Press, 1991.

Zimovets, Sergei. *Molchanie Gerasima: Psikhoanaliticheskie i filosofskie esse o russkoi kul'ture*. Moscow: Gnozis, 1996.

Zunshine, Lisa. *Why We Read Fiction: Theory of Mind and the Novel*. Columbus: Ohio State University Press, 2006.

Index

Aikhenval'd, Iulii, 153
Aksakov, Konstantin, 103
Alter, Robert, 35, 60, 183n45
Annenkov, Pavel, 132
anonymous authorship, 25
Apuleius, 11, 43

Baisky, Porfirii. *See* Somov, Orest
Baker, Geoffrey, 90
Bakhtin, Mikhail, 10–11, 171–72, 182n34; on authorial "outsideness": *see under* narrative positioning; on novelistic discourse, 15, 17, 23, 31–32, 54–55, 58–59
Baldwin, William, 197n5
Balzac, Honoré de, 18, 63–64, 75–83, 85–86, 194–95nn43–45, 194n50; ambition and mania in, 80–82, 85; desire in, 77–82, 86
  WORKS: *The Black Sheep*, 77; *Cousin Bette*, 195n65; *Lost Illusions*, 80; *The Old Girl*, 76; *The Wild Ass's Skin*, 79
Banfield, Ann, 12, 91–92
Barthes, Roland, 89
Basom, Ann Marie, 99–100
Begichev, Dmitry, 3
Behn, Aphra, 21
Belinsky, Vissarion, 84, 88, 94, 199n42
Bestuzhev-Marlinksy, Aleksandr, 16, 53; dueling in, 68
  WORKS: *Ammalat-Bek*, 23–24, 28, 67; *The Clock and the Mirror*, 21, 69; *Cuirassier*, 183n46; *Evening at the Caucasian Waters in 1824*, 42, 104; *Evening on a Bivouac*, 42, 104; *A Night on a Ship*, 21, 64–65, 192n7; *Novel in Seven Letters*, 27; "A Page from the Diary of a Guard Officer," 200n57; *The Red Veil*, 64–65, 73; *A Second Evening on a Bivouac*, 104
Blic, Göran, 195n50
Boccaccio, Giovanni, 43, 44–45, 185n14
Bocharov, Sergei, 55, 189nn58–59, 190n75
Booth, Wayne, 15, 179n45
Borowec, Christine, 210n41
Brooke-Rose, Christine, 199n41
Brooks, Peter, 194n50
Budgen, David, 176n22, 180n2
Bulgarin, Faddei, 3, 94
Burling, William, 182n28
Butkov, Iakov, 93–94
Byron, George Gordon, Lord, 106, 194n43

Casanova, Pascale, 175n19
Castle, Terry, 202n77
Caucasian tales, 17, 23, 63, 66–68, 192n17
Cervantes, Miguel de, 43, 47, 186n26
characterization: in Balzac, 18, 63–64, 75–78, 80, 82–83, 194n43; doubles, 18, 89, 105–7; monstrosity, 97–98, 105; in *Oblomov*, 145–46, 151, 156–57; in society tales, 18, 64, 84; in Tolstoy, 166; types, 18, 89, 95–98, 140, 156–57
Chaucer, Geoffrey, 44–47, 184n12, 184n14
Chernyshevsky, Nikolai, 173n4, 210n48
Chulkov, Mikhail, 176n22
cognitive theory, 113–14, 138, 203n15
Cohn, Dorrit, 8, 9, 11, 12, 13, 91, 110, 111, 115, 128, 137, 179n45, 183n42
Congreve, William, 182n28
consciousness, presentation of, 9–12, 13, 19–20, 80, 90–91, 93, 109–15, 119, 121, 137–38, 142, 144, 160, 177n31; in Goncharov, 146–48, 151–58; omniscience and, 11–12, 92, 177n29, 178n35; in the society tale, 63–64, 76; in Tolstoy, 160,

162, 167, 171; in Turgenev, 123–24, 129–30, 131, 133, 135, 204n21. *See also* interiority
Contemporary, 4, 19, 88, 139
"corners," 93–95, 97–98, 108
Cornwell, Neil, 185n20, 191n1
Costlow, Jane, 12
Culler, Jonathan, 33, 34, 183n39

Dal', Vladimir, 3, 96
Davis, Lennard, 29, 35, 60, 180n3, 181n27
de Armas Wilson, Diana, 5
Defoe, Daniel, 21, 29
Delaney, Consolata, 130
Dickens, Charles, 112, 115
Diment, Galya, 150, 208n11, 209n24
Di Salvo, Maria, 176n22
Dobroliubov, Nikolai, 140, 150, 207n5, 210n48
Dolinin, Aleksandr, 175n17
Donovan, Josephine, 43, 44, 46, 184n8, 185n16
Doody, Margaret Anne, 177n31
Dostoevsky, Fyodor, 4, 5, 16, 181n23, 191n2, 199n39
dream narratives, 19, 141–45
Druzhinin, Aleksandr, 192n17, 208n12, 211n57

Efebovsky, Pavel, 95–96
Ehre, Milton, 139, 146, 148–50, 151, 211n57
Eikhenbaum, Boris, 3, 7, 42–43, 53–54, 61, 83, 84, 173n3, 173n5, 193n41, 196n73
Eliot, George, 33
Emerson, Caryl, 213n7
Emin, Fedor, 176n22, 180n2
epistolary form, 27, 181n23
Epshtein, Mikhail, 101, 199n42
estrangement, 160–67, 214nn25–26, 212n1, 212–13nn6–7

Fanger, Donald, 175n17
fantastic (and supernatural tales), the, 18, 89, 92, 98–105, 107–9, 143, 199n39, 199n41, 200n57, 202n77
fictionality, 8, 22, 29, 30, 33, 34–35, 60, 80, 136, 143–44, 159, 176n26, 180n5
fictional vs. nonfictional discourse, 33–34, 80, 183n42

Fielding, Henry, 21, 35, 112, 183n45
Flaubert, Gustave, 90, 112, 206n67
folklore and folktales, 7, 24, 102
Fontane, Theodor, 90, 112, 115
Foucault, Michel, 9
"found manuscript" device, 17, 25, 26–27, 47–53, 65, 84, 87, 126–27, 186n26
frame-tales. *See* prose cycles
Frazier, Melissa, 84, 106, 174n10, 175n17, 176n22, 179nn43–44, 181n25, 187n35, 201n72, 214n25
Freeborn, Richard, 4, 12
free indirect discourse, 92, 130, 137, 160
Freud, Sigmund, 33, 34, 77
Frost, Edgar, 116–17, 118, 121, 136

Gall, Franz Joseph, 75
Gallagher, Catherine, 8–9, 13, 22, 30, 35, 136, 143
Gan, Elena, 24
Garden, Patricia, 213n13
Gasperetti, David, 176n22
Gaston, Patricia, 187n46
Geiro, L. S., 208n14
Genette, Gérard, 178n37, 183n44
Gilroy, Marie, 196n72
Ginzburg, Carlo, 162
Gippius, Vasilii, 100
Givens, John, 154, 211n54
Gogol, Nikolai, 3, 16; the demonic in, 100–102, 211n57; folklore in, 24; and Hawthorne, 179n44
WORKS: *Dead Souls*, 4, 101, 199n42; *Evenings on a Farm near Dikan'ka*, 4, 14–15, 24, 42, 44, 45, 47, 55, 56, 58, 59–60, 98, 100–102, 104, 185n22, 199n45, 201n62; "The Fair at Sorochintsy," 98, 100–104, 199n45, 200n47, 200n56; *Mirgorod*, 201n62; "The Night before Christmas," 104; *The Overcoat*, 201n61; *The Portrait*, 99–100, 101; "A Terrible Vengeance," 101, 104; "Vii," 101, 201n62
Goncharov, Ivan, 16
WORKS: *A Common Story*, 88, 173n4, 191n2; *A Lucky Mistake*, 191n2; *Oblomov*, 4, 19–20, 139–43, 145–58, 208n12; "Oblomov's Dream," 4, 19–20, 139, 140–43, 145, 208n11, 208n15, 209n24

Goody, Jack, 21, 22, 180n8
Goscilo, Helena, 192n19, 193n39, 194n44, 195n67
Goulet, Andrea, 195n50
Grebenka, Evgenii, 96, 98
Grech, Nikolai, 3
Greenleaf, Monika, 106
Gregg, Richard, 190n70
Griffiths, Frederick, and Stanley Rabinowitz, 176n22
Grigor'ev, Apollon, 76, 189n58, 210n46
Grigorovich, Dmitrii, 93
Grossman, Leonid, 130, 131

Hadfield, Andrew, 197n5
Hamburger, Käte, 91
Heier, Edmund, 75, 83, 193n43, 194n44
Herald of Europe, 131–32
Hoisington, Sonia Stephan, 49–50, 53, 188n49, 189n59
Holmgren, Beth, 210n37
Holquist, James, 101, 104
Holquist, Michael, 202n77, 213n7
Hunter, J. Paul, 43

Iakubovich, Dmitrii, 49, 50–53, 83, 188n49
Iezuitova, R. V., 180n2
interiority (internal-external divide), 9–11, 13, 19, 41, 63–68, 73, 111–15, 128–29, 133, 136, 137, 141, 145, 160, 178n33; in ancient novels, 177n31; in Goncharov, 152, 155; in Lermontov, 69–76, 84–87, 113, 127; in the society tale, 63, 83; in Turgenev, 115–16, 119–21, 123–25, 127, 129, 130–31, 134–35, 203n21

Jaffe, Audrey, 176n29
James, Henry, 4, 112, 203n21
Jameson, Fredric, 18, 76–82, 90
Jung, Carl G., 209n23

Kahler, Erich, 202n2
Kahn, Andrew, 176n22
Kalashnikov, Ivan, 3
Kleespies, Ingrid, 154, 207n10
Klein, Joachim, 208n15
Kliger, Ilya, 175n19, 213n7
Kolotaev, Vadim, 121–22
Komarov, Matvey, 176n22
Kropf, David, 188

Labov, William, 33
Lavater, Johann Kaspar, 71, 74, 87, 194n44, 204n21
Layton, Susan, 192n17
Lazhechnikov, Ivan, 3
LeBlanc, Ronald, 175n17, 211n54
Lermontov, Mikhail, 3, 16
  WORKS: *A Hero of Our Time*, 3, 4, 7, 10, 18, 42, 63–64, 67, 83–87, 195n67, 196n72; *Princess Ligovskaia*, 3, 10, 18, 63, 69–76, 83–85, 86, 113, 115, 127, 141, 192n19, 193n39, 193nn41–42, 194n44
Le Sage, Alain-René, 11
Levine, George, 197n11
Library for Reading, 201n72, 208n12
Likhachev, A., 98
Literary Gazette, 96
Lkhovsky, Ivan, 140
Lodge, David, 29
Lotman, Yuri, 175n19
Lounsbery, Anne, 146, 150, 151, 153, 179n44
Lukács, György, 196n75

Mahlik, Madhu, 199n45
Malina, Debra, 35
Mander, Jenny, 48, 174n14, 186n26
Manley, Delarivier, 9, 182n28
Mann, Iurii, 95, 97
Marguerite de Navarre, 44, 185n16
Marlinsky, Aleksandr, 3
Masal'sky, Konstantin, 3
Mashkov, Petr, 3
Maslov, Boris, 175n19
McKeon, Michael, 6, 29–30, 43, 174n13, 180n5, 182n31
Meijer, Jan, 189n59, 191n76
Merezhkovsky, Dmitrii, 100
Mersereau, John, 194n43
metalepsis, 35–36, 41, 183n44
Meyer, Priscilla, 194n43
Miller, D. A., 9, 12, 80–81, 178n33
Millgate, Jane, 188n50
mimesis, 29, 91, 197n11
Moeller-Sally, Stephen, 24
Molière, 139
Moretti, Franco, 175n19
Morson, Gary Saul, 213n6, 213n13
Moscow Telegraph, 23
Mouhy, Charles de Fieux de, 48

narrative positioning, 7–16, 18, 22, 25, 30–31, 178n37; authenticity claims, 21–23, 25–29, 35–36, 38, 126, 180nn2–5, 180n8; autopsy trope, 75; disclaiming authorship, 15, 23, 24–27, 29, 35–36, 60; "discursive perspective," 7–8, 16–17, 60, 80, 89, 91, 136, 142, 144–45, 170–71, 209n25; exemption from temporal and spatial constraints, 13, 79, 81–82, 92–93, 95, 98, 106, 108–9, 124; first-person (*Ich-Erzählung*), 7, 10, 37, 38, 112, 178n31; framing narrators, 17, 25–32, 36–37, 44–53, 55–61, 65, 84, 103–4, 182n34; intrusive (self-conscious) narrators, 35, 60; invisibility, 70, 74, 83; optical instruments and, 66, 70; "outsideness," 13–14, 92–93, 98, 106, 107–8, 171–72, 213n7; point of view, 33, 183n39
naturalism (and the "natural school"), 16, 18, 88–89, 92–98, 105, 107–8, 196n3; Goncharov and, 140, 145, 156–57, 208nn14–15
Navas, Ana Rodriguez, 47–48, 188n49
Nekrasov, Nikolai
WORKS: *The Life and Adventures of Tikhon Trosnikov*, 97; "Petersburg Corners," 93, 94, 97; *Physiology of Petersburg* (ed.), 18, 94
Nelles, William, 47, 186n24
Nerval, Gérard de, 147
Notes of the Fatherland, 139
Novak, Daniel Akiva, 197n12
novel, the: form, 6, 16; nomenclature, 4, 12, 141, 145, 177n30; origins and rise of, 5–7, 8, 10, 22, 29–30, 34–35, 43, 60, 89, 136–37, 143, 144, 159, 171, 175n19, 176n22, 182n31, 197n5; sociohistorical influences, 5–7, 68, 89, 160, 175n22. *See also* consciousness; fictionality; interiority; narrative positioning; realism; reliability in fiction

Odoevsky, Vladimir, 3, 16, 18, 24, 42
WORKS: *The Apparition*, 36, 38–40, 99, 190n64; *Imbroglio*, 21, 25–26; *Motley Tales*, 42, 44, 45–46, 48, 53, 56–57, 185n20, 186n28, 190n64; *Notes of a Coffin-Maker*, 42; *Orlakh Peasant Girl*, 42, 184n3; *The Possessed*, 42, 184n3; *Princess Zizi*, 28, 38; *Russian Nights*, 42, 184n2; *The Sylph*, 40–41, 99
Olin, Valer'ian, 103
Orwin, Donna, 203n21

Palmer, Alan, 114–15, 203n15, 203n19
Paperno, Irina, 209n25
Pavlov, Nikolai, 26–27
Peace, Richard, 139, 140
Perovsky, Aleksei. *See* Pogorel'sky, Antonii
Peterson, Dale, 130
Phillips, Delbert, 200n57, 201nn61–62
physiognomy, 18, 67, 71, 74, 75–76, 78, 83, 87, 193–94nn43–44, 204n21
physiological sketches, 18, 89, 92, 95–98, 108, 140, 141, 184n1, 193n39
Physiology of Petersburg. *See* Nekrasov, Nikolai
Pogodin, Mikhail, 24
Pogorel'sky, Antonii, 3, 18, 24
WORKS: *The Convent Girl*, 37–38, 40; *The Double*, 42, 105, 107, 200n57, 202n75
Polevoi, Nikolai, 3, 14–15, 23, 24
Powelstock, David, 196n72
prose cycles (frame-tales), 3, 4, 9, 10, 14–15, 29, 41, 42–61, 83, 86, 115–16, 125, 171, 184n1, 184n4, 184n8, 185n17, 185n23; as a progenitor of the novel, 17, 42–46, 60–61; Russian formalists on, 17, 43
pseudonymns, 24–25
Puckett, Kent, 174n12
Pushkin, Aleksandr, 3, 16, 53–54, 106, 173n1, 194n43; influence on Tolstoy, 62, 173n2; on propriety, 66, 68, 192n10
WORKS: *Eugene Onegin*, 3, 4, 191n76; *A Novel in Letters*, 27, 188n50; *The Queen of Spades*, 199n39; *Tales of Belkin*, 3, 24, 42, 45, 46, 48, 49–53, 55–56, 59–61, 187n45, 188nn49–50, 188n54, 189nn58–59, 190n64, 190n70, 190n75
Putney, Christopher, 101, 200n47, 200n56

Raven, James, 25
realism, 11–12, 16, 18, 22, 29–30, 88, 89–92, 93, 108–10, 112, 159, 162, 177n31, 197nn11–12, 202n77; and the fantastic,

18, 104, 108–10; 201n61, 202n77; formal, 6, 89–90; transparency and, 124, 137; Turgenev and, 13, 115, 137
Reid, Robert, 69
reliability in fiction, 8–9, 15–16, 87, 172, 177n30, 179n45
representation, 16–17, 18, 19–20, 23, 31–32, 34, 55, 60, 73, 78, 79–80, 136–37, 143–44, 156, 178n33; realist, 89–91, 109–10
Reyman, Irina, 68
Richardson, Samuel, 21, 29
Robinson, Douglas, 213n7
romanticism, 88–89, 90, 92, 98, 105–8, 179n44, 196n3, 202n72
romantic novellas, 18
Rostopchina, Evdokiia, 28, 184n58
Rudnev, Vadim, 214n26

Saint-Beuve, Charles Augustin, 47–48, 188n49
Schmid, Wolf, 188n54, 189n59
Schwarz, Roberto, 6–7, 175nn18–19
Scott, Walter, 14–15, 17, 49–53, 58–59, 83, 187n35, 187nn45–46, 188n50, 194n43
WORKS: *Ivanhoe*, 52; *The Monastery*, 52, 187n45; *Rob Roy*, 187n45; *Tales of My Landlord*, 49–53, 187nn45–46; *Waverley*, 52, 187n45
Seeley, Frank, 205n34
Senkovsky, Osip, 3, 42, 201n72
Setchkarev, Vsevolod, 211n57
Shepard, Elizabeth, 62–63, 66, 75, 82
Shklovsky, Viktor, 43–44, 46, 160–61, 175n17, 212n1, 213n7
Shpilevaia, Galina, 97
Shryok, Richard, 186n23
siuzhet vs. *fabula*. *See* story-discourse relationship
Smith, Barbara Herrnstein, 33–34
Smollett, Tobias, 21
society tales, 17–18, 24, 62–76, 82–87, 191nn1–2
Somov, Orest, 18, 24
WORKS: *The Kikimora*, 21; *Matchmaking*, 21; *Novel in Two Letters*, 27; *The Sign*, 28, 38, 40
Sophocles, 33
States, Bert, 142, 144
Stepanov, Aleksandr, 3
Sterne, Laurence, 35
story-discourse relationship, 18, 33–36, 41, 60, 79, 84, 108, 136–37, 144–45, 159–60, 183n42; in *Oblomov*, 142
Sue, Eugene, 157
Swift, Jonathan, 35
symbolization, 166–70

tales and novellas (*povesti*), 9, 10, 12, 21, 177n30
Thousand and One Nights, The, 43
Todd, William Mills, 5, 7, 67, 84, 175n22, 181n23, 196n75
Todorov, Tzvetan, 98–99, 103, 106, 108, 143, 199n39, 199n41
Tolstoy, Leo, 140–41, 214n25, 212n1
WORKS: *After the Ball*, 20, 167–72, 214n27; *Anna Karenina*, 62, 173n2; *War and Peace*, 4, 160–66, 169–70, 212n6, 213n13, 214nn25–26
Tosi, Alessandra, 173n3
Trail, Nancy, 202n77
Trollope, Anthony, 90
Tseitlin, Aleksandr, 94–95, 98, 140
Turgenev, Aleksandr, 76
Turgenev, Ivan, 16, 112, 191n2, 206n67
WORKS: *Asia*, 210n48; "Chertopkhanov and Nedopiuskin," 126, 130, 131–32, 206n51; *The Diary of a Superfluous Man*, 86; "The End of Chertopkhanov," 19, 113, 116, 125–36, 155; *Fathers and Sons*, 4; "A Living Relic," 131; *Mumu*, 12–13, 19, 113, 115, 116–25, 136, 141, 155, 204–5nn31–34, 205n42; *A Nest of the Gentry*, 4; *Rudin*, 4, 12, 19, 116; *A Sportsman's Sketches*, 4, 12, 19, 29, 115–16, 125–26, 129, 130–33, 184n1; "There Is a Clattering!," 131; *Two Generations*, 4, 12, 115
Tynianov, Iurii, 173n3

Vel'tman, Aleksandr, 3, 18, 26, 27, 36–37, 127, 191n7
verse novels, 3, 173n1
Veselovsky, Aleksandr, 7, 175n19
Vinitsky, Ilya, 202n77
Vinogradov, Viktor, 14–15, 18, 95, 97, 98, 175n17

Voltaire, 39, 162
Voskresensky, Mikhail, 3

Wasiolek, Edward, 212n6
Watt, Ian, 5–6, 22, 43, 89–90, 174nn13–14, 197n11
Weir, Justin, 214n27
Weststeeijn, Willem, 204n21
wish-fulfillment, 77–80
Woloch, Alex, 6, 174n12, 197n11

Zagoskin, Mikhail, 3, 18, 42, 49, 53, 57–58, 103
Zhukova, Mariia, 24, 26, 42, 48–49, 53, 57, 183n48
Ziegler, Vickie, 185n23
Zimovets, Sergei, 117
Zola, Émile, 196n3
Zunshine, Lisa, 113, 203n17